STRATEGIC ISSUES IN MICROFINANCE

Contemporary Perspectives on Developing Societies

John Mukum Mbaku, Series General Editor, Weber State University
Mwangi S. Kimenyi, Series Associate Editor, The University of Connecticut

Between 1989 and 1991, there were several changes in the global political economy that have had significant impact on policy reform in developing societies. The most important of these were the collapse of socialism in Eastern Europe, the subsequent disintegration of the Soviet Union, the cessation of superpower rivalry, and the demise of apartheid in South Africa. These events have provided scholars a new and challenging research agenda: To help the peoples of the Third World participate more effectively in the new global economy. Given conditions in these societies, the first line of business for researchers would be to help these countries establish and maintain transparent, accountable and participatory governance structures and, at the same time, provide themselves with more viable economic infrastructures. The *Contemporary Perspectives on Developing Societies* series was founded to serve as an outlet for such policy relevant research. It is expected that books published in this series will provide rigorous analyses of issues relevant to the peoples of the Third World and their efforts to improve their participation in the global economy.

Also in this series

Hope, K. R., Sr. (ed.) (1997), *Structural Adjustment, Reconstruction and Development in Africa.*
John Mukum Mbaku and Julius O. Ihonvbere (eds.) (1998), *Multiparty Democracy and Political Change: Constraints to Democratization in Africa.*

Strategic Issues in Microfinance

Edited by
MWANGI S. KIMENYI
Department of Economics
The University of Connecticut & African Educational
Foundation for Public Policy and Market Process, Inc.
Storrs, Connecticut, USA

ROBERT C. WIELAND
International Economics-Washington
Washington, DC, USA

J.D. VON PISCHKE
Internationale Projeckt Consult GmbH
Frankfurt am Main, Germany

Routledge
Taylor & Francis Group
LONDON AND NEW YORK

First published 1998 by Ashgate Publishing

Reissued 2018 by Routledge
2 Park Square, Milton Park, Abingdon, Oxon, OX14 4RN
711 Third Avenue, New York, NY 10017, USA

Routledge is an imprint of the Taylor & Francis Group, an informa business

Publisher's Note
The publisher has gone to great lengths to ensure the quality of this reprint but points out that some imperfections in the original copies may be apparent.

Disclaimer
The publisher has made every effort to trace copyright holders and welcomes correspondence from those they have been unable to contact.

A Library of Congress record exists under LC control number: 98071958

ISBN 13: 978-1-138-34862-2 (hbk)
ISBN 13: 978-0-429-43657-4 (ebk)

Contents

Tables

Figures

List of contributors

DALE W ADAMS, professor emeritus at The Ohio State University, is a consultant on topics of development finance, and lives in Park City, Utah. He completed his graduate work at Michigan State University and has since worked on development finance problems in numerous countries. These problems include deposit mobilization, transaction costs in financial markets, interest rate policies, informal finance, and reform of development banks. He has published several books and a number of professional papers and articles on these topics.

LYNN BENNETT is an anthropologist who is Sector Manager for Social Development in the World Bank's South Asia region. She spent 16 years in Nepal and India where she studied the social and symbolic role of women in Hindu culture, and led research on women's economic role in Nepal and India. In 1982 with UNICEF in Nepal, she designed and implemented a group-based program called Production Credit for Rural Women. This interest continued in her work as Program Officer with the Ford Foundation in India (1984–87) and later when she joined the World Bank. In addition to her position as Gender Coordinator for South and East Asia, she designed and then co-managed the Bank's global study on 'Sustainable Banking with the Poor' which has produced *A Global Inventory of Microfinance Institutions*, *The Practical Guide to Microfinance*, and the *Technical Handbook on Microfinance* in addition to more than 25 case studies of MFIs from all over the world and a series of papers drawing lessons from the case studies.

BRIAN A. BRANCH is Director of Programs, Latin America and Caribbean, for the World Council of Credit Unions (WOCCU). He has been engaged in development field research and project implementation for over 16 years. In his present capacity he identifies, designs and assists the implementation of programs that enable credit unions to improve their services to achieve market-based sustainability, savings protection and funding self-sufficiency. These programs include innovative savings and loan products for members with low incomes and/or microentrepreneurs. In 1990 he received his Doctor of Philosophy in Economics at the University of Wisconsin in Madison. He received his Master of Arts in Latin American Studies at the University of Texas-Austin, and worked as a research consultant for the United States Agency for International Development in Lima, Peru. He was a visting researcher at the Centro de Investigaciones, Universidad del Pacifico in Peru and received his B.A. in Government and Spanish from Bowdoin College in Maine.

ROBERT PECK CHRISTEN directs the Microfinance Training Program at the Economics Institute in Boulder, Colorado where he also serves as Editor of the Microbanking Bulletin. Mr. Christen is based in Chile and operates a private consulting practice oriented towards the development of commercially based microfinance services in several countries around the world. Previously, he worked for several years with Accion International through which he founded and operated microcredit programs in Bolivia, Cost Rica and Chile. He is author of *Banking Services for the Poor: Managing for Financial Success* (ACCION, 1997), as well as a number of short papers in the areas of design, management and the regulation and supervision of microfinance services. Mr. Christen was born in the United States and received his BA from Beloit College and his MS from Ohio State University in Agricultural Economics where he did his research in the area of development finance.

CARLOS E. CUEVAS is technical manager for the World Bank's Sustainable Banking with the Poor Project, which conducts research on microfinance institutions and clients. He is also a co-leader of the Bank's Rural and Micro Finance Thematic Group. Prior to joining the World Bank in 1995, Dr. Cuevas was a senior microenterprise specialist for two years at the Inter-American Development Bank. In this capacity he developed policy guidelines, provided advisory assistance to operations units and participated in the coordination of that Bank's microenterprise operations. From 1986 to 1993 he was assistant professor at the Ohio State University, where he had previously earned his Ph.D. in agricultural economics. He has conducted extensive applied research on rural, micro and small enterprise finance in Africa, Asia and Latin America.

MIKE GOLDBERG is a microfinance specialist with the Secretariat of the Consultive Group to Assist the Poorest, a multi-donor initiative to support microfinance retail and wholesale operations around the world. Mr. Goldberg manages partnerships with leading microfinance institutions in Kenya, Uganda, Central America and China. He is also responsible for providing technical training to World Bank staff members. Before joining CGAP, Mr. Goldberg provided assistance to World Bank projects in Sri Lanka, India, and China, and led a study of five South Asian group-based microfinance institutions. His previous work experience includes project management with CARE in Guatemala and Appropriate Technology International. Mr. Goldberg also served as a Peace Corps Volunteer in Ecuador, working with ACCION International. Mr. Goldberg holds Masters degrees in Economic Development and in Business Administration and a Bachelors degree in International Relations from Johns Hopkins University.

CLAUDIO GONZALEZ-VEGA is a professor of Economics and of Agricultural Economics and Director of the Rural Finance Program at The Ohio State University. He was formerly Dean of the Faculty of Economic Sciences at the University of Costa Rica. He has degrees in Law and in Economics from the University of Costa Rica, a Masters degree from the London School of Economics, and a Ph.D. from Stanford University. He has been a consultant to the World Bank, USAID, and other international organizations and has published widely on topics of rural and microfinance, international trade, political economy, poverty, and macroeconomic management in developing countries.

OTTO HOSPES is a lecturer in the Netherlands on credit systems and self-help organizations at the Wageningen Agricultural University (WAU), department of Social Sciences, Center for Agrarian Law and Legal Anthropology. He studied rural sociology at WAU. In 1989–90, he carried out his Ph.D. field research on 'Changing Credit Relations on Rural Ambon, Indonesia,' focusing on the role and dynamics of informal financial arrangements. He is one of the editors of *Financial Landscapes Reconstructed: The Fine Art of Mapping Development.* Currently, he is the principal research coordinator of a FAO-WAU research Programme on 'The Cooperative Management of Scarce Resources in Africa.' He is also convenor of CERES, the Dutch inter-university Research School for Resource Studies for Development.

MWANGI S. KIMENYI is Associate Professor of Economics at the University of Connecticut where he has been since 1991. Previously, he was an assistant professor of economics at the University of

Mississippi. He was born in Kenya and received his B.Ed. in Chemistry from the University of Nairobi, an M.A. in International Affairs and an M.A. in Economics from Ohio University, and the Ph.D. in economics from George Mason University. He is the Vice President and Chief Financial Controller of the African Educational Foundation, Inc., and Managing Director of the African Institute for Public Policy and Market Process, Kenya. He is the author of *Economics of Poverty, Discrimination and Public Policy* (South-Western, 1995), *Ethnic Diversity, Liberty and the State: The African Dilemma* (Edward Elgar, 1998). His current research focuses on public choice and institutional reforms in developing countries.

BARRY L. LENNON is a senior financial advisor in the Microenterprise Development Office of the U.S. Agency for International Development (USAID). In 1969 he began working in financial market development as a Peace Corps volunteer in the Western Highlands of Guatemala. After two years as a regional credit union extension agent in Guatemala, Mr. Lennon transferred to Mali, where he worked as a Peace Corps volunteer credit manager for three years. Since 1975, Mr. Lennon has been involved with cooperatives and credit unions, public sector banks, and many different non-bank financial intermediaries in Africa, Latin America, and more recently, Eastern Europe and the Newly Independent States. In his present position, he helps USAID Missions design new financial service programs for micro and small business clients, and he evaluates the financial service programs of U.S. and international private voluntary organizations (PVOs) having grants from USAID.

DAVID C. RICHARDSON is senior technical advisor for the World Council of Credit Unions (WOCCU) in Madison, Wisconsin. He provides technical assistance to WOCCU's projects world-wide, including technical troubleshooting, new product development, and executive training. From 1987 to 1994 he was chief financial advisor for WOCCU's rehabilitation project in Guatemala that transformed credit unions and other cooperatives into profitable, service-oriented businesses, replacing a subsidy-based operating strategy that had been followed for 25 years. From 1978 to 1987 David Richardson was an agricultural investment director for Mutual Life Insurance Company of New York, managing a diversified $200 million agricultural loan portfolio in 26 states. Prior to that he was a credit and operations officer for the Farm Credit Administration. He received his B.S. in agricultural economics/Latin American studies from Brigham Young

University and his M.A. in agri-banking/business management from Texas A&M University.

MARGUERITE S. ROBINSON holds a Ph.D. in social anthropology from Harvard University. She served as a Professor of Anthropology and Dean of the College of Arts and Sciences at Brandeis University before becoming an Institute Fellow of the Harvard Institute for International Development, where she has worked since 1978. She has conducted extensive fieldwork in rural and tribal areas and among the urban poor in Asia and also worked in Latin America and Africa. Beginning in 1979, Dr. Robinson has served as advisor to the Ministry of Finance, Government of Indonesia, and to the Bank Rakyat Indonesia (BRI) on the development of its local banking system. She has also served as advisor to the Bank of Tanzania, the Vietnam Bank for the Poor, BancoSol in Bolivia, the Kenya Rural Enterprise Programme (K-REP), and numerous other institutions. Her publications include: *Local Politics: The Law of the Fishes, Development Through Political Change in Medak District, Andhra Pradesh* (South India), Oxford University Press, 1988; *Political Structure in a Changing Sinhalese Village*, Cambridge South Asian Studies No. 15, Cambridge University Press, 1975.

REINHARD H. SCHMIDT studied business administration and economics at the Goethe University in Frankfurt. He has been a professor of finance at the Universities of Frankfurt, Gottingen and Trier, and a visiting professor at Stanford University, Georgetown University and at the University of Pennsylvania. He currently holds the Wilhelm-Merton Chair of International Business and Finance at the University of Frunkfurt and is a member of the academic advisory board of Internationale Projekt Consult GmbH. He is the author or co-author of several books and academic articles in the fields of financial economics and development finance, and has worked as a consultant in Africa and Latin America.

LAURA VIGANÒ is an assistant professor of banking at the University of Bergamo, Italy, and a permanent consultant to 'Giordano Dell'Amore' Foundation (Finafrica-Milan). Dr. Viganò graduated in Economics and Business Administration in 1987. In 1992, she completed her Ph.D. in Business Economics, Finance and Capital Markets at the University of Bergamo. In 1990, she was a visiting instructor at the Ohio State University. She worked in several African countries and in the Middle East doing research for international development agencies. She has presented papers at international conferences and published articles and a book on various aspects of financial markets and intermediaries.

ROBERT C. VOGEL, who received his Ph.D. in Economics from Stanford University, is currently Executive Director of IMCC and an Adjunct Professor at The Ohio State University. He has been a professor of economics at Syracuse University and the University of Miami, director of the World Banking and Finance Program at the Economics Institute in Boulder, Colorado, a financial economist with the World Bank, and a senior staff economist with the Council of Economic Advisors. Dr. Vogel's writings on finance and development have appeared in leading professional journals. He was one of the principal authors of the World Bank's 1989 *World Development Report: Financial Systems and Development* and of *Maximizing the Outreach of Microenterprise Finance: The Emerging Lessons of Successful Programs* for USAID. Dr. Vogel has been a consultant to USAID, the World Bank, the Inter-American Development Bank and various government and private clients. He has worked on financial sector policy issues in several Latin American countries, Swaziland, Ukraine, Bulgaria, Hungary, and Romania. He has directed projects in Costa Rica, Peru, Guatemala, Honduras, Bolivia, and the Philippines.

J. D. VON PISCHKE is affiliated with Internationale Projekt Consult GmbH, a German firm that offers management services for small and microenterprise lending programs. From 1993 to 1995 he was with KPMG's Barents Group as Director of USAID's Financial Sector Development Project, implemented by Barents as a contractor. Dr. Von Pischke spent 20 years at the World Bank as a financial analyst. He obtained his Ph.D. at the University of Glasgow, was a commercial banker with Chase Manhattan, and a Peace Corps volunteer in Ethiopia. Current research interests include market-based deposit insurance, capital enhancement guarantees, improving disclosure of the financial performance of donor-funded credit projects.

ROBERT C. WIELAND is an economist working with the consulting firm International Economics—Washington. His work has focused on rural and microfinance issues since 1983, when he undertook a portfolio review of the World Bank's agricultural credit loans. He wrote a chapter on informal finance for the 1989 *World Development Report* and has undertaken research in a number of developing countries examining finance costs, demand for services, and policy constraints to expanded financial services. His current areas of focus include transaction costs, non-financial policy constraints to microenterprise development, and regulatory avoidance in the provision of financial services.

CLAUS-PETER ZEITINGER is the founder and managing director of Internationale Projekt Consult (IPC) GmbH, a Frankfurt-based firm which specializes in consultancy support for financial systems and financial institutions in developing countries and countries in transition. He studied economics at the University of Frankfurt, where he earned a doctorate. He has acted as a consultant to several donor agencies and financial institutions in many countries, in particular Latin America and Eastern Europe, where IPC has gained experience in 'upgrading' target group-oriented financial institutions and 'downscaling' commercial banks.

Acknowledgments

Financial sector development was the theme of two conferences at the Brookings Institution in the fall of 1994. Each was sponsored by the United States Agency for International Development (USAID). One was directed primarily at macroeconomic issues of financial liberalization and stabilization, summarized in *Sequencing? Financial Strategies for Developing Countries*, edited by Alison Harwood and Bruce L.R. Smith, and published in 1997 by Brookings Institution Press.

The other meeting, titled Financial Services and the Poor: U.S. and Developing Country Experience, provided the impetus for this book. Key papers on financial services in developing countries that were originally prepared for that conference are presented here, revised and updated. They deal with strategic issues in microfinance that remain at the center of research and informed debate, public policy, and institutional strategy for delivering financial services to the poor.

USAID sponsorship was provided through the Office of Emerging Markets under the Financial Sector Development Project, Phase II (FSDP II). These activities were managed by Barents Group of KPMG Peat Marwick as prime contractor to USAID. The project consortium assembled by Barents Group included the Brookings Institution. J.D. Von Pischke, one of the editors, served as FSDP II project manager at Barents Group from 1993 to 1995.

Many people made possible this book and the conference at which earlier versions of these papers were presented. The core group included Russell Anderson, Monica McKnight and Rebecca Maestri of USAID's Office of Emerging Markets. Brookings scholar Bruce L.R. Smith headed the Brookings team and helped to shape the program. Donna James and Jennifer McAllister at Barents Group and the late LeeAnn Sonnergren and Susan Williams at Brookings provided administrative support.

This book is published by Ashgate as part of a series organized by the African Educational Foundation, Inc., which was founded by economists from African countries who are faculty members of universities in the United States. Professor Mwangi S. Kimenyi, a presenter at the Brookings conference and one of the editors of this volume, is vice president of the Foundation and associate editor of the

Ashgate series. Professor John Mukum Mbaku, president of the Foundation and general editor of the series, oversaw the preparation of the final copy.

The views expressed in the chapters that follow are those of the authors and should not be ascribed to the United States Agency for International Development or to the trustees, officers or other staff members of the Brookings Institution, the Barents Group, or the African Educational Foundation.

Mwangi S. Kimenyi
Robert C. Wieland
J.D. Von Pischke

1 Introduction

MWANGI S. KIMENYI, ROBERT C. WIELAND & J.D. VON PISCHKE

Promoting development from the bottom up, in ways that enable the poor to create income and wealth for themselves, is a widely shared ideal within the development community. Many or even most development specialists and institutions would identify animation of development by the poor as a principal objective. This is the context that amplifies the call for microfinance, based on the fact that increased income and wealth are promoted by access to capital used productively. Finance is the business of accumulating financial capital and spreading it around, and microfinance consists of doing this at the small end of financial markets, where the poor are most likely to participate.

The clientele Marguerite Robinson describes in the introduction to her chapter in this collection is the dream team for development specialists:

> people who farm or fish or herd; who operate small or micro-enterprises where goods are produced, recycled, repaired or traded; provide services; who work for wages or commissions; gain income from renting out small amounts of land, vehicles, draft animals, or machinery and tools; and other individuals and groups at the local levels of developing countries, in both rural and urban areas.

Directly assisting this group by improving their access to financial services and their ability to create wealth is an attractive proposition. Accordingly, it has attracted considerable and increased investment from donor institutions and attention from others involved in development. The Brookings Institution seminar, sponsored by USAID, *Financial Services and the Poor: U.S. and Developing Country Experiences*, aimed to take stock of this effort by providing a forum for practitioners and analysts to report their findings.

Key issues

This book seeks to complete that task by making available to a wider audience a selection of papers from that seminar. These essays provide a range of perspectives on important microfinance issues in developing countries. Beyond the goal of improving access to financial services, the authors do not speak with one voice and frequently contradict each other. Key issues that emerge from this volume are:

- *The role of credit*: Why is credit such a popular instrument and high priority among donor organizations? What are the limits of the contributions that financial services can make to poverty alleviation? At what point does disregard of these limits impede the development and sustainability of the financial institutions using donor or other official funds?
- *Outreach modalities*: How should relationships between lenders and borrowers be organized? Are, or under what conditions are, programs that lend to individuals more effective and capable of greater, more efficient growth than group-based arrangements? How can, or should, social services be linked to financial services? Should microlenders offer financial services only, or should they also provide nonfinancial assistance such as training, business advice and social services? Is provision of savings facilities, and their linkage with credit services, essential for institutional growth and sustainability of microlenders?
- *Risk*: What is the nature of risks inherent in microlending? How can risks be identified and managed? What are the interactions between borrower selection and credit methodology in controlling risk? What microcredit pricing strategies are required to cover microlending risks?
- *Lessons from informal finance*: What insights can the informal financial sector offer to microlenders seeking outreach and sustainability? Are informal operators generally competitive or are informal arrangements typically severely segmented and not highly competitive by the very nature of their limited markets? Do monopolistic providers offer, at least in part, potentially attractive models for formal microlenders to emulate?
- *Governance and incentives*: Are donor-supported microfinance ventures likely to succeed generally, or is lack of sustainability more probable because of muddled objectives and a lack of suitable institutions at the field level, such as uninterested commercial

banks, incompetent state-owned institutions, and NGOs lacking sufficiently businesslike orientation?

* *Keeping score*: How can accountability be encouraged in microfinance? Can regulation and supervision by government authorities suffice? What can be done to promote transparency? Why have donors been so reticent to disclose meaningful financial data regarding the performance and condition of their credit project portfolios? What forces, self-correcting or imposed through intervention, stimulate efficient strategic reorientation, policy reforms and institutional rehabilitation? What could donors do to promote transparency? How can institutional change be implemented and managed?

All of the papers presented in this collection are grounded in field experiences. It is striking that, even with an empirical basis, interpretations differ across the papers. These differences are evidence of an industry that is still sorting out its fundamentals. The short list of questions in the preceding paragraph contains just a few of the issues addressed differently by authors in this collection. If one compared the papers delivered at this conference to the content of a hypothetical conference ten years earlier, one would see that some basic concepts, such as the importance of cost efficiency and cost recovery, have been more or less accepted.

While still a relatively new subject area, microfinance is old enough to have an 'old view' and a 'new view'. The old view characterized earlier attempts to intervene in financial markets on behalf of the poor and the small-scale. It treated finance as an input to production which one could enlarge and accelerate without worrying too much about overall financial sector policy or the commercial sustainability of the institutions that were used to deliver this stimulant. Enjoying donor and other government support, this view was put to the test in the 1970s and early '80s and was found wanting. Despite the commitment of massive resources for agricultural and other targeted credit around the world, a consensus evolved among most observers that these operations provided inefficient benefits to limited populations and that in some ways they even undermined economic development.

As the results of this experiment became apparent, many analysts—some represented in these pages—began to draw attention to the importance of the sustainability of financial institutions and to the importance of the legal and regulatory environment within which they operate. These issues are now widely accepted as being important and there is, again, something approaching consensus in the ways that they are addressed. Still, as one reads these essays and considers the implications of the position argued, it will be apparent that much remains to be done in developing cogent and effective approaches for microfinance.

Organization

The book is divided into three sections, starting with a collection of three papers which address the microfinance market in the broad context of economic development for the poor. These papers provide descriptions of how the microfinance market is related to broader strategies of economic development and, particularly, financial intermediation. They lay the groundwork for the discussions in following sections on design strategies and on accountability and sustainability.

Claudio Gonzalez-Vega provides an overview of the links between financial markets and development efforts aimed at the poor. His strategic insights are based on the application of economics to historical efforts to make financial systems work for the poor. He concludes that finance is a specialized tool and that it can promote development only if it is applied within the boundaries of its usefulness. In this respect, using financial institutions to allocate capital by some decision rule other than gaining the highest rate of return on investments might be tantamount to giving a stone to a man who has no bread. On the other hand, he also recognizes and reports several ways in which appropriate and new technologies can expand the use of formal finance by the poor.

Harry Schmidt and Claus-Peter Zeitinger also address the links between financial market development and efforts aimed at improving the lot of the poor, but with a highly specific focus on the application of donor resources. Their analysis starts from the proposition that external funding is highly useful in making financial services more broadly accessible to the poor and they describe the terms and conditions under which such funding might be most effective. They caution about unrealistic expectations regarding how quickly sustainable financial institutions can be created. These authors provide a useful summary of issues surrounding several lending technologies and approaches for providing sustainable financial services, which leads them to favor individual rather than group-based lending. They also address deposit services in the context of commercial sustainability and the development of microfinance institutions. This institutional orientation is further developed in a discussion of business strategies for improving the supply of financial services to the poor.

Marguerite Robinson's chapter provides an analysis of a wide range of factors in the sustainable delivery of financial services to the poor. Beginning with a list of ways in which microfinance is important to social and economic development, she also enumerates: why credit subsidies are ineffective; the main reasons why strategic thinking has shifted away from credit delivery and toward financial intermediation; and factors underlying success among microfinance institutions. The author also provides an outline of the basic concepts that generated the 'old paradigm' of subsidized credit and the principles that support the 'new paradigm' of sustainable financial intermediation. Each of these factors is analyzed through interpretation of empirical results from Indonesia and other successful microfinance operations.

While each of the papers in the first section differs somewhat in emphasis and interpretation, they provide a consistent set of reasons for viewing microfinance as a valid tool for improving the productivity of the poor in developing countries. From this platform, the papers in the second section focus on strategies and approaches by which microfinance can more effectively achieve its potential. Strategic issues include: implementation vehicles and mechanisms, the interface between the institution and the clientele, and alternative institutional arrangements and their implications for microfinance programs.

The lead chapter is by Dale Adams, a long-time opponent of the old paradigm of targeted credit and an architect of the view that is now current. He addresses the effect on donors of the shift to a new approach. He asks whether donors have been hasty in embracing NGOs and PVOs as vehicles for microfinance operations. Framing his argument in terms of the economic goals of production credit versus the social welfare goals of many NGO-based finance programs, this question and its consequent analysis leans against the wind, forcing a re-examination of some important and fundamental microfinance issues.

Lynn Bennett broadens the discussion by linking financial intermediation with social intermediation. Scope for borrower participation and its significance for the success of programs invites a multidisciplinary approach to microfinance. The importance of borrower participation in microfinance is obvious, but analysts' (especially economists) preference for simple choice sets and their need to separate suppliers from buyers in analyses of these markets has perhaps been a barrier to broader discussion of this issue. This chapter provides a basis from which further analysis of this topic can and should develop.

Otto Hospes addresses the social elements of financial intemedia-tion from an anthropological perspective, pointing out that in many parts of the developing world targeted for microfinance interventions, economies are just becoming monetized, and have no more than rudimentary financial services. Newly monetized societies can be expected to have a great deal of flux in their social and cultural characteristics and the author points out that many cultural attributes that served a society well before monetization are no longer applica-ble, nor so useful, once money becomes the arbiter of exchange. These issues are important to the development of broadly applicable approaches to microfinance and they receive insufficient attention generally.

In his discussion of market niches and the relevance of informal finance, Carlos Cuevas proposes that, regardless of what microfinance institutions might learn from informal intermediaries and their financial instruments, the two sets of service providers (formal and informal) are fundamentally different even though they provide complementary services to overlapping clienteles. In making this argument, he identifies three different types of informal financial arrangements and describes the ways in which they serve the poor. He then addresses three different successful 'alternative' financial institutions and shows how the services that they provide differ in character from those of informal intermediaries. While the services and institutional forms of alternative and informal financial interme-diaries differ, he argues that they share many of the same limitations, including the absence of adequate regulation and supervision and limited opportunities for spreading financial risks.

In their comparative study of several credit programs targeting poor and small-scale clients in Nepal Lynn Bennett, Michael Gold-berg, and J.D. Von Pischke describe the features of 'non-sustainable' credit operations. They also provide a detailed discussion of the changes in strategic objectives that are required to turn these opera-tions around and what would need to be done to effect these changes. The authors outline the role of groups and social intermediation in sustainability and they list performance factors useful for evaluating microfinance clients.

The evaluation of microfinance customers using credit rating and scoring systems is taken up in greater detail by Lauro Viganò. Her chapter reports the findings of a statistical study of the likelihood of loan repayment given 'symptomatic variables' based on readily available borrower information. Standardized credit evaluation systems which reduce lending risk in a cost-effective manner would be extremely useful to microfinance operations. The research on which the chapter is based is an important contribution to the development of such systems.

The third and final section presents four papers which address financial sustainability in microfinance and how to ensure it. These include discussions of why financial sustainability is imperative, what is required to achieve it in terms of both internal, institutional incentives and in the broader context of donors and external regulators. These papers cover a broad range of issues from the implications of financial sustainability for management and regulation to the use of information by microfinance institutions and their supporters. Following the three theoretical papers, the section ends with a case study which gives added weight to the arguments for sustainable business practices in financial operations. This description of the reform and stabilization of the Guatemalan credit union system shows how the arguments made in the preceding papers for business-like services and the importance of cost recovery in microfinance can help to build better systems.

Robert C. Christen discusses in his overview chapter why financial sustainability should be considered essential to success in microfinance. He identifies factors that help to generate financial sustainability and links these to the development of microfinance institutions. He says that financial sustainability is a prerequisite for large-scale outreach on the credible assumption that donor funds will never be adequate to support growth beyond the start-up phase. Program expansion will therefore have to be based on retained earnings and access to commercial financial markets, both of which require financial sustainability. The chapter also provides a broad-ranging discussion of the implications of financial sustainability for interest rate policies, lending standards, organizational efficiency, and liquidity management.

Robert C. Vogel develops an argument for regulation and supervision in his paper, pointing out that these are important to alternative financial institutions in terms of their own self-interest. If the quest for funds (i.e., deposit mobilization and financial leverage) is the primary factor motivating alternative financial institutions to seek 'formality', the case for regulation and supervision becomes self-evident. The importance of improved financial information and the need to control volatility are discussed, along with the problems that are likely to arise in regulation of microfinance. But the main

story is about microfinance institutions' need to access additional
resources through deposit mobilization and commercial borrowing
from domestic and international financial markets.

J.D. Von Pischke broadens the context in his discussion of
performance evaluation of microfinance operations and the role of
the donors that support them. He notes that adequate financial
statements are an important, if not sufficient, indicator of sustainability
in microfinance and that attention to financial accounting has been
lacking in most donor supported microfinance operations. He
identifies the parameters that need to be tracked and how one might
do so. Cash flow, accounting for income and losses, subsidy dependence, and consistency of program strategies are addressed in the
context of donor objectives and the goals of microfinance institutions.
The chapter also addresses the issue of incentives for accounting and
reporting reform in microfinance.

The final chapter is a case study by David Richardson, Barry
Lennon, and Brian Branch of a successful attempt to rebuild a
microfinance operation—in this case a national credit union system.
The authors document the decline of the system which created the
need for rehabilitation and reform. With technical assistance and an
infusion of additional capital to stabilize credit unions' financial
health, Guatemala's credit union system has achieved growth in
membership and business and has gained a more sustainable financial
footing. One of the most important steps taken in this exercise was to
shift the focus of the credit unions away from their earlier bias toward
borrowers and toward improved returns for savers. This change
generated a large increase in membership and savings and, given the
demand among microfinance customers for savings services that is
identified in the preceding papers, returned the institutions to their
original objective of serving their member-clients more effectively.

PART I

THE MICROFINANCE MARKET

2 Do financial institutions have a role in assisting the poor?

CLAUDIO GONZALEZ-VEGA

Concerns about poverty and finance

Growing concerns about poverty stand out in political agendas all over the world, as the stubbornness of poverty even in the richest nations is being met with increasing impatience. Governments of diverse ideological persuasions are trying to do something for the poor, while international donors offer, again, their support to these efforts. From good intentions to actual remedies, however, there is a long way, and practitioners are looking for successful operational approaches to deal with poverty. In this context, the old question re-emerges: what about credit?

The extent to which the reduction of poverty and/or the alleviation of its consequences has been a policy issue has differed across countries and over time. In the United States, poverty was at the top of the nation's agenda when the War on Poverty was declared 30 years ago (Harrington, 1962). By the early 1980s, however, many chose to highlight the counterproductive nature and high fiscal costs of some of the poverty alleviation programs (Reagan, 1982). Recently, public attention has focused again on the potential role of both government and the publicly-supported non-government organizations (NGOs) in directly alleviating the continuing plight of the poor.

Among recent initiatives, specialized credit programs for the poor are becoming increasingly popular (Jordan, 1993; Minsky et al., 1993). Because many believe that a more effective design of poverty alleviation programs will prevent their earlier shortcomings, it becomes critical to identify lessons from those earlier experiments. As experience accumulates about the performance of credit programs explicitly designed to assist the poor, therefore, there is a growing opportunity to take stock of which policies have worked and which have not. A substantial volume of experience on credit programs for the poor, positive and negative, has been accumulated in low-income countries. Many of the lessons learned are relevant for the United States as well.

The history of anti-poverty policy has not been different in the developing nations, where poverty has been so conspicuous. Leaving behind the basic needs paradigm of the 1970s, for most of the developing world the 1980s were a decade of structural adjustment, dominated by stabilization efforts designed to bring national expenditure in line with national income and by attempts to increase national income through policy reforms that promote a more rapid accumulation of capital and more efficient use of resources.

There is a strong professional consensus that the adjustment programs of the 1980s were successful in moving many countries toward internal and external macroeconomic balance. The debate is intense, however, about whether these objectives could have been achieved 'while better protecting the poor and providing the basis to incorporate them in the growth process' (Grootaert and Kanbur, 1990).

Regardless of whether the poverty outcomes of the 1980s stemmed from past policies which militated against growth or from the adjustment policies that inevitably followed as the earlier strategies failed (Morley, 1994), there is no doubt that low-income country governments and international donors have been increasingly concerned with poverty alleviation.

There are two dimensions to this preoccupation. A first type of concern relates to the need to achieve growth with equity over the long term. This requires policies and programs that foster the participation of the poor in processes of economic growth by creating employment opportunities, by increasing the access of the poor to income-generating assets, by raising the productivity of their assets, both physical and human, and by allowing them to manage risk better (Grootaert and Kanbur, 1990). If efficiently provided, financial services may play an important role in this task of incorporating at least some of the poor in processes of economic growth.

A second type of concern relates to the need to mitigate the transitional costs of the adjustment for the most vulnerable groups of society. *Formal* financial services can play a very limited role in this effort, if any. Other fiscal mechanisms provide a more cost-effective approach to assist those who have no productive opportunities and, therefore, no debt capacity. The use of credit in these cases carries an excessive social cost and is easily counterproductive, as one would not want to burden the economically nonviable with additional debt they cannot repay (Adams, 1994).

In dealing with poverty issues it is always difficult to bridge the gap, on the one hand, between moral obligations calling for private and public charity and, on the other, the economic requirements that could improve the lot of the poor (Schultz, 1992). It appears, nevertheless, that financial services can have a *sustainable* economic role only when the opportunities for improvement exist. To understand why this is the case, one needs to examine the nature of finance and the importance of its economic contributions.

Functions of finance

The financial system is a key component of the institutional infrastructure required for the efficient operation of all markets. The most important contribution of finance is its ability to support a larger size and to foster a greater degree of integration of the markets for goods and services, factors of production, and assets and liabilities. This enlargement of markets is a precondition for powerful processes of productivity growth resulting from more division of labor and specialization, greater competition, the use of modern technologies, and the exploitation of economies of scale and of scope. As noted by Adam Smith, these are the processes that increase the productivity of available resources and lead to economic growth.

The expansion and integration of markets is achieved through the provision of monetization services and the efficient management of the payments system, the development of services of intermediation between surplus and deficit economic agents, and the establishment of opportunities for the accumulation of stores of value, the management of liquidity, and the transformation, sharing, pooling, and diversification of risk (Long, 1983).

Particularly important are the services of financial intermediation, which transfer purchasing power from agents with resources in excess of those needed to take advantage of their own internal opportunities (surplus agents, such as savers), to those with better opportunities but not enough resources of their own (deficit agents, such as investors). By making this division of labor between savers and investors possible, financial intermediaries channel resources from producers, activities, and regions with limited growth potential to those where more rapid expansion of output is possible.

Since there are always more economic agents who claim that they have superior uses for resources than there is purchasing power available, financial markets contribute to the selection of the best possible uses of resources. These markets offer monitoring services, ensuring that funds are profitably used, as promised, and they contribute to the enforcement of contracts, making sure that those who have borrowed repay the loans (Stiglitz, 1993). After all, finance is about promises to pay in the future that are expected to be fulfilled. The conditions under which such repayment takes place influence, in turn, who bears what risks.

The efficient provision of financial services is extremely critical for the operation of the economy at large. Because financial markets so influence the allocation of resources, Stiglitz has compared them to the 'brain' of the entire economic system, the central locus of decisionmaking: 'if they fail...the performance of the entire economic system may be impaired.' There is clearly a major social interest at stake here. Most governments have recognized this and many have gone to extremes in order to prevent a collapse of their financial systems. Frequently, however, while recognizing but misunderstanding their powers, governments have intervened in financial markets in the pursuit of a varied range of worthy non-financial objectives, but with negative consequences.

Finance and poverty: lessons from the past

A number of initiatives to directly assist the poor with financial services fall under the category of unsuccessful interventions. A key question to address, therefore, is the potential cost of such interventions in terms of the reduced efficiency of the financial system at large. This is a cost that a country might find to be worth enduring if the expected benefits were sufficiently large. Unfortunately, this is typically not the case, given the very nature of financial markets.

This is one of the most important lessons from earlier attempts to use formal financial markets to ostensibly promote particular activities, to compensate producers for other repressive policies, to free them from the grip of moneylenders, or to redistribute income towards the poor (Gonzalez-Vega, 1993). Subsidized interest rates, administrative loan allocations, and targeted credit programs did not displace informal sources of financial services and hardly promoted anything. They only redistributed income, but in reverse, from poor to rich (Gonzalez-Vega, 1984). Despite the best of intentions, these interventions frequently turned out to be harmful for the particular segments of the population that they had intended to help (i.e., the marginal clientele).

These outcomes are well known and have been extensively documented for dozens of countries (Adams et al., 1984). Too much effort was spent in small farmer credit programs, for example, for the meager results obtained. The primary objective of increasing the farmers' access to formal credit was poorly met and a reduction in the cost of borrowing was achieved only for a few large borrowers. Despite artificially low interest rates, formal credit did not become cheap for small rural producers and most credit portfolios became concentrated in a few hands.

More importantly, government-sponsored credit programs distracted attention from the technological innovation, infrastructure building, institutional development, and human capital formation that directly increase the productivity of resources. Finance, instead, can only contribute to this goal indirectly, by making it possible for some agents to take advantage of opportunities created by those other growth-inducing processes. In the absence of such opportunities, there is only a limited role for finance to play.[1]

There is an increasing body of evidence confirming that economic growth and reductions in poverty go hand in hand. Clearly, a substantial improvement in living standards requires economic growth (Biggs et al., 1988). Further, securing full participation of the poor in such a process is a long-term effort and it involves improving their employability, expanding the educational opportunities for their children, improving the performance of labor markets, creating a hospitable environment for their productive activities and much more. An efficient provision of the financial services that they demand is part, but only a part, of this process.

So, to the question 'can financial services be used to assist the poor in improving their lot?' the answer is 'only when finance is allowed to do what finance is supposed to do.' That is, only:

(a) when finance allows a transfer of purchasing power from uses with low marginal rates of return to uses with high marginal rates of return;

(b) when finance contributes to more efficient inter-temporal decisions about saving, the accumulation of assets, and investment;

(c) when finance makes possible a less costly management of liquidity and the accumulation of stores of value; and

(d) when finance offers better ways to deal with the risks implicit in economic activities.

Otherwise, financial interventions such as subsidized and targeted credit programs are a weak instrument to achieve non-financial objectives and frequently lead to unexpectedly negative outcomes (Gonzalez-Vega, 1994). This section can be summarized with the proposition that many ingredients are needed for the poor to come out of poverty and that credit is only one of them. Credit is an important ingredient, but it is not even the most important one. Financial services play the key role of facilitating the work of growth-promoting forces, but only when the opportunities exist.

Lessons about loans and deposits

A second important lesson from experience is that, among financial services, credit is not the only one that is important for the poor. In particular, deposit facilities provide valuable services for liquidity management. Researchers are always surprised by the intensity of the demand for deposit facilities in the rural areas of poor countries (Gonzalez-Vega et al., 1992). Satisfaction of this demand has been a distinctive feature of programs that have been successful in delivering financial services to the poor (Robinson, 1994). An outstanding example is the *unit desa* or village unit program of Bank Rakyat Indonesia, with over 12 million small depositors and somewhat more than two million small borrowers (Patten and Rosengard, 1991). Thus, not all producers demand loans, and among those who do, not all demand credit all of the time. However, most if not all economic agents demand deposit and other facilities for liquidity management and reserve accumulation all of the time. In some countries the demand for facilities to transfer funds is also high.

A third lesson from experience is that the demand for credit is not just a demand for loanable funds. Finance plays a critical role not only in savings and investment but also in dealing with the lack of synchronization between income-generating (production) and spending (consumption and input use) activities. Finance is also closely associated with risk management. It facilitates the accumulation of reserves for precautionary reasons (to be able to survive emergencies) and for speculative purposes (to be able to take advantage of unexpected future opportunities). For this, being creditworthy is critical.

Being creditworthy is equivalent to possessing a credit reserve. Poor people do not necessarily want a loan now; they want the opportunity to get a loan if and when they need it (Baker, 1973). They want their access to credit to be reliable, to result in a timely and flexible disbursement of funds, to be always there. Because the informal sources of credit offer this quality of service, poor people are reluctant to substitute formal sources of funds, no matter how subsidized, for the flexible and reliable informal financial arrangements that have served them well over the years.

What matters is not access to loanable funds but the development of an established *credit relationship*. This, in turn, implies a sense of permanence of the financial institution. A fourth lesson learned, in this connection, is that a financial intermediary cannot project an image of permanence if it does not provide valuable services of high quality to its clientele and if it is not financially and institutionally viable.

Institutional viability and the poor

The most severe deficiency of earlier interventions to provide financial services to the poor was the lack of institutional viability of the organizations created for that purpose. Why does viability matter? Concern with viability springs from a clear recognition of the scarcity of resources. If resources are limited, without self-sufficient financial institutions there is little hope for reaching the numbers of poor firm-households that are potential borrowers and depositors. The amounts required are beyond the ability and willingness of governments and donors to provide (Otero and Rhyne, 1994).

The alternative to viable organizations are expensive, nonviable quasi-fiscal programs that reach only a few select beneficiaries. Thus, viability matters a lot from this equity perspective: to be able to reach more than just a privileged few. Moreover, if the objective were just a one-time, transitory injection of funds, then lump-sum transfers are always a more efficient way of accomplishing this. If in contrast sustainability is important, then the viability of the financial organization matters.

The most important contribution of a concern for institutional viability is that it elicits appropriate incentives among all the participants in financial transactions. In this sense, concerns for financial viability are a potential substitute for an appropriate structure of property rights in generating compatible incentives both among the staff and among the clients of the organization.

Thus, for example, while poor loan recovery rapidly destroys viability, an image of viability improves repayment discipline. A reputation as a good borrower in an established intermediary-client relationship is a more valuable intangible asset if the financial institution is expected to be permanent rather than transitory. When this intangible asset is sufficiently valuable, it helps to elicit punctual repayment. In contrast, when the organization's survival is questioned, default follows in stampede force and institutional breakdown becomes a self-fulfilling prophecy. Viability matters when repayment matters.

A concern for viability makes it possible to identify one of the ways in which interest rates and default rates are linked. Interest rates that are too low and cause intermediary losses are perceived by borrowers as signals of lack of permanence of the organization. Delinquency follows. Moreover, in the same way that very high interest rates may induce adverse selection (Stiglitz and Weiss, 1981), too low rates tend to attract rent seekers who eventually default (Gonzalez-Vega, 1993). Thus, both too high or too low interest rates may reduce the lender's expected profits through higher than expected default rates.

Targeting hurts viability in several ways. It reduces the scope for portfolio diversification in already highly specialized lenders. It limits the lender's degrees of freedom in screening loan applicants, and it reduces incentives for vigorous loan collection. These constraints, in turn, shift accountability for default from the lender to the donor that imposes conditions on the availability of funds by directing their use toward specific targets (Aguilera-Alfred and Gonzalez-Vega, 1993). Restrictions on loan uses, irrelevant because of the fungibility of funds (Von Pischke and Adams, 1983), increase lender and borrower transaction costs. They also reduce the quality of the services supplied by the intermediary, and they lower the value of the intermediary-client relationship. Many donors, more interested in monitoring compliance with the targets, for a long time ignored this potential impact of targeting on delinquency. However, they were *surprised* when rampant default destroyed the institutions that had been (ab)used in order to channel donor funds easily.

Deposit mobilization is also intimately linked to the importance of institutional viability. Deposits provide information to the lender about potential borrowers, create a basis of mutual trust, and facilitate the accumulation of a downpayment that can serve as a deductible in any future loan contract. Deposits contribute, therefore, to the solution of difficult information and incentive problems frequently encountered in financial markets. Moreover, deposit mobilization creates an image of institutional viability that promotes repayment. Thus, while donor-funded loans may not be repaid, those funded with the neighbor's deposits usually are (Aguilera-Alfred and Gonzalez-Vega, 1993).

Most importantly, depositors create institutional independence from the whims of donors and politicians; they shield the financial organization from political intrusion (Poyo et al., 1993). In general, deposit mobilization contributes to sustainability and to an organizational environment or corporate culture where permanence becomes an important (compatible) incentive to attract and retain competent managers and to induce the intermediary's staff to behave in ways that foster the viability of their organization. For them, the value of their relationship with the organization increases when deposits are an important source of funds. Deposit mobilization, nevertheless, is not an easy task. It requires an appropriate organizational design, liability management techniques, and prudential supervision to protect depositors. The mobilization of small deposits can be very costly (Schmidt and Zeitinger, 1994).

In summary, the following lessons have been learned about finance and the poor:

(a) The poor require more than just financial services; the non-financial ingredients of growth and development matter.

(b) The poor demand more than just credit; deposit facilities may matter even more.

(c) The poor want more than just loanable funds; they need a permanent, flexible, and reliable credit relationship.

(d) In consequence, the poor seek viable, efficient, profitable, well-managed financial intermediaries with which to establish permanent relationships.

Formal and informal finance

One important additional lesson is that informal financial arrangements are pervasive and very successful in providing some types of financial services among the poor (Bouman and Hospes, 1994). They are timely, reliable, and levy low transaction costs on their clients, mostly for loans of small amounts and for short periods of time. The value and importance of these informal financial arrangements have been increasingly recognized. The allegations and stigma of exploitation have been replaced by the flattery of imitation in attempts either to replicate their features or to link informal lenders to national financial networks (Adams and Fitchett, 1992). As Pirela (1990) has asked, however, 'if this is the case, why would additional (semi-formal and formal) financial intermediaries be needed to do a job that indigenous, informal arrangements are already doing too well?' The fact is that, despite their valuable contributions, informal financial arrangements suffer from several limitations.

These shortcomings stem from the very features that make informal transactions competitive in the first place. They are grounded in the local economy and are thereby limited by local wealth constraints and the covariant risks of the local environment. As a result, their frontier is narrow; they do not go far enough in scope: geographically, over time, and across products. Informal finance provides valuable services, but in small amounts, for short periods of time. These services are not always good vehicles for long-term investment. More importantly, because they are cost-effective only in the immediate neighborhood, informal transactions do not overcome market segmentation and do not contribute much to the most important function of finance: the integration of markets. For this task, formal financial institutions with a national scope are required.

The costs of finance

Developing national financial systems is not an easy task. The main reason is that the provision of financial services is expensive. Formal financial services are almost equivalent to a luxury good. Their production requires valuable human and material resources with high opportunity costs. Moreover, mistakes in the evaluation of creditworthiness are costly both for the intermediary and for society.

Some of these costs are associated with getting the transacting parties together. In this task, formal finance usually implies high fixed costs; this is certainly the case with bank branches. Their fixed costs loom particularly high when the clients are small, heterogeneous, and dispersed in sparsely populated areas (Gonzalez-Vega et al., 1996). The key to the level of these costs is market size, and this is not unique to financial services. It is expensive to provide health, education, or entertainment in remote areas with a low population density. In informal finance, in contrast, these costs are low, given the nature of the technologies used and the proximity of the transacting parties.

Moreover, successful finance requires inputs for screening loan applicants (information management for signaling contract terms, creditworthiness evaluation, and loan approval), for monitoring borrowers, and for the efficient design and enforcement of contracts. These costs are a function of distance (geographic, occupational, cultural) and of feasible technologies used to produce these services. In addition, alternative technological arrangements result in specific comparative advantages in the provision of financial services in specific market niches. The choice of appropriate technology is critical. And finally, as the poor are so heterogeneous, so are the financial services that they demand, creating opportunities for different types of intermediaries to satisfy their demand.

Much innovation has taken place in microfinance technologies (Christen et al., 1995). The key to success is to design an intervention that is properly dimensioned to the size of the market and compatible with the nature of the clientele (Chaves and Gonzalez-Vega, 1996). Traditional banking technology, based on property as collateral and on financial statements, is prohibitively expensive for loans to the poor. Both lender and borrower transaction costs are too high in this case. Banks may, of course, adopt more information-intensive technologies than those that rely on traditional collateral (Gonzalez-Vega, 1997). That is, banks may embark on downscaling strategies (Krahnen and Schmidt, 1994).

There are major advantages in using banks as intermediaries. In their efforts to reach marginal clientele, they can operate with a national scope, under a clear regulatory framework, and they can leverage their equity with deposits from the public to achieve economies of scale and of scope (Gonzalez-Vega and Graham, 1995; Baydas et al., 1997). Banks need, however, a genuine technological revolution. Other non-bank organizations, in contrast, may possess comparative advantages in information and contract enforcement among these clienteles. These organizations may eventually be upgraded to become more like banks and thus overcome the weaknesses of their institutional design.

In either case, the challenge is to bring together those who have the informational and enforcement advantages (usually local agents) and those with sufficient resources and a willingness to lend and to accept the risks implied (governments and donors). This generates significant agency costs, as governments, donors, apex organizations, or bank headquarters have to monitor the decentralized operations of branches, credit unions, NGOs and the like (Jensen and Meckling, 1976). While decentralization can improve intermediary performance through better use of information, it complicates the tasks of internal control.

The role of organizations

There are two possible approaches to the question of improving access to credit for particular groups such as the poor:
(a) One may mandate portfolio quotas at banks and create special targeted lines of credit within existing formal intermediaries. Most likely this will not be the appropriate technology to reach the poor. One may even mandate subsidized loans for the target group; this has always been counterproductive, in the end hurting the intended beneficiaries.
(b) Alternatively, one may promote the development of viable intermediaries with a vocation for and a comparative advantage in the specific market niches where the poor operate. The desired clientele then would be reached indirectly, by targeting the development of organizations that typically serve these groups. In this way, the problem will be addressed by the development of appropriate technologies within sustainable organizations.

For this second approach to be successful, however, some strict conditions must be met. Experience has shown that no constraints on risk management should be placed on the lender, which should have full flexibility in evaluating creditworthiness and in collecting loans. In general, these intermediaries should be allowed to operate on market terms. These are common features of successful interventions, which have worked with, not against, the market (Von Pischke, 1991; Chaves and Gonzalez-Vega, 1996).

Appropriate technology is clearly a necessary condition for reaching the poor with sustainable financial services. It is not, however, a sufficient condition. While policies, procedures and technologies matter, policies will not be enacted, procedures will not be revised, and technologies will not be adopted unless it is in someone's interest to do so. In the end, all decisions are made by individuals who pursue their own objectives, given existing constraints.

Institutions constrain individual behavior, define property rights and incentives, and embody the rules of the game (North, 1992). Organizational design matters a lot because individual choices are induced and/or constrained by the structure of incentives within the organization. In this way organizational design influences behavior which, in turn, influences performance. If what matters is not just loanable funds but viable organizations, emphasis on designing efficient and viable organizations is critical. The dilemma is that a flood of donor and government funds tends to destroy adequate organizational designs. Building organizations rather than destroying them with excessive or misplaced donor funding is a major challenge.

The most difficult remaining question in the provision of financial services to the poor is thus the design of organizations with the correct structure of incentives and governance rules. As this depends so much on the structure of property rights of the organization, there are serious questions about the extent to which intermediaries with attenuated property rights structures (such as the earlier state-owned development banks and the new NGOs) or with conflicting governance rules (such as credit cooperatives) will be able to generate sustainable financial intermediation. The greatest challenge for the progress of finance for the poor, therefore, is in the institutional design of such organizations. This is, according to Krahnen and Schmidt (1994), the most promising and critical area for future donor assistance.

Moreover, because of several limitations of locally-based financial arrangements, such as limited opportunities for risk diversification and for intermediation, appropriate linking of local intermediaries to the aggregate financial system must be established in order to increase the viability of enforcement-effective and informationally-advantaged agents and to overcome the local, covariant, systemic risks and limited opportunities for intermediation that they face. Ultimately, what matters is the further development of financial systems and networks (e.g., new ways of economic organization). As markets grow and institutions are developed, formality will increase (although informality will not disappear), and the introduction of modern institutions will be required. For this, appropriate policies, cost-effective technologies, and viable organizational designs will still be needed.

Note

1   Even in stagnant economies, nevertheless, finance plays a role in consumption smoothing. This role is frequently performed well by informal financial arrangements (Udry, 1990).

References

Adams, D.W (1994), 'Altruistic or Production Finance? A Donor's Dilemma,' Economics and Sociology Occasional Paper No. 2150, The Ohio State University: Columbus, OH. Also presented as Chapter 5 of this book.

Adams, D.W and Fitchett, D.A. (eds.) (1992), *Informal Finance in Low-Income Countries*, Westview Press: Boulder, CO.

Adams, D.W, Graham, D.H. and Von Pischke, J.D. (eds.) (1984), *Undermining Rural Development with Cheap Credit*, Westview Press: Boulder, CO.

Aguilera-Alfred, N. and Gonzalez-Vega, C. (1993), 'A Multinomial Logit Analysis of Loan Targeting and Repayment at the Agricultural Development Bank of the Dominican Republic,' *Agricultural Finance Review*, Vol. 53, pp. 55–64.

Baker, C. (1973), 'The Role of Credit in the Economic Development of Small Farm Agriculture,' *Small Farmer Credit Analytical Papers*, Agency for International Development Spring Review of Small Farmer Credit: Washington, DC.

Baydas, M., Graham, D.H. and Valenzuela, L. (1997), 'Commercial Banks and Microfinance: New Actors in the Microfinance World,' Microfinance Best Practices Paper, Development Alternatives Inc., Bethesda, MD.

Biggs, T., Grindle, M.S. and Snodgrass, D.R. (1988), 'The Informal Sector, Policy Reform, and Structural Transformation,' in Jenkins, J. (ed.), *Beyond the Informal Sector: Including the Excluded in Developing Countries*, Institute for Contemporary Studies: San Francisco, CA, pp. 131–171.

Bouman, F.J.A. and Hospes, O. (eds.) (1994), *Financial Landscapes Reconstructed: The Fine Art of Mapping Development*, Westview Press: Boulder, CO.

Chaves, R.A. and Gonzalez-Vega, C. (1996), 'The Design of Successful Rural Financial Intermediaries: Evidence from Indonesia,' *World Development*, Vol. 24, No. 1 (January), pp. 65–78.

Christen, R.P., Rhyne, E., Vogel, R.C. and McKean, C. (1995), 'Maximizing the Outreach of Microenterprise Finance: The Emerging Lessons of Successful Programs,' USAID Program and Operations Assessment Report No. 10, AID Center for Development Information and Evaluation: Washington, DC.

Gonzalez-Vega, C. (1984), 'Cheap Agricultural Credit: Redistribution in Reverse,' in Adams, D.W, Graham, D.H. and Von Pischke, J.D. (eds.) (1984), *Undermining Rural Development with Cheap Credit*, Westview Press: Boulder, CO, pp. 120–132.

Gonzalez-Vega, C. (1993), 'From Policies, to Technologies, to Organizations: The Evolution of The Ohio State University Vision of Rural Financial Markets,' Economics and Sociology Occasional Paper No. 2062, The Ohio State University: Columbus, OH.

Gonzalez-Vega, C. (1994), 'Stages in the Evolution of Thought on Rural Finance. A Vision from The Ohio State University,' Economics and Sociology Occasional Paper No. 2134, The Ohio State University: Columbus, OH.

Gonzalez-Vega, C. (1997), 'Non-Bank Institutions in Financial Sector Reform,' in Harwood, A. and Smith, B.L.R. (eds.), *Sequencing? Financial Strategies for Developing Countries*, The Brookings Institution Press: Washington, DC, pp. 127–146.

Gonzalez-Vega, C. and Graham, D.H. (1995), 'State-Owned Agricultural Development Banks: Lessons and Opportunities for Microfinance,' GEMINI paper, Development Alternatives Inc.: Bethesda, MD.

Gonzalez-Vega, C., Guerrero, J.A., Vasquez, A. and Thraen, C. (1992), 'La Demanda por Servicios de Deposito en las Areas Rurales de la Republica Dominicana,' in Gonzalez-Vega, C. (ed.), *Republica Dominicana: Mercados Financieros Rurales y Movilizacion de Depositos*, The Ohio State University: Santo Domingo.

Gonzalez-Vega, C., Schreiner, M., Meyer, R.L., Rodriguez, J. and Navajas, S. (1997), 'The Challenge of Growth for Microfinance Organizations: The

Case of Banco Solidario in Bolivia,' in Schneider, H. (ed.), *Microfinance for the Poor?* Organization for Economic Co-operation and Development: Paris, pp. 129–167.

Grootaert, C. and Kanbur, R. (1990), 'Policy-Oriented Analysis of Poverty and the Social Dimensions of Structural Adjustment,' The World Bank SDA Working Paper, World Bank: Washington, DC.

Harrington, M. (1962), *The Other America: Poverty in the United States*, MacMillan: New York.

Jensen, M.C. and Meckling, W.H. (1976), 'Theory of the Firm: Managerial Behavior, Agency Costs, and Ownership Structure,' *Journal of Financial Economics*, Vol. 3, No. 4, pp. 305–360.

Jordan, J.L. (1993), 'Community Lending and Economic Development,' *Economic Commentary*, Federal Reserve Bank of Cleveland, November, 15.

Krahnen, J.P. and Schmidt, R.H. (1994), *Development Finance as Institution Building: A New Approach to Poverty-Oriented Banking*, Westview Press: Boulder, CO.

Long, M. (1983), 'A Note on Financial Theory and Economic Development,' in Von Pischke, J.D., Adams, D.W and Donald, G. (eds.), *Rural Financial Markets in Developing Countries: Their Use and Abuse*, The Johns Hopkins University Press: Baltimore, MD, pp. 22–28.

Minsky, H.P. et al. (1993), 'Community Development Banking,' Public Policy Brief No. 3, The Jerome Levy Economics Institute of Bard College: Annandale-on-Hudson, NY.

Morley, S.A. (1994), *Poverty and Inequality in Latin America: Past Evidence, Future Prospects*, Essay No. 13, Overseas Development Council: Washington, DC.

North, D.C. (1992), *Transaction Costs, Institutions, and Economic Performance*, International Center for Economic Growth: San Francisco, CA.

Otero, M. and Rhyne, E. (eds.) (1994), *The New World of Microenterprise Finance: Building Healthy Financial Institutions for the Poor*, Kumarian Press: West Hartford, CT.

Patten, R.H. and Rosengard, J.K. (1991), *Progress with Profits. The Development of Rural Banking in Indonesia*, International Center for Economic Growth: San Francisco, CA.

Pirela Martinez, H. (1990), 'The Grey Area in Microenterprise Development,' *Grass Roots Development*, Vol. 14, No. 2, pp. 33–40.

Poyo, J., Gonzalez-Vega, C. and Aguilera-Alfred, N. (1993), 'The Depositor as a Principal in Public Development Banks and Credit Unions: Illustrations from the Dominican Republic,' Economics and Sociology Occasional Paper No. 2061, The Ohio State University: Columbus, OH.

Reagan, R. (1982), 'Remarks Before the National Black Republican Council,' *Weekly Compilation of Presidential Documents*, 18, September 14, 1152–1157, GPO: Washington, DC.

Rhyne, E. and Otero, M. (1994), 'Financial Services for Microenterprises: Principles and Institutions,' in Otero, M. and Rhyne, E. (eds.), *The New World of Microenterprise Finance: Building Healthy Financial Institutions for the Poor*, Kumarian Press: West Hartford, CT, pp. 11–26.

Robinson, M.S. (1994), 'Savings Mobilization and Microenterprise Finance: The Indonesian Experience,' in Otero, M. and Rhyne, E. (eds.), *The New World of Microenterprise Finance: Building Healthy Financial Institutions for the Poor*, Kumarian Press: West Hartford, CT, pp. 27–54.

Schmidt, R. and Zeitinger, C.-P. (1994), 'Critical Issues in Small and Microbusiness Finance,' paper presented at the International Donor Conference on Financial Sector Development, Vienna.

Shultz, T.W. (1992), 'Foreword,' in Castañeda, T. (ed.), *Combating Poverty: Innovative Social Reforms in Chile During the 1980s*, International Center for Economic Growth: San Francisco, CA.

Stiglitz, J. E. (1993), 'The Role of the State in Financial Markets,' *Proceedings of the World Bank Annual Conference on Development Economics*, World Bank: Washington, DC.

Stiglitz, J.E. and Weiss, A. (1981), 'Credit Rationing in Markets with Imperfect Information,' *American Economic Review*, Vol. 71, No. 3, pp. 393–410.

Udry, C. (1990), 'Credit Markets in Northern Nigeria: Credit as Insurance in a Rural Economy,' *The World Bank Economic Review*, Vol. 4, No. 3, pp. 251–71.

Von Pischke, J.D. (1991), *Finance at the Frontier: Debt Capacity and the Role of Credit in the Private Economy*, The World Bank: Washington, DC.

Von Pischke, J.D. and Adams, D.W (1983), 'Fungibililty and the Design and Evaluation of Agricultural Credit Projects,' *American Journal of Agricultural Economics*, Vol. 62, No. 4 (November), pp. 719–26.

3 Critical issues in microbusiness finance and the role of donors

REINHARD H. SCHMIDT & CLAUS-PETER ZEITINGER

Introduction

The conceptual basis of the study

Although the international donor community has, over the years, made numerous serious attempts to make financial services available to the poor segments of the economically active population of developing countries, it is fair to say that something approaching a consensus on goals and methods has only recently begun to emerge. This 'new view' has its roots in a longer tradition of development finance policy and thinking about the broad issues it addresses.[1]

After the Second World War and into the 1970s, development finance was not particularly concerned about poor target groups. This started to change when it became obvious that the channeling of massive amounts of foreign funds to large projects in the developing countries did not lead to the 'trickle down effect' which had been expected. In the early 1970s, the concept of target group orientation began to emerge. As far as financing was concerned, donors started a wave of small, diverse projects which were meant to make credit available to the poor.

An early mechanism for broadening access to finance was through funding for publicly-owned financial institutions. However, these efforts failed almost everywhere. This failure of formal directed credit institutions led to the evolution of a more radical version of target group-oriented financing. This new approach gained particular prominence in the 1980s and consisted of setting up credit programs largely outside of the banking sector as well as outside of the reach of governments. Under this approach, non-governmental organizations (NGOs) and self-help groups (SHGs) were used as conduits for donor funds. Their ability to reach the small and very small borrowers, which is unmatched by other types of institutions, was seen as their main strength.

The main drawbacks of these efforts were that such financing schemes proved extremely costly for donors and, at least in some cases, for the borrowers as well; they inevitably failed to reach large numbers of their target group; and, most importantly in our view, these foreign injections of funds did not lead to the creation of institutions which would have been able to play a lasting role in the lives of their 'beneficiaries'.[2]

The 'new view' that has emerged in the 1990s responds to the 'blind spots' exhibited by a development strategy which was *only* target group-oriented.[3] In addition to a clear gearing of efforts to *poorer target groups* in urban as well as rural environments, the new view consists of a fruitful combination of three main elements:

A focus on *institution building*: Aid efforts should not be directly oriented to the provision of financial services to the target group, but rather to the creation of financial institutions which would be both able and motivated to cater to the relevant target group or groups. Setting up or strengthening such institutions should therefore be the primary objective of aid projects in the field of development finance.

A *commercial approach*: The essential elements of a commercial approach are that the institution tries to keep its costs as low as possible and is able—and also formally permitted—to charge interest rates and fees which are commensurate with its total costs. A commercial approach to small and micro-lending is necessary because only an institution which, at least over the medium term, is able to cover its costs can hope to remain in existence and to provide benefits to its clients on a continuing and predictable basis.

A *financial systems orientation*: Activities geared to improving the access of poor target groups to financial services need to look at things in the broad perspective of countries' entire financial systems. The most important consideration in this is that an improvement of the overall financial system is likely to bring the greatest benefit to the target group over the long term.

This chapter is based on this new view of small and micro-business finance and, accordingly, incorporates the financial systems perspective, the commercial perspective and the institution-building perspective.

Purpose, orientation and structure of the chapter

In our view, donor agencies and the experts working for them should try to make maximum use of the new view outlined above. However, we realize that it will not be easy to follow this recommendation. In fact, the starting point for this chapter is the proposition that putting the general principles into practice turns out to be much more difficult than some of their advocates seem to believe—and also more difficult than some donor agencies have probably been led to believe. Given these difficulties, we find it appropriate to strictly limit the focus of this chapter to what we consider to be the most important questions in the field of small and micro-business financing. The purpose of this concentration is to provide an orientation for donor institutions which, through their funding decisions, essentially determine the nature of the development projects in the field discussed here.

This chapter contains three main sections, each dealing primarily with one main problem. The first is the credit business of a target group-oriented financial institution. The focus is on the choice of a credit technology and on the imperative of keeping costs low and achieving cost coverage which forces such institutions to adopt a special credit technology. This technology is discussed and its efficiency is compared with that of the 'group lending approach.'

The second is the provision of deposit facilities to members of the target group. The discussion centers on the role the deposit business should play in the process of building a financial institution which is clearly target group-oriented, cost-conscious and innovative in its efforts to lend to small and micro entrepreneurs.

The third is institution building using downscaling and upgrading strategies. Its main message is that institution-building projects are useful and that they can be successful, but that they tend to take much more time and require much more effort and commitment on the part of the donors than they usually think or seem willing to acknowledge.

Credit

Credit technologies for target group-oriented lending

The feasibility of issuing credit to a target group comprised of poor people who rarely have adequate financial records and who cannot furnish conventional types of credit security has been questioned for as long as such efforts have been attempted. However, the costs and risks entailed in lending to this target group are not a 'given'; instead, they are a function of the *credit technology* which is being employed. One objective of this section is to dispel the general doubts concerning lending to the target group. The second objective is to undertake a comparison of two 'competing' credit technologies.

Generally speaking, 'credit technology' covers the entire range of activities carried out by a lending institution having to do with: selecting borrowers; determining the type of loan to be offered, the loan amount and maturity and the way in which it is to be secured; and the monitoring and recovery of loans. A given credit technology is characterized by some configuration of these features. One can distinguish two classes of credit technologies which we characterize here as 'individual-based' and 'group-based' technologies.

The non-conventional individual-based credit technology

As conventional banking technology is asset- and document-based, its applicability in the case of the target group of small and micro entrepreneurs is obviously quite limited. The alternative individual-based credit technology we shall call the *non-conventional credit technology*. It is being applied by certain formal financial intermediaries and NGOs in Asia, Latin America and Eastern Europe, and is different from the first one insofar as it has been adapted to the special situation of borrowers from the small and micro-business sector. The non-conventional credit technology retains the advantages of dealing with each individual case separately and is tailored to the situation of the individual borrower, but it uses direct inspection to acquire information about the borrower rather than documents.

The advantage of the individual-based credit technology from the point of view of the borrower is lower transaction costs. This is the case because the financial institution externalizes neither the risk-induced nor the administrative costs. However, from the point of view of the lender, an individual-based credit technology will prove to be competitive only if it succeeds in minimizing loan loss risk and administrative costs or at least reducing them to a level which does not jeopardize the financial viability of the lending institution. How does the non-conventional credit technology attempt to achieve this result?

The default risk is reduced by using non-conventional methods of analyzing the borrowers' debt capacity, and by supplying a product that is tailored to the situation of the target group. The credit analysis is based on an assessment of the 'family enterprise' in its totality, and in particular its *ability* to repay even if the borrowed funds have no impact on the earnings potential of the family business. This limits the credit risks and obviates the need to monitor the specific uses to which loans are put, which would not be feasible in any event. Loan sizes as well as maturities and repayment patterns are also determined in such a way that the risk for lenders and borrowers is limited.

Although an attempt is also made *ex ante* to ascertain the *willingness* of the borrower to repay the loan, the credit technology still has to include unambiguous penalty mechanisms which reduce moral hazard. This means, among other things, that borrowers are asked to pledge assets as collateral which they can easily provide but which would be relatively expensive or difficult for them to replace if they were seized. With this type of collateral policy, the primary goal of the lending institution is to make the borrowers take seriously their payment obligations. The non-conventional technology also provides for the utilization of rigorous credit monitoring and recovery procedures in the case of arrears, complementing the penalty mechanisms mentioned above.

The credit technology would fail to have the desired effect if it were not backed up by control and organizational structures at the lending institution which ensure incentive-compatible implementation. Accordingly, an institution utilizing the individual-based credit technology will make a single loan officer responsible for the entire loan-granting process as well as its relationship with the client after disbursement of the funds. This enables the officer to develop a quasi-personal relationship with 'his' or 'her' borrowers which gives access to significantly more information about clients and their businesses over time. The effectiveness of this system can be enhanced by introducing performance-based pay programs for the lending staff.

A significant reduction in administrative costs is achieved by offering only a limited range of standardized products and by introducing as many standardized, routine procedures as possible into the credit process. Special computer software packages designed to meet the specific requirements of the credit technology are often employed.

Group-based credit technologies

The other class of credit technologies are those which involve groups of borrowers in one form or another in the process of issuing and recovering loans. Two variants are of special importance here. One uses what may be characterized as 'groups as loan guarantors'; in the other variant, the group plays more of a social role, and it may be characterized as the 'group as social network' approach.

The individual-based credit technology gives rise to specific risk-induced and administrative costs which the lender should strive to minimize. The group-based credit technology seems to imply that the lending institution can avoid incurring precisely these kinds of costs by employing group pressure or formal group liability, and by shifting a considerable portion of its administrative costs onto its borrowers.

Therefore, it is not too surprising that group loans to members of economically disadvantaged target groups are fairly popular not only among certain new financial institutions and a great many credit-granting NGOs; they are also generally viewed favorably by most of the international donor community. Taking their cue from the Grameen Bank, a number of institutions, especially in Latin America, are using some features of this model. Accordingly, given the fact that the Grameen Bank is considered to be the most outstanding positive example of a successful group-lending program, it is advisable to take a closer look at how this bank really goes about its lending activities and how other institutions which apply a group-based credit technology differ from this model.

Most surprisingly, closer inspection reveals that the Grameen Bank does not make use of any kind of formal group liability. Nor does it rely very much on 'peer pressure', which is alleged to be the distinguishing characteristic of group lending systems of all types, to influence the borrowers' repayment behavior. In fact, it does not impose any penalties whatsoever on a group if one of its members is either unable or unwilling to pay. The group merely has a moral obligation to act as a social support system for its members and to try to induce a delinquent borrower to make her payments. Thus, the bank chooses not to exploit the potential of the group as a means of enforcing group liability. Instead, it appears that the institution prefers a more individualistic form of liability reflected, for example, in its policy of requiring that its individual members secure their loans with tangible assets whenever this is technically feasible.[4]

Group-based lending approaches have been popular for a number of years in Latin America, and more and more credit-granting institutions have developed approaches which appear to be similar to the one used by the Grameen Bank without, however, being able to achieve a comparable degree of coverage of their target groups.

In our view, there are three major differences between the group-based credit technology used in Latin America and the one developed by the Grameen Bank.

Differences in the process of forming groups: This process can take up to six months in Bangladesh and is carried out with extreme care. Yet, group formation would appear to be relatively easy since the target group is defined in extremely narrow terms and most of the members of that target group live in small villages with rigid, traditional social structures and normally have known each other for quite some time. As a consequence, the borrower groups of the Grameen Bank tend to be very stable. In Latin America, on the other hand, group formation usually does not take much longer than a week although there tends to be less social cohesion among the group members to begin with. Consequently, the groups are quite unstable.

Differences in the concept of group liability: The Latin American version of the group-based credit technology adheres much more strictly to the principle of group liability and indeed, requires the use of a formal joint and several liability arrangement.

Differences in the cost of loans: The loans issued by Latin American financial NGOs using this group-based credit technology rarely carry an effective interest rate of less than 50% per annum in real terms, which is significantly higher than the costs incurred by the Grameen Bank's borrowers.[5]

In our view, the group-based credit technology as it is used in most cases in Latin America represents a kind of inverted, 'mirror-image' version of the system used by the Grameen Bank which misses the point of what the intermediary in Bangladesh has done.

Comparing group-based and individual-based lending

This section compares elements of the group-based and the non-conventional individual-based credit technology. The criteria for such a comparison must relate to both the demand side, i.e. the borrowers, and the supply side, namely the financial institutions.

Considered from the point of view of institutions, a credit technology can be called 'efficient' if it makes it possible to reach the target group more effectively and to do so at a lower total cost to the lending institution than would be possible with other credit technologies. This definition focuses on the productivity and the cost-efficiency of the technology.[6]

For the purpose of comparing efficiency, we have compiled and analyzed data from a number of formal and semi-formal financial credit-granting institutions in Asia and Latin America which cater mainly or exclusively to small borrowers and use one of the two approaches. The institutions included in the comparison are generally considered to be very positive examples of users of the respective technology.

We have derived three hypotheses concerning the relationship between the productivity and cost-efficiency of the two credit technologies and tested them on the basis of the data:

Group lending has an advantage over individual-based lending in that *at an early stage* of the life of a credit program, group lending is more productive and cost-efficient.

The reason for this hypothesis is that, according to the claims made by advocates of the group-based lending approach, and based on what we know about the way in which groups are in fact being formed in Latin America, the process of setting up groups takes less time and is less costly than the corresponding learning and training process which is required in the case of an individual-based credit technology. On the basis of the available evidence this hypothesis could not be rejected.

In the course of time, however, the productivity and cost-efficiency of an institution using group lending increases only moderately, while a bank or NGO lending on a strictly individual basis can increase its efficiency rather quickly.

The reason for this hypothesis is that the group lending technology shifts a considerable part of the burden of selecting customers and monitoring their repayment behavior onto the target group and thus 'externalizes' bank functions. In so doing, a bank using this technology deprives itself of the opportunity to learn from its experience and thereby to reduce its administrative costs. In contrast, the notion of learning, of getting to know customers better and developing routine procedures for issuing, monitoring and collecting loans is at the core of the individual-based lending technology. By comparing pairs of institutions of similar age, nature and location, and by evaluating the limited data on time series which we were able to gather, we found strong empirical evidence that this hypothesis is correct.

The efficiency of a *relatively old institution* using groups is still higher than that of a bank or NGO of comparable age which employs the individual-based credit technology.

The reason for this hypothesis is that shifting important functions of the financial institution onto the borrower groups is assumed to lead to cost savings for the institution, as this is a central part of the rationale of the group lending approach. Thus, even a bank which has had substantial experience in the utilization of the individual-based credit technology would presumably not be able to compensate for this cost advantage of the group approach. Although the evidence on this hypothesis is mixed and somewhat inconclusive, there are some indications that it is wrong.

Empirical testing of these hypotheses on the basis of scant information from a handful of institutions is difficult. Nevertheless, we consider the results of our preliminary analysis to be highly revealing: If the first hypothesis were correct and the third one wrong, this would imply that, due to increases in efficiency over time caused merely by institutional learning of the kind that can take place with the individual-based technology, an individual-oriented bank would eventually outperform a comparable group-oriented bank or NGO in terms of efficiency. What appears to be a strength of the group-based technology at first sight, namely the externalization of vital banking functions, turns out to be a weakness in the longer run, as it prevents the financial institution from learning and reducing its operating costs. Given a sufficiently long time horizon, which is called for in development finance projects, the discounted value of the total administrative costs of an individual-based-technology bank might then be lower than those of a comparable bank employing the group-based lending approach.

The assessment from the perspective of the lending institution has to be supplemented by an assessment from the *perspective of borrowers*. Both groups of institutions which we have compared have the same target group and are equally accessible. However, with respect to the speed with which a loan can be obtained, flexibility regarding the terms of the loan, and most importantly with regard to transaction costs, the non-conventional individual-based technology is definitely superior to all kinds of group-lending technologies for small and micro entrepreneurs. Even if a difference in cost-efficiency at the level of the suppliers of credit is difficult to establish, the balance of both kinds of costs would seem to show quite clearly that the individual-based non-conventional credit technology is the better of the two. Thus, donors should reconsider the preference which some of them seem to have for the group lending approach.

Savings

The relevance of saving

Fortunately, saving is no longer *the forgotten half of development finance* (Vogel, 1984). In order to avoid any misunderstanding of the main proposition which we advance in this section, we will begin by emphasizing the significance of saving in a macro and a micro-economic perspective and, at the same time, the significance of deposit-taking as a service to clients and as a source of funds for financial institutions:

From a macroeconomic perspective, saving is necessary as the basis of capital accumulation.

From the perspective of the customers, deposit facilities provide a service which is needed by all groups in society, namely, carrying over stores of wealth from one period to the next. Demand for deposit facilities includes poor people and small and microentrepreneurs.

From the perspective of *all* financial institutions, deposit mobilization is an important means for funding the lending operations of the banking system. However, the new view of small business finance takes a financial systems perspective. This perspective provides the straightforward insight that no single institution should be viewed or treated as though it were the entire system. The three benefits to savings listed above apply without qualification to the financial sectors of countries and regions. But they do not necessarily apply to all institutions at all stages of their development. For example, we do not think that deposit facilities are a necessary element of innovative urban-based financial institutions which direct most of their lending to small and microentrepreneurs. For them and their credit customers, specialization in lending may be more advisable as long as they are still growing rapidly and can fund this growth independently of deposit taking.

As neither macroeconomic nor demand-side considerations make it imperative that *all* institutions develop a deposit business, we must look all the more closely at the supply side and ask why target group-oriented financial institutions should be or should become full service banks. The question is worth asking for the simple reason that most donor agencies seem to have developed a strong preference for target group-oriented full service banks in recent years. They have come to consider the full service bank model as an ideal from a development policy perspective.

Two models of a target group-oriented full service bank

There are, in fact, two different models of a 'full service bank'. One model can be called the *intra-sectoral full service bank*. Such a bank would mobilize the bulk of its deposits from the same target group to which it directs most of its lending. Some observers would regard such a full service bank as the absolute ideal. The relevant question in relation to this model is simply: Is it realistic for an institution which considers poor people, and in particular small and microentrepreneurs, as its target group to gather deposits from its clients?

The other model would be an *inter-sectoral full service bank* which tries to lend to people poorer than those from which it collects the bulk of its deposits. The most interesting question in relation to this model is this: Is it beneficial to members of the target group that 'their' financial institution mobilizes deposits from other segments of society?

Empirical evidence

It is useful to examine the available empirical evidence in order to assess the feasibility and the advisability of the two models of a full service bank. Unfortunately, there are few well-documented case studies of successful savings programs at target group-oriented financial institutions. The relevant literature, fascinated by the sheer ability of small savers to put aside money, rarely contains hard empirical data which would allow one to evaluate the concept of a target group-oriented full service bank. Such data would tell us about:

- the size distribution of savings as an indicator of where deposits come from;
- the interest costs and administrative costs of mobilizing savings from different groups of depositors;
- the stability of the deposit base; and
- the relationship between the volume of deposits and the volume of lending.

Examining empirical data on the deposit mobilization efforts of some well-known development finance institutions in Asia and Latin America, we note that certain Asian institutions like BKK and the BRI Village Units in Indonesia have the reputation of being very successful in this field. But considered in detail the success of BKK is quite limited as far as *voluntary* savings are concerned. BKK's mobilization of *small savings* is insufficient to fund its lending operations to any appreciable extent. The Village Unit system is more successful. There appear to be several interesting reasons for its success. First of all, its deposits are guaranteed by the big government-owned bank BRI, of which the Village Unit Program is a part. Secondly, it offers considerably higher interest rates than, say, BRI itself, thus raising the possibility that many deposit customers of BRI may simply have shifted their deposits to another part of the same conglomerate. In macroeconomic terms as well as in terms of improving the supply of deposit facilities, the value of these savings services may therefore be quite limited.

Although we do not have data on administrative costs, the high interest costs alone would support the hypothesis that mobilizing savings is an expensive proposition in Asia.

The experience of certain target group-oriented financial institutions in Latin America points in the same direction: even when normal market interest rates are offered, *voluntary* saving by members of the *target group* contributes only a small volume of deposits. Thus, a rapidly expanding target group-oriented financial institution clearly needs alternative sources of funding. If it seeks to obtain these additional funds on the local market for deposits, it will find it difficult to quickly attract savings capital from members of the middle class even if it offers a substantial interest rate premium. This is so because it takes a new independent bank several years to gain the trust of potential savings customers and because competition among financial institutions for their business is intense in cities and for this group of clients.

The Peruvian municipal savings banks are an interesting case which shows how difficult it is to implement the model of an inter-sectoral full service bank. Over the last few years these institutions' savings deposit volume has been equivalent to more than 100% of their outstanding loans. The savings banks' growth in recent years has been a function of their ability to attract deposits, which has proved to be a rigid constraint to their growth. A considerably higher growth in savings would have been needed to satisfy the credit demand of the target group and to enjoy economies of scale which could have been exploited with additional funding.[7]

The case of the Peruvian municipal savings banks provides the rare opportunity to analyze the administrative costs of mobilizing savings. Rochus Mommartz's[8] (1994) study conducted in the context of GTZ's support to the Peruvian savings banks finds that in 1993 the full costs of savings mobilization exceeded 10% of the stock of total deposits. A large part of these deposits came from big savers and institutions. The full costs of mobilizing small savings, defined as balances of less than US$ 500, amount to a surprising 40% per year, despite the fact that these banks have, with foreign assistance, gone a long way in introducing cost-saving administrative procedures and that they make ample use of electronic data processing techniques.

Implications

The evidence provides additional confirmation of what has become common knowledge: there is a demand on the part of small savers for appropriate deposit facilities. And this implies that a target group-oriented institution, as well as the people who run it and the donors who support it, must seek to ensure that there is a supply available to meet this demand.

In marked contrast to the situation in many rural areas, where a development finance institution is often the only one that offers formal deposit facilities, in the urban environments in which most of the financial institutions that lend to small and micro entrepreneurs operate, there are in most cases deposit facilities available 'in the market'. Therefore, these institutions need not provide complicated and costly deposit services for borrowers from their main target group *at an early stage of their lives as institutions*, and they should not be forced to restrict the scale of their credit operations to that dictated by the volume of funds generated by their mobilization of small savings.

A possible objection to this proposition is that there are synergies between the lending and the deposit business of a bank. But the discussion of credit presented above shows that credit technologies for reaching this target group can be placed on a cost-minimization path and substitutes can be found for these synergies. Evidence implies that the benefits of deposit mobilization are not necessarily important enough to offset the high costs of administering such facilities. In particular, the limited quantity of funds mobilized in the form of small savings will not provide the basis for robust growth among institutions targeting poor people and small and microentrepreneurs.

In regard to the model of the inter-sectoral full service bank, what are the implications of gearing savings operations mainly to middle- and upper-class depositors? How will this effect the quality of the lending operations, which are directed mainly at lower-class borrowers?

The most important consequence of efforts to attract savers from the middle class is that the institutions incur high funding costs as middle-class savers often must be induced to switch banks. Savings from the middle class are also relatively more volatile and force the

institution to hold higher liquidity reserves. In addition, the mobilization of a sufficient volume of savings from the middle class induces
the institutions to make changes in their credit business and in the
general orientation of their business policy as they must have at least
some of the attributes of a normal full service bank in order to attract
these customers. Thus, securing the business of middle-class savings
customers cannot be expected to lead to an increase in the quality of a
target group-oriented intermediary's credit business with its primary
clientele.

With respect to the way in which a target group-oriented
intermediary defines its basic mission, one possible consequence of
this attempt to accommodate a different social class is a gradual shift
away from the target group it was originally designed to serve. A
similar case can be made against efforts to attract big savers, including
institutions. Thus, the inter-sectoral full service bank is also a concept
which proves to be difficult to implement on an economically sound
basis and one which is questionable from a development-policy
standpoint.

This raises the question of where the bulk of the funding required
for onlending will come from: funds must be attracted. The precise
extent to which large local deposits should be sought will be a
function of the institution's size and age. We feel that new and clearly
target group-oriented institutions should be able to rely primarily on
long-term borrowing from bilateral and/or multilateral financial
cooperation programs. In view of the total costs of other sources of
funds, it is evident that access to foreign aid funds at normal, market-
oriented rates is in itself a valuable form of assistance for the
institutions which we are considering here. There is no need to
provide these funds at concessionary rates. Foreign funding does
create a form of dependence, but overall we feel that this dependence
has fewer negative consequences for a consistent, long-term target
group-orientation than a dependence on the savings deposits of other
social strata.

Institution building

Assumptions and evaluation criteria

A strategy of development finance as institution building is based on
three assumptions:

The economic and social situation of the target group can be improved if more and better financial services are offered to them. Providing more and better financial services requires that there be institutions which can supply these services on a continuing basis and which are motivated to do so.

An institution can provide adequate financial services to the poor only if it is financially viable, or can at least become financially viable over the medium term.

From an institution-building perspective, financial institutions should meet two requirements. They should be target group-oriented and they should be financially sound. These two requirements are not in conflict in the long run, although there may be conflicts in the short run.

In accordance with the general thrust of our chapter, this section will concentrate on an issue which can be considered to be of particular importance and practical relevance from a donor perspective: How can viable financial institutions be created, and what does this require in terms of donor support? The general message of this section is that institution-building projects are so worthwhile and so difficult that it seems to be advisable for donors to treat them as projects in their own right and not to consider institution building merely as something which is added on to projects which basically have a different focus.

Selecting partner institutions

The ideal institution which donors might select or create as a partner institution would be: socially close to the target group; professional as a bank and therefore able to keep its costs relatively low; on good terms with but not too close to the respective government; and efficiency-oriented without being profit-oriented.

In an explicit institution-building approach to lending to targeted groups, the selection of a partner institution is regarded as a problem of choosing among various alternatives mainly on the basis of the first two criteria mentioned above, i.e., target group-orientation and professionalism.

A crucial aspect of partner selection is ownership and governance structure. Institution building typically entails the task of finding a suitable owner or creating an ownership position. This task consists of assigning the function of being responsible for the project to some specific person or institution. We will call this person or group of persons or institution 'the owner'. In doing so we employ a

functional or economic concept of ownership.[9] The owner in this
broad sense assumes that ultimate responsibility for the success or
failure of the project resides in the developing country.

Ownership in this sense does not necessarily imply legal
ownership, but legal ownership may be the basis of functional
ownership; and, of course, a private commercial bank or the
government of the respective country can be an owner, too. How
problematic the implications of private or public ownership will prove
to be depends in large part on the governance structure. The
governance structure consists of the specific regulations which define
the responsibilities and powers of the owners in relation to the project
and the local institution which carries it out.[10]

It is important to point out that the governance structure of the
partner institution should not be treated as a given but should be
designed carefully as part of project design. This is why there are no a
priori grounds for considering only certain types of institutions, with
certain ownership and governance structures, as eligible and suitable
partners and 'objects' of institution-building projects. In particular,
neither government-owned banks nor private commercial banks
should be ruled out as partners, although it will probably be more
difficult to shape the governance structure in an appropriate way with
these kinds of owners than, for example, in cases where an NGO is the
partner institution.

The concept of 'downscaling': how to make a financial institution
more target group-oriented

Downscaling as one of the standard strategies in the field of financial
institution building[11] presupposes that there is a formal financial
institution which could in principle provide financial services,
especially credit, to the target group, but which has so far not served
this market segment. It assumes that the institution's owners have an
interest—for one reason or another—in reaching this target group.

The financial sector reforms initiated in many countries during
the last decade have created an environment which makes the
provision of financial services to entrepreneurs from the small
business community, if not an attractive proposition, at least
conceivable from the point of view of commercial banks. There are
now market forces in place which would in principle induce existing
banks to go 'down market' in their efforts to expand their customer
bases. As these forces are still weak, however, it may be worthwhile to

strengthen them through additional incentives to induce formal institutions to better serve the financing activities of the target group.

There are certainly banks which will, over the medium to long term, adopt or develop on their own the credit technology and the organizational structures to serve this new type of client. And it is precisely these banks which are most likely to be interested in becoming partners in a downscaling project. Facilitating this process may be especially attractive if it involves an existing branch network that could quickly reach a broad client base.

This raises the question of whether it is legitimate from a development-policy standpoint to accelerate a process which will take place anyway. Our answer to this question is clearly affirmative: if a development project speeded up this process in a bank with a large branch network by five years, many small entrepreneurs could get access to formal credit five years earlier.

On a practical level, the concerns which even innovation-minded banks may have with regard to the risks and costs of small-business and informal-sector lending are an obstacle to the successful implementation of a downscaling strategy. There is, however, a sizable body of empirical evidence indicating that loans to microenterprises can indeed exhibit lower arrears and default rates than loans to large enterprises, provided that a suitable incentive structure is in place and that an appropriate credit technology is employed. Downscaling requires, first of all, that this empirical information be made available to prospective partner institutions.

The core of donor activities in a downscaling project is the transfer of a lending technology like the one described above, and the considerable start-up costs of introducing such a technology and implementing the organizational structures which this technology presupposes. It is precisely these start-up costs which may pose an almost insurmountable obstacle to the initiation of small and micro lending activities by institutions that are in principle willing to do so. International donor organizations should be prepared to provide short-term support to enable participating institutions to overcome their reservations. Such assistance, which amounts to a short-term subsidization program, would provide incentives for a bank which is generally willing in principle but still reluctant in practice, and also ensure that the start-up costs are not passed on in full to the institution's small and micro credit customers, even though in some cases this would be feasible.

The practical experience acquired by the Inter-American Development Bank (IDB) and the European Bank for Reconstruction and Development (EBRD) illustrates the potential of, and the problems posed by, an explicit downscaling strategy. The strategy appears to work well now. Nevertheless, in the beginning a great many reservations had to be overcome at the level of the donor institution, the participating banks and the respective governments. As an outcome of a lengthy learning process, the donor institutions are now less concerned than they were initially about the fact that, through the cooperation program they do interfere with the internal structure of the participating banks to a substantial degree.

'Upgrading': how to build an NGO and turn it into a small bank

In this section, we present some stylized facts relating to the process of how an institution which tries to concentrate on providing credit to small and micro businesses is born, grows up and becomes a formal financial institution. Formalization provides the potential to play a lasting role as an element of the financial system and as a provider of financial services to persons who have traditionally not had access to formal credit. Based on the experience of GTZ, the German Agency for Technical Cooperation, in specific projects in Latin America with the strong support of the Microenterprise Division of the IDB, three messages are conveyed about the upgrading strategy:

Creating or supporting an NGO and converting it into a formal institution with a consistent target group orientation is a process which takes a long time to complete. During this time, the institution has to be able to rely on continuous and appropriate support from the donor or donors.

The most crucial aspects of the process are finding the appropriate combination of technical and financial assistance, and ensuring that the different forms of support, and especially the provision of funds for onlending, are forthcoming at the right time and in the right quantities.

The process of building a financial institution should lead to a situation in which the institution's operating income is sufficient to cover its full costs. There is no way around the fact that, before this stage is reached, there is a need for donors' subsidies. Even in the final stage the operating costs passed on to the institution's customers are likely to be high when measured by conventional standards.

For ease of exposition—and because this proves to be advisable in practice—we assume that the partner organization is, or will be, an NGO. This is the typical case. In cases where this is not so the substance of our arguments still applies.

The creation of a financial NGO

In the first phase, an NGO is created or modified. Four elements are needed in order for this to take place. These four elements have to be designed very carefully and, typically, with considerable involvement of the relevant donor or donors. They are:

A legal form: The institution should be a non-profit organization (NPO), preferably constituted under private law. Its formal status should allow it to have a certain degree of independence from the people behind it, and it should be legally able to conduct serious lending business and to receive donations from foreign institutions. These considerations make the legal form of a foundation more advisable than the alternative form, which would be an association.

A governance structure and by-laws: At the heart of the governance structure is the definition of the institution's mission. In our case, it consists of providing appropriate financial services to a specific target group on a financially sound basis. In the by-laws, the mission should be formulated explicitly, and expressed in operational terms to the greatest degree possible.

The governance structure gives a board of trustees supreme authority to determine the institution's business policy and ultimate responsibility for internal control, yet provides for its business operations to be run by a management (preferably a team) which must perform its functions with a high degree of professional competence and whose members should not simultaneously sit on the board of trustees.

Key individuals: A foundation's governing body is its board of trustees. It is composed of individuals who are ultimately the project partners. The board's composition should above all reflect the interests and objectives which will shape the character of the future financial institution. Ideally, it should include a number of individuals with a successful track record in business, some with experience in banking, and others experienced in the field of social services.

Money and commitment: With this type of donor-supported NGO it is neither necessary nor desirable for the initial capital to be raised by the founders and/or board members themselves, and this for two reasons. First, very few of the people who have the qualifications required for board membership would be capable of providing a significant contribution relative to the amounts that would be needed very soon after the start of an NGO's operations. And second, significant disparities in individual capital contributions would tend to rob the group of its all-important internal cohesiveness. This has an important implication: in order to guarantee from the outset that all members of the board of trustees enjoy equal status, it is essential that the start-up and original endowment capital be provided by a donor organization (albeit subject to conditions).

The growth and transformation process

Assuming that a new NGO has been set up, or, as the case may be, that an existing NGO has been chosen as the basis for the project, the following scenario illustrates the possible economic and technical development of a donor-supported financial NGO. The scenario shows the sequence of steps and the extent of the institution's funds budgeted for onlending, as well as the optimal timing for such injections. Funding should be covered by the donor or donors in addition to the technical cooperation component they provide.[12]

The scenario covers a time span of *ten* years. The first *four years* are the time needed for the NGO to reach financial sustainability. This is taken as a precondition for transformation into a formal financial institution. The remaining six years can be roughly divided into a phase of rapid efficiency growth and a subsequent phase of slower growth in efficiency. From the tenth year on, further growth is assumed to be possible only by a purely quantitative expansion of operations.

During the first year the institution's lending operations will be on a small scale, with a small portfolio and a small number of employees, each of whom is responsible for only a small number of customers and a limited portfolio. The funds used for lending are essentially endowment capital. The initial loans are very small, not only because of the particular target group involved, but also because the institution needs to exercise caution while learning to deal with the new borrowers. Despite high interest income of 40% per annum on the average outstanding portfolio, the institution will not cover its costs during this first year. The technical assistance component during the first year, as well as during the two following years, should include support by several international and local experts and the donation of computer hardware and fixed assets.

In the second year it will be possible to treble the volume of lending, since both the absolute number of staff members and their efficiency will have increased. (The new institution is assumed to use a lending technology similar to the one which we have called the non-conventional technology.) The specific advantage of this lending technology is that it enables the institution and its loan officers to learn from experience, and by so doing to achieve a rapid and substantial increase in productivity.

Once the institution is more experienced in working with the target group, the average size of the loans will rise slightly. During the second year, the institution must receive additional funds from the donor or donors in order to secure its growth and productivity increase. But this time the funding should take the form of an interest-free loan, not of a grant.

The third year will see another large increase in the number of borrowers, and they can be served more effectively due to the opening of new branch offices. Average loan sizes and maturities will again rise slightly. A combination of the increased number of employees, the further improvement in their efficiency and the rise in the average loan amount, together with a constant level of interest rates, leads to an earnings situation which, for the first time, enables the institution to cover all its operating and risk-induced costs. To ensure that the institution grows optimally, it needs to receive an additional injection of funds from outside in the form of a 'soft' loan (e.g., 6% per annum in US$).

In its fourth year the NGO achieves a breakthrough financially en route to becoming a cost-covering financial institution. In this phase, it is strongly recommended that the financial NGO initiate the transition to a formal financial intermediary and change its legal structure to that of a corporation. The legal form of a foundation will pose an obstacle to receiving the funds it needs in order to realize its future growth prospects. Its funding from year 5 on can and should be met by loans provided by international development institutions at their normal 'commercial' rates. From year 4 on and with a portfolio size of more than US$ 10 million, the combined administrative and risk costs of the institution will drop below 20% and slowly approach 12% per annum.

The original endowment capital of the foundation, together with donated fixed assets, will form the equity base required for the establishment of a formal financial institution—or part of it. The foundation, the original NGO, becomes the principal owner of the bank. The donor organization(s) can and should also acquire a formal stake by converting a portion of the soft loan provided in year 2 into equity.

Once a bank has been founded, the focus of the technical assistance component can be gradually changed and shifted to other activities, e.g., the launching of a deposit-taking business. As we have demonstrated above, deposit business should be developed gradually with due consideration given to its costs. The deposit business should be seen primarily as an activity designed to provide a service to the customers of the bank. That opening up this second line of business will convert the institution into a 'complete' bank is of secondary importance. During this phase of the institution's development, the role of deposits—in particular from the target group of small and micro businesses—as a source of loanable funds should not be overestimated.

Implications

On the basis of practical experience, the entire process of first creating an institution, then bringing it up to a level at which it can cover its costs, and finally converting it into a formal bank without giving up its target group orientation represents a realistic approach. But it requires a long-term vision and a long-term commitment on both sides. Donors who want to be partners and supporters of this process have to be prepared to play a more lasting and, at the same time, more flexible role and to make their own future behavior more predictable and reliable for their partners in the developing countries, than they are used to doing, and also than they would really like to.

One anticipated problem is that commitment to long-term involvement can create incentives and opportunities for local partners to abuse the participation of the foreign partner. We propose keeping this problem under control by designing active participation of the foreign partner into the decisionmaking process of the local partner. We recognize, however, that this type of participation is not customary for donor organizations and that they might have reservations about such an approach.

We conclude by pointing out four widespread deficiencies in the way that donor institutions consider and handle institution-building projects. These observations are based on our consulting experience gained in cooperation with several major donor organizations. The general thrust of our critical remarks is that donors are reluctant to consider institution building as a genuine and legitimate type of project and that they do not take them as seriously as they need to be taken.

Donors seem to feel that it is difficult to justify pure institution-building projects in the field of finance, and more specifically in conjunction with the provision of credit to a target group which is difficult to deal with. As a consequence, they quite frequently incorporate elements of direct support for the target group into an institution-building project, even if these elements water down the project strategy and lessen its chances of success. Rigid requirements with respect to loan sizes or interest rates are features of this tendency to undermine the institution-building effort[13] of a project with ancillary objectives.

In practice, donors tend to burden institution-building projects with multiple and inconsistent objectives. In part, this tendency seems to be grounded in the assumption that creating an institution and transforming it into a viable and professional financial intermediary is not a particularly difficult task, leaving the project management staff or the institution itself with plenty of capacity for doing other things at the same time. The preference on the part of donors for an 'integrated promotion' of small and microbusiness people as well as a tendency to demand too early that their partner institutions become something like full service banks are manifestations of this widespread misconception.

Many donors follow a general policy of very limited intervention. As a matter of principle, there can be no doubt that less intervention is preferred to more. However, in building financial institutions, the real issue is how much non-intervention is feasible if the objective of the project is to be achieved. In our experience, institution-building projects require a much higher degree of intervention and long-term commitment on the part of the donors than other types of projects.

A certain uneasiness about the responsibility they have in the context of an institution building project is a likely reason why donations and loans play a much bigger role in such projects than equity. Donors should understand that equity is in many cases the appropriate financial instrument for building an institution. They should not be too concerned that, by providing equity where it is needed, they become owners, and thus 'responsible'.[14] In fact, their actual position is very much like that of an owner in the first place and they do assume responsibility for the success of the projects they support.

Acknowledgments

This chapter summarizes the main results of a longer study (Schmidt and Zeitinger, 1994) which was prepared for the Donor Coordination Conference in Vienna, September 1994. Financial support from the Dutch Ministry of Foreign Affairs, Swiss Development Cooperation and the German Ministry for Economic Cooperation is gratefully acknowledged. However, the views expressed here are those of the authors and their views alone, and should not in any way be attributed to the institutions which commissioned the study. Copies of Schmidt and Zeitinger (1994) are available from the authors.

Notes

1   For a critical assessment, see J. D. Von Pischke, 1991, Part II, and Krahnen and Schmidt, 1994, pp. 9–27.
2   For an empirical study of the efficiency of credit-granting NGOs, cf. Schmidt and Zeitinger (1996).
3   The new view is alternatively labeled a 'financial sector perspective' (Von Pischke, 1991), a 'commercial approach' (Jackelen and Rhyne, 1991) and an 'institution building approach' (Krahnen and Schmidt, 1994). The different labels are not a reflection of substantive differences, but at most a matter of emphasis.
4   This 'revelation' is certainly not intended to detract from the impressive achievements of the Grameen Bank!
5   See Schmidt and Zeitinger (1996), where it is reported that a sample of Latin American NGOs which regarded themselves as efficiency-oriented offered standard loan contracts to their clients with an average inflation-adjusted rate of 88% (on an annualized basis) in 1991.
6   For details and a list of the institutions, see Schmidt and Zeitinger (1994), pp. 70–75.
7   See Lepp (1994), pp. 222–280, and most recently Bredenbecker (1997).
8   The study of Bredenbecker (1997) supports these findings with more recent data from selected Cajas.
9   For a detailed study of this concept of ownership, see e.g., Fama and Jensen (1983).
10   The concept of 'governance structure' which we use in this chapter is influenced by the writings of O.E. Williamson; see e.g., Williamson (1985), pp. 64–84.
11   On the standard classification of institution-building strategies (and its deficiencies), see Krahnen and Schmidt (1994), pp. 81–86.
12   For details, including a numerical example, see Schmidt and Zeitinger (1994), pp. 37–43.
13   In contrast to those requirements which are mentioned in the text, performance requirements which put pressure on the partner institutions to bring their costs down to a certain level would be in the spirit of the institution building approach.
14   See Schmidt and Zeitinger (1994 and 1996) for a detailed discussion of why donors should take seriously, and live up to, the responsibilities which they incur in their role as de facto owners of many of the projects which they support.

References

Bredenbecker, K. (1997), 'Savings Mobilization: Lessons From the Peruvian Savings Banks in Trujilo and Sullana,' *Savings and Development*, Vol. 21, pp. 87–109.

Fama, E. and Jensen, M. (1983), 'Separation of Ownership and Control,' *Journal of Law and Economics*, Vol. 26, pp. 301–326.

Jackelen, H.R. and Rhyne, E. (1991), 'Towards a More Market-Oriented Approach to Credit and Savings for the Poor,' *Small Enterprise Development*, Vol. 2, No. 4, pp. 4–20.

Krahnen, P. and Schmidt, R.H. (1994), *Development Finance as Institution Building: A New Approach to Poverty-Oriented Banking*, Westview Press: Boulder, CO.

Lepp, A. (1994), Finanzsektorpolitik und der Zugang klein(st)er Unternehmen zu Finanzdienstleistungen—Ein Untersuchung am Beispiel von Peru, Diss. Univ. Frankfurt/M., Germany.

Mommartz, R. (1994), 'Eficiencia economica de las Cajas Municipales de Ahoro y Credito (CMAC) del Peru, mimeo, IPC: Frankfurt, Germany.

Otero, M. and Rhyne, E. (1994), *The New World of Microenterprise Finance: Building Healthy Financial Institutions for the Poor*, Kumarian Press: West Hartford, CT.

Schmidt, R.H. and Zeitinger, C.-P. (1994), *Criticial Issues in Small and Microbusiness Finance*, mimeo, IPC, Frankfurt.

Schmidt, R.H. and Zeitinger, C.-P. (1996), 'The Efficiency of Credit-Granting NGOs in Latin America,' *Savings and Development*, Vol. 20, pp. 353–384.

Vogel, R.C. (1984), 'Savings Mobilization: The Forgotten Half of Rural Finance,' in: Adams, D.W, Graham, D.H. and Von Pischke, J.D. (eds.), *Undermining Rural Development with Cheap Credit*, Westview Press: Boulder, CO, pp. 248–265.

Von Pischke, J.D. (1991), *Finance at the Frontier: Debt Capacity and the Role of Credit in the Private Economy*, EDI Development Studies, World Bank: Washington, DC.

Williamson, O.E. (1985), *The Economic Institutions of Capitalism*, Free Press: New York.

PART II

MICROFINANCE PROGRAM DESIGN STRATEGIES

4 Microfinance: the paradigm shift from credit delivery to sustainable financial intermediation

MARGUERITE S. ROBINSON

More than 80% of the world's population does not have access to financial services from formal institutions, either for credit or for savings (Christen, Rhyne and Vogel, 1995; and Rosenberg, 1994). Among them, of course, are nearly all the poor of the developing world. Although there is massive demand for microfinance worldwide, banks typically believe that providing small loans and deposit services would be an unprofitable activity for them. The problem is exacerbated by the low level of influence of the poor who require microfinance. Accordingly, institutional commercial microfinance has remained at a low level (Rosenberg, 1994, p. 2). From the borrower's point of view, the crucial words in microcredit *are access and cost.* Subsidized loan programs provide cheap credit, but they do not provide lower-income households with widespread *access* to credit. Informal moneylenders, in aggregate provide wide access, but generally at very high cost to the borrower. On the savings side, the poor need secure, convenient, voluntary savings services, with instruments that provide liquidity and returns. These are frequently unavailable at the local level—from either the formal or the informal sector.

Since government and donor funds can supply only a tiny fraction of global microfinance demand, financial intermediation by self-sufficient institutions is the only way that financial services can be supplied to lower-income people worldwide.

Microfinance refers to small-scale financial services for both credit and deposits—that are provided to people who farm or fish or herd; operate small or microenterprises where goods are produced, recycled, repaired, or traded; provide services; work for wages or commissions; gain income from renting out small amounts of land, vehicles, draft animals, or machinery and tools; and to other individuals and local groups in developing countries, in both rural and urban areas.

Where available, sustainable institutions providing microfinance increase the options of the working poor by helping them reduce risk, improve management and productivity, obtain higher returns on investment, and improve the quality of their lives. Savings services permit people to store excess liquidity for future use, and to obtain returns on their assets. Credit services enable the use of anticipated income for present investment or consumption. However, institutions providing commercial financial intermediation at the local level are very rare.

Financial institutions, of course, cannot serve all of the poor. Destitute, food-deficit people at the lowest levels of the poor are often not yet bankable, even by the standards of institutions that provide microfinance. Such people need food, and they need employment and/or government or donor assistance in starting or improving microenterprises. Over time they can become clients of institutions providing commercial microfinance.

This chapter concerns the vast number of the 'working poor' who already have microenterprises or other income sources that would enable them to participate in, and benefit from, commercial institutions providing microfinance. However, it is important also to draw attention to the relations between sustainable microfinance and poverty alleviation—both direct and indirect. When microfinance is provided at commercial rates through profitable, sustainable institutions, it can facilitate:

(a) a direct improvement in the economic activities, political empowerment, and the quality of life of the working poor;

(b) increased employment of the poor; and

(c) a shift of government and donor support from credit subsidies to poverty alleviation. The productivity, incomes and quality of life of hundreds of millions of people could be substantially increased by access to institutional savings and credit facilities delivered locally.

This chapter documents that self-sufficient institutions can provide microfinance profitably, with large scale outreach to lower income clients, demonstrating a recent shift in the microfinance paradigm from credit delivery to commercial financial intermediation. It analyzes the reasons that financial institutions can provide credit to the working poor at lower interest rates and total costs than many informal commercial lenders; discusses the development of sustainable microfinance systems in Indonesia; contrasts the approach used in Indonesia with that of the Grameen Bank in Bangladesh; and considers the policy implications of the new paradigm.

The paradigm shift

A shift from subsidized delivery programs to commercial intermediation is underway internationally. We examine here the rise and decline of the old approach and the emergence of a new paradigm.

The rise and decline of the old paradigm in subsidized credit

During the 1960s and 1970s, governments and donors promoted large-scale subsidized rural credit programs in developing countries around the world. Since it was assumed that subsidized credit was required to stimulate agricultural growth, agricultural finance came to be treated essentially as a subsidized crop input. This approach was based on the (unexamined) assumptions that poor farmers need credit for productive inputs, that they cannot save enough for the inputs they require, and that they cannot afford to pay the full cost of credit. Therefore, subsidized credit programs would be required for the adoption of new agricultural technologies, enabling farmers to produce more crops, increase their incomes, and repay their loans. It was further assumed that, in general, lower-income people do not save, or prefer to save in non-financial forms. Therefore, savings mobilization would require that people be taught financial discipline. As a result, compulsory saving is often required as a condition of obtaining a subsidized loan.

The assumptions, however, were at variance with reality. By the late 1960s and early 1970s, serious difficulties with subsidized credit programs had begun to become apparent; by the late 1970s, criticisms of the rationale behind these policies filled development literature (Donald, 1976; Von Pischke, Adams and Donald, 1983; Adams, Graham and Von Pischke, 1984; Von Pischke, 1991; Gonzalez-Vega, 1993). The distortions and failures of the subsidized rural credit programs included the following:

(a) credit subsidies tend to encourage corruption and to be captured by wealthier and more influential households;

(b) the diffusion of many agricultural innovations in developing countries does not depend on formal credit;

(c) subsidized credit programs frequently have high default rates and large losses;

(d) credit subsidies, channeled to local elites, buy political support for governments and once offered, are difficult to dislodge; and
(e) in many cases subsidized credit depresses savings mobilization and the development of sustainable financial institutions.

It later became evident that subsidized credit has similar effects on small and microenterprises and leads to the perpetuation of a policy environment in which most lower-income borrowers, both rural and urban, are typically unable to gain access to institutional credit (Costello, Stearns and Christen, 1991; Robinson, 1992, 1994a; Rhyne and Rotblatt, 1994).

Perhaps the most deleterious aspect of subsidized credit is that, by definition, it restricts the range of financial services available and the number of clients served. In developing countries, successful mobilization of voluntary savings and effective microcredit programs have tended not to occur together. This is largely because of the long-prevailing mode of credit subsidies. For example, the Grameen Bank in Bangladesh has been successful in lending to the poor; however, since Grameen does not mobilize voluntary savings effectively and is not sufficiently viable to attract commercial investment, the Bank remains subsidy-dependent. The subsidy-dependent microcredit model can work for particular institutions at particular times, but it is not sustainable in the long term and not affordable on a global scale. Since subsidy-dependent institutions are capital constrained, they cannot meet demand.

The opposite model is also prevalent—mobilizing rural savings that are invested elsewhere. For example, many rural bank branches in India and China have mobilized large amounts of voluntary savings. Yet in China, and until 1996 in India, the spread between the interest rates on loans and deposits was too small for profitable lending to small borrowers. Therefore, most of these savings have been invested or deposited in urban banks, while microcredit demand remains largely unmet.

Under both models, financial institutions have not—and cannot—meet the demand for *microfinance*: i.e., credit *and* savings services. Even the best of the institutions that operate with subsidized loan portfolios are effective either in capturing savings or in providing micro-loans. *They cannot afford to be effective in both because they do not have a large enough spread to cover the operating and financial costs that would be required. Sustainable microfinance has occurred only in systems that provide commercial financial intermediation.*

The emergence of the new paradigm: sustainable financial intermediation

In the last two decades, Indonesia has turned on its head the conventional wisdom about local finance. Bank Dagang Bali (BDB), a private bank in Indonesia, first demonstrated that banks serving the microfinance market can be profitable without subsidy. The Bank Rakyat Indonesia (BRI), a large state-owned commercial bank, demonstrated that the demand for microfinance can be met on a large scale by sustainable institutions; and Indonesia's village-owned banks demonstrated that commercial microfinance can be provided profitably on a small scale by community-owned financial institutions. Together, they have demonstrated that widespread, locally available services can have important effects on social and economic development. The combination of the wide outreach of these institutions and their financial viability has made Indonesia the center of sustainable microfinance.

Microcredit: access and cost

Substantial evidence exists to show that sustainable financial institutions can profitably deliver microcredit to large numbers of borrowers at about 5% to 30% of the interest rates charged by informal commercial lenders to lower-income borrowers. Informal lenders in many developing countries currently charge a 'flat' monthly interest rate of about 5% to over 40% on the original loan balance (Germidis, Kessler and Meghir, 1991; Robinson, 1994a). They typically offer the lower rates to better-off and more influential borrowers, while in general, the higher rates are charged to the poorer borrowers, who have the fewest alternatives. In contrast, BRI provides loans through its local banking system at a flat monthly interest rate that is at or below 1.5% on the original balance of the loan. A flat interest rate on the original balance of 1.5% per month (approximately equivalent to a 32% annual effective rate on the declining balance for a 12-month loan) was charged from the beginning of BRI's general purpose credit program (KUPEDES) in 1984 until 1995. In 1995, a range of flat interest rates from 1% to 1.5% per month was instituted (equivalent to annual effective rates from 26% to 32%). Inflation remained at or below 10% throughout this period. No additional fees are charged to borrowers who repay on time.

The crucial point is that lower-income borrowers who borrow from moneylenders generally pay much higher interest rates for credit than would be necessary if commercial microfinance were widely available through institutions. This is of particular significance because the high rates of informal lenders tend to constrain microenterprise growth, and also because the volume of informal commercial credit is very large in developing countries worldwide (Germidis, Kesler and Meghir, 1991; Von Pischke, 1991; Hoff, Braverman and Stiglitz, 1993; and Ghate et al., 1992).

Why do informal commercial lenders charge high interest rates?

Informal lending is of two main types: commercial (loans from moneylenders, traders, employers, commodity wholesalers, landlords) and non-commercial (loans from friends, relatives, neighbors, and some forms of rotating savings and credit associations). While non-commercial loans from friends, kin, neighbors, etc. are common and usually carry no (or low) financial interest, they often entail other kinds of social, political, and economic obligations. Non-commercial informal credit tends to be available for small amounts for short terms—for emergencies; or for special occasions and specific purposes, such as land purchase, weddings, or house construction for a young couple. However, the funding for such loans is usually limited and the amounts are often inadequate and/or the terms inappropriate for production credit for agriculture, local industries, trade or services.

Informal commercial lenders, however, typically provide credit that can be used for both production and consumption—but at high cost to the lower-income borrower. The prevalence of high interest rates in informal credit markets is so well documented that the literature is filled with debates as to why these rates are so high. There are two main arguments (Von Pischke, 1991; Germidis, Kessler and Meghir, 1991).

The first, and older, view is that informal credit markets are noncompetitive and that monopolistic moneylenders charge high interest rates, extracting substantial profits. A variant of the monopolistic moneylender is the lender whose primary aim is not to extract interest payments but to force the borrower to default. However, the so-called 'malicious moneylender' is widely viewed as a myth (Von Pischke, 1991, p. 174). Yet there is considerable evidence, dating from at least the 1920s until the present, in support of the argument that some informal commercial lenders gain monopoly profits, collected in financial form, land, or labor (Darling, 1978; Indian School of Social Sciences, 1976; Rao, 1977; Sharma, 1978; Vyas, 1980; Marla, 1981; Kamble, 1982; Roth, 1993; Robinson, 1988 and 1994a).

There is also substantial evidence to support the opposing position that most rural lenders are neither exploitive nor malicious (Von Pischke, Adams and Donald, 1983; and Von Pischke, 1991). It is argued that they are providers of important financial services in rural areas. Operations of moneylenders:

> are frequently more cost-effective and useful to the poor than those of the specialized farm-credit institutions, cooperatives and commercial banks that governments use to supplant moneylenders.... The emerging perspective is that informal financial arrangements are generally robust and socially useful.... Widespread use of informal finance suggests that it is well suited to most rural conditions (Von Pischke, Adams and Donald, 1983, p. 8).

This conclusion assumes that the high interest rates for informal commercial loans reflect the lenders' transaction costs and risk (Bottomley, 1975; Tun Wai, 1980; Adams and Graham, 1981; Wilmington, 1981; Singh, 1983; Von Pischke, Adams and Donald, 1983; Vogel, 1984; Adams and Vogel, 1986; Bouman, 1989; Von Pischke, 1991; Floro and Yotopoulos, 1991). One view is that, 'The high cost of administering small loans and persistent repayment problems lead to higher interest rates in informal rural money markets in the developing world' (Bottomley, 1975, p. 243). Another view, also widespread, is that risk premiums and transactions costs do not explain the high interest rates charged because, in fact, these costs are low! Thus 'informal intermediaries ... survive on the basis of competitiveness, financial viability and low cost operations' (Bouman, 1989, p. 9). Germidis, Kessler and Meghir (1991) also find that transaction costs and risks in the informal sector are low. Reasons cited include low overhead; low default risk—good cheap information on the creditworthiness of potential borrowers—and interlinked credit contracts.

Are the transaction costs and risks of informal commercial lenders high or low? The answer, of course, is both—depending upon the circumstances. Lenders' transaction costs can be expensive, and lenders may charge high prices when they cannot diversify risk. Transaction costs and risks, especially for repeat borrowers, can also be low. There is considerable variation in informal financial markets, as was pointed out three decades ago:

> In most Asian countries, the agricultural credit markets ... are not classifiable either as fully competitive or fully monopolized. Competition may prevail in one village while the next is under the control of a single lender. Even within a village one borrower may have several sources of loans, while another lacking alternatives may be forced to pay monopolized rates (Long, 1968, p. 276).

The presence or absence of 'malicious moneylenders' is not an issue of myth or reality; such lenders represent one end of a continuum within informal financial markets. It has been extensively documented that some informal moneylenders are malicious and exploitive, and that many are not. The latter provide useful financial services; the relevant question is: does the borrower need to pay such high interest rates?

'Malicious moneylenders,' transaction costs, and risk premiums can all be causes of high interest rates. However, none of these, nor even all of them together, explains satisfactorily the widespread persistence of high interest rates in informal rural credit markets. The reason that informal commercial lenders charge high interest rates, especially to lower-income borrowers, is that *informal credit markets are not competitive as is widely assumed, but are in fact explained by a variant of monopolistic competition.*

Informal credit markets tend to consist of many small monopolies or quasi-monopolies generated by the dynamics of local-level socioeconomic processes and associated information flows. The dynamics of these markets are best explained by monopolistic competition, except that in this case monopoly profits can be maintained over the long term. Lenders, even over time, do not usually compete for the same borrowers. Therefore, the constraint on lenders tends not to be the availability of funds; the constraint is on the number of borrowers over whom the lender can maintain sufficient control to minimize the default rate.

Informal commercial lenders of all types understand well that lending beyond their sphere of influence and control of information can lead to high default, and thereby to a lowering of the quality of their loan portfolio. Such lenders typically provide credit to their commodity suppliers, employees, tenants, and others with whom they have interlinked transactions. These linkages, combined with local political alliances, create information flows that are both channeled and constrained by local-level social processes. It is the networks through which these interlinked transactions are conducted, and the associated political, business, social, and kin-based relationships of the locality, that typically provide the information flows and controls that enable lenders to recover their loans with relatively low risk.

While local business networks and political alliances provide control mechanisms, they also provide constraints that effectively limit the number of borrowers per lender. The prevalence of loans linked to transactions in other markets is related to a widely reported characteristic of local credit: informal commercial lenders typically provide credit to relatively small numbers of borrowers, usually well under 50, often under 20, and rarely over 100 (Robinson, 1994a).[1] Credit rationing is practiced by moneylenders all over the world—not necessarily because of capital constraints, but because of limits on the number of potential borrowers from whom the lender can collect. Aleem points out from a study of the Chambar rural credit market in Pakistan:

> Each lender in this environment is perceived by borrowers to be offering a different product ... which gives him some flexibility to price according to his own circumstances. Equilibrium in this model involves a distortion in the market; there are too many lenders in relation to the size of the informal credit market .... (Aleem, 1993, pp. 148–149).

Thus, local politics, market interlinkages, and the structure of information transfers often serve to limit the number of borrowers per lender, and to maintain high interest rates in the informal commercial credit market. Aleem makes the important point that, 'Because of these [information] imperfections [in the market] the lender does not have an incentive to cut interest rates to increase his market share, even when rates are well above his marginal cost of lending' (Aleem, 1993, p. 150).

For lenders, market entry is limited primarily by their access to borrowers operating within the area in which the lender holds political influence and controls good information, and by the number of individuals with whom the lender can maintain transactions in other markets. Under these general conditions, lenders and borrowers tend to maintain long-term relationships. Borrowers face risks in changing informal lenders and are widely reported to do so only rarely (Robinson, 1988; Aleem, 1993; Siamwalla et al., 1993). Thus, informal commercial lenders tend not to compete for clients, or to compete imperfectly. The pattern of numerous relatively small quasi-monopolies reflects primarily local information flows and lenders' perceptions of their abilities to collect loans with low risk.

Yet despite massive documentation to the contrary, the widespread assumption of a competitive informal credit market persists. For example, 'One should not expect monopoly profits to be terribly important [in informal rural finance] since there are few barriers to entry into informal financial intermediation and competitive forces generally prevail' (Bouman, 1984, p. 243). There is considerable evidence to demonstrate that while the first of these reasons is generally true, the second is not. A similar view is: 'Monopoly profits of the sort implied by these examples would surely attract vigorous competition that would severely erode returns' (Von Pischke, 1991, p. 185). But this generally does not happen. Since lenders typically do not want to expand their market shares, they often have no incentive to lower interest rates. Therefore, loan terms that translate into high annual interest rates are widespread, well-entrenched, and accepted by the many poor borrowers who have no better options.

Lower-income borrowers generally have no other credit options for financing their productive activities because: (1) if such a borrower turns to another informal lender, he or she is likely to face significant risk for similar credit terms (the new lender may choose not to lend to the borrower, while the old lender may hear about the defection and cut off the borrower's credit (Robinson, 1988); (2) subsidized credit programs tend to bypass most lower-income borrowers; and (3) institutional commercial credit is typically unavailable for microfinance. While non-commercial loans from friends, kin, and neighbors may be available, such loans are normally unsuited to ongoing finance of the borrowing household's productive activities. In the absence of an institutional alternative that provides access to commercial credit, such borrowers tend to stay with their informal commercial lenders, despite the high cost the borrowers pay for credit. The extensive evidence of monopolistic competition seems to have been largely ignored in the enthusiasm of the 1970s and 1980s for the elimination of intervention in rural credit markets, since the assumption of a competitive informal credit market was an important part of that argument. In their seminal statements opposing credit subsidies, Adams, Von Pischke and other sometimes lost sight of the difference between intervention and subsidy, and tended to assume that removal of formal-sector interventions would leave behind local, informal competitive credit markets. As Siamwalla commented:

> This critical literature [in Von Pischke, Adams and Donald, 1983] stressed the distortions introduced by government policies [for credit subsidies] and, in doing so tended to idealize the informal credit markets that did exist or that might have existed in absence of the massive government intervention in the credit market. There was a presumption that an intervention-free rural financial market would approximate the perfect competition model (Siamwalla et al., 1993, p. 170).

Interventions and subsidies should not be confused. Removal of credit subsidies is essential for the development of competitive credit markets. However, removal of subsidies will not, in itself, generally result in competitive microfinance. Interventions in local financial markets are important, primarily because the information that institutional microfinance can be profitable has not yet reached most parts of the developing world. Thus, Indonesia began to have competitive credit markets at the local level only *after* the government intervened in order to enable BRI's local banking system to become profitable; BRI's success then motivated other financial institutions to compete in the same market.

The widespread pattern of monopolistic competition in the informal market provides an important reason for institutional participation in local financial markets. In most developing countries, however, the reason for such intervention has rarely been understood. The result is that the poor pay far higher total costs for credit than would be required if conveniently located financial institutions were to provide them microcredit at commercial rates. *The difference to a poor borrower between paying a moneylender a flat monthly interest rate on the original loan balance of 20% or 30%, or paying a financial institution a monthly flat rate of 1.5%, can be the growth of the borrower's enterprise.*

However, governments and donor agencies have little incentive to build sustainable institutions providing microfinance at the local level because of many widespread, but mistaken, assumptions. A policymaker is unlikely to give priority to the development of sustainable microfinance institutions if he or she believes that institutions cannot provide financial services at the local level because informal lenders have better information, meet demand, and benefit the poor; that the institution will adversely select its borrowers and have a high level of default; and that the working poor cannot or will not save in a financial institution, and that therefore the institution cannot be funded from savings. Throughout Indonesia, and increasingly in other countries, all these assumptions have been shown to be wrong. The success of BRI in operating a profitable system of financial intermediation at the local level has, for the first time, engendered extensive competition from other financial institutions of many types. *It is thus the formal sector, not the informal sector, that has the potential to make local financial markets competitive.*

How can commercial microfinance institutions charge interest rates much lower than those of informal commercial lenders?

There are three main reasons:

(a) In contrast to informal commercial lenders, institutions providing commercial microfinance have an incentive to attain wide client outreach. Such institutions, for which the lending of money is a business (and not a way of retaining commodity suppliers, employees, or political supporters), price their loan products on commercial principles. They also provide incentives and training to staff in order to expand the institution's microfinance business and its profitability.

(b) Banks and other formal-sector institutions providing commercial microfinance can benefit from financial intermediation, from economies of scale, and from better protection against covariant shocks.

(c) Financial institutions with well-trained and motivated staff can attain better information about large numbers of lower-income borrowers than can an individual moneylender. This is because:

- As institutions, banks are not subject to the same kinds of local political, social and informational constraints that limit the scale at which moneylenders can operate with low risks.
- Voluntary savings services can provide good information about the economic activities and the character of large numbers of savers—who are also potential borrowers. This helps to keep loan repayment rates high and to lower the bank's costs for loan transactions.
- Moneylenders are often bank clients and may be willing to trade information for prime customer status.
- Staff of bank branches are generally local people who maintain social and political relationships and who, in aggregate, have access to multiple local information flows.

For these reasons, institutions providing commercial microfinance can offer loans to creditworthy lower-income borrowers at much lower interest rates than the latter would normally pay to moneylenders. Because such institutions maintain many small branches located in areas convenient for their customers, and because they offer loans with simple procedures, borrowers' transaction costs tend to be relatively low. While these costs may still be higher than the transaction costs of borrowing from moneylenders, the total cost of borrowing from banks, especially for poorer borrowers, is generally far lower than the cost of borrowing from informal commercial lenders.

From the perspective of the financial institution, three aspects of sustainable microfinance—all apparently counter-intuitive to many bankers, politicians, and policy makers—are crucial to the new paradigm.

First, in order to combine wide coverage with institutional sustainability, interest rates from small loans must be significantly higher than the rates charged by large urban bank branches. This reflects the inescapable fact that the delivery of microfinance services at scattered locations is more expensive than providing larger loans and deposits in centrally-located urban banks. Thus, the spread between loan and deposit interest rates must be sufficient to cover all the (non-subsidized) financial costs, non-financial costs, and risk.

Second, the interest rates of self-sufficient microfinance institutions are highly attractive to lower-income borrowers at the local level because they represent a small fraction of the rates typically charged by informal lenders.

Third, there is vast unmet demand in developing countries for savings services that are delivered at the local level and that offer a combination of security, convenience, liquidity, confidentiality, access to loans, returns, and good service. In Indonesia, BDB and BRI finance all their loans from locally mobilized savings.

The development of sustainable microfinance in Indonesia

Indonesia, with a population of 193 million, is the world's fourth most highly populated country. It has a diverse economy, and the average annual economic growth since 1980 has been about 8%. In 1996 GDP per capita was US$ 980. There has been a sharp reduction of those below the poverty line, from over 60% in the 1960s to about 11% in 1996.

Viable microfinance comes in different forms. The three Indonesian financial institutions discussed below provide microfinance profitability without subsidy: Bank Dagang Bali (BDB) is a small private bank, Bank Rakyat Indonesia (BRI) is a large state-

owned commercial bank, Badan Kredit Desa (BKD) is a century old
network of village-owned banks, now supervised by BRI.

Bank Dagang Bali, a small private bank

Bank Dagang Bali was opened in 1970 by I Gusti Made Oka and Sri
Adnyani Oka, a husband and wife who had experience as microentrepreneurs and informal commercial lenders (Robinson, 1995b). In
1968 the Okas used this knowledge to create Bank Pasar Umum
(BPU), a small secondary market bank, to provide financial services to
lower-income people.

Starting with initial capital of US$ 350, BPU provided loans for a
one-month term, with interest of 8% a month and a 3% fee for each
loan. Loan repayments were collected in daily installments, and
collections were immediately relent. BPU became profitable very
quickly because the Okas, with their extensive knowledge of the local
financial market, knew that there was a large demand for both savings
and credit services and they could undercut moneylenders by a wide
margin.

By 1970, after two years of operation, the BPU had US$ 41,345 in
profits and the Okas decided to open a private bank in addition to the
BPU. They borrowed an additional US$ 13,782 from the local
provincial bank. With their initial capital of US$ 55,127 from the BPU
profits and the bank loan, the Okas opened Bank Dagang Bali—the
second private bank in Bali—in September 1970. As of December 31,
1996, DBD operated eight branches, 18 sub-branches and four
smaller offices that serve as deposit collection points. Six branches are
located in Bali; the other two are in Jakarta and Surabaya, Indonesia's
largest cities. The bank, which serves over 350,000 clients, had about
US$ 115 million in deposits and about US$ 95 million in loans
outstanding as of December 31, 1996. The annual effective rates on
most small loans is about 30% and repayment rates are typically
above 98%. BDB has been profitable every year since it opened and is
fully self-sufficient. During the 1990s annual before-tax profits have
ranged from about US$ 1 million to about US$ 1.7 million.

BDB is extremely active on the savings side of its microfinance
activities and provides many services, including the maintenance of
daily routes to visit customers at home or place of work. All savings
are voluntary; compulsory savings are not required to obtain loans.

Bank Rakyat Indonesia (BRI): a large state-owned commercial bank

As a state-owned commercial bank, BRI's special assignment has been the provision of agricultural credit in rural areas. The bank also provides commercial, corporate, and international banking services. Since this chapter concerns BRI's local banking division, the term BRI refers here only to the bank's local banking system.[2] In the early 1970s, BRI established over 3600 small bank units at the sub-district level throughout the country. Savings accounts were offered in BRI's bank units beginning in the mid-1970s. However, the annual interest rates set by the government (12% for loans and 15% for most deposits) discouraged the units from undertaking effective savings mobilization.

BRI's bank units were originally set up as a channeling agent for subsidized loans to farmers under BIMAS, the credit component of Indonesia's massive program to achieve rice self-sufficiency that began in 1970. Originally all units were located in rural areas. However, in 1984 the system was restructured and in 1989 unit banks were added in lower-income urban areas.

The initial approach to financial intermediation at the local level through BRI's unit banking system was similar to that found in many developing countries having rural banking programs designed under the old paradigm: institutional credit was subsidized, the credit program was poorly planned, the low-interest BIMAS loans typically bypassed the poor, arrears and losses were high, and deposits were low. During 1983, BRI's unit banking system sustained a loss of US$ 28 million, and the bank gave serious consideration to closing the system. However, the Indonesian government began a series of major financial reforms in 1983. The first of these, in June 1983, permitted government banks to set their own interest rates on most loans and deposits. Subsequent financial deregulation provided an enabling environment in which BRI could transform its subsidized local banks into a sustainable system of financial intermediation, operating at the sub-district level in both rural and urban areas.

Since January 1984, BRI's local bank units have offered the KUPEDES program of general rural credit. Most Indonesian households have multiple income sources, and KUPEDES loans are provided for any viable productive activity, including services and trade. The loans are often used for financing several activities within one household. KUPEDES loans from about US$ 10 to about US$ 10,650 (in 1996 dollars) are available to anyone deemed creditworthy. Loan terms up to two years for working capital and three years for investment capital are available.

In 1985, new deposit and savings accounts were introduced at BRI's unit banks. These offer the depositor security at convenient bank locations, and customers can choose among instruments offering different ratios of liquidity and returns. BRI's local banking system broke even at the end of 1985 after only two years of commercial operation, and the system has been profitable every year since 1986. At the end of 1996 BRI's 3595 local bank units had US$ 1.7 billion in KUPEDES credit outstanding to about 2.5 million borrowers (Table 4.1). The KUPEDES long-term loss ratio as of the same date was 2.2%. The low rate of arrears is attributable primarily to the fact that borrowers repay promptly because they want to retain the option to reborrow: there is also a monetary incentive for prompt repayment. For many KUPEDES borrowers, the only alternative is to borrow from the informal commercial market at much higher interest rates.

Table 4.1 Bank Rakyat Indonesia's unit banking system: performance indicators (1993–1996)

	1993	1994	1995	1996
Total value of loans outstanding (US$ billion)	0.94	1.14	1.42	1.74
Total number of loans outstanding (million)	1.90	2.10	2.30	2.50
Long-term loss ratio*	3.1%	2.6%	2.3%	2.2%
Total value of savings (US$ billion)	2.07	2.43	2.68	3.0
Total number of deposit accounts (million)	11.4	13.1	14.5	16.1
Return on assets	3.4%	5.2%	6.5%	5.7%
Total number of units	3,267	3,388	3,512	3,595
Percentage of profitable units	89.3%	93.7%	95.7%	94.9%

Notes: *The ratio of the cumulative amount due but unpaid since the opening of the unit, to the cumulative amount falling due.

From the early 1970s until the financial deregulation of June 1983, BRI's unit banking system had mobilized only about US$ 18 million in savings nationwide in over 3600 unit banks. This was widely attributed within the government and the formal financial sector to the lack of local demand for financial services, absence of 'bank-mindedness,' and mistrust of banks that were assumed to characterize Indonesia's rural population. These assumptions were wrong. As of December 1996, the unit banking system held deposits of about US$ 3 billion in about 16.1 million deposit accounts.

BRI's success in local banking since 1984 is based on:
(a) an extensive organizational reform within the bank that created a unit banking division;
(b) use of scarce, high-level management resources for microfinance development;
(c) a spread between loan and deposit interest rates that permits institutional profitability;
(d) convenient, secure unit bank locations at the local level;
(e) a simple, uniform, and appropriately designed and priced set of instruments and services;
(f) simple, transparent reporting procedures;
(g) a system under which each unit operates as a 'profit center,' with the staff receiving performance incentives based on the unit's outreach and profitability;
(h) a well designed and implemented internal supervision process;
(i) the creation of a specialized staff training program that emphasizes knowledge of local markets and responsibility at the local bank level, and
(j) respect for, and close relations with, the units' predominantly rural, lower-income clients.

The Badan Kredit Desa: BRI supervised network of village banks

In additional to the activities of its local banking system, BRI supervises and in some cases provides commercial loans to fund traditional village banks in Java and Madura. Begun in 1896 under the Dutch colonial government, these banks, known as *Badan Kredit Desa* (BKDs), are owned by their respective village governments. At the end of 1996, the BKD system served over 750,000 clients. There are 4806 BKDs in active operation; each provides financial services on a commercial basis within its own village, usually on a weekly basis. BRI's units are located at subdistrict level, serving the villages of the sub-district, while the BKDs reach deeper into their own villages. Most BKD loans are short term, usually for 10–12 weeks and for amounts below US$ 75. Interest rates set by the respective local governments are typically at least double the BRI unit bank rates. Compulsory savings are required as a condition of receiving a loan.

While most BKDs finance their loans from retained earnings, they can borrow at a commercial rate from BRI to finance their loan portfolios. BKDs with excess liquidity (derived mostly from profits) can deposit these at BRI and obtain interest on the deposits. Adjusted profits in 1996 for the total BKD network were about US$ 6 million.

Sustainable microfinance in Indonesia: summary

Financial services are widely available to lower-income clients throughout Indonesia. BDB finances the greatest range of clients, while BRI's local banking system serves by far the largest number. Village banks (BKDs) provide loans and offer deposit facilities to even poorer clients than those typically served by BDB and BRI. These financial institutions represent widely varying institutional structures, but they have important underlying commonalities:
(a) They provide financial services profitably to large numbers of the working poor.
(b) Interest rates for loans are higher than those normally charged by large urban Indonesian banks, reflecting the higher costs of financial services delivered at the local level.
(c) Loan arrears are low, due to a number of factors. The most important is that the terms of the loan are attractive to borrowers, who want to repay so that they can retain the option to reborrow.
(d) In BRI and BDB, where compulsory savings are not required, deposits finance all loans. In the BKDs, retained earnings and commercial loans finance the loan portfolio.
(e) Activities are restricted entirely to financial services: no community development, social services, client training or other non-financial activities are carried out by these institutions.
(f) All the institutions are self-sufficient and operate without subsidy.

BRI's local banking system and Grameen Bank: a comparison

BRI's local banking system and Grameen Bank in Bangladesh are the two largest indigenous banks in the world providing microfinance. A comparison will be useful in helping to explore policy issues. Grameen is a well-known, donor-driven model of successful microfinance delivery, and it represents a different approach from that of the Indonesian banks.

Since Grameen essentially provides only microfinance, while BRI's local banking activities are carried out by a division of a large commercial bank, the comparison made here is between Grameen Bank and BRI's local banking division. In order to provide comparability, most of the data used here are from Yaron, Benjamin and

Piprek (1997), where uniform adjustments to the financial reports from both institutions have already been made. Information has also been included from Christen, Rhyne and Vogel (1995), Morduch (1997), and data from BRI's local banking division and the Grameen Bank.

The Grameen figures are difficult to obtain and to interpret. There are discrepancies among the various recent sources, and terms used are not always clearly defined. Despite the difficulties with data, the overall comparison between the two institutions is clear-cut and important. There are substantial similarities and fundamental differences in the philosophies and the operations of these two banks.

In 1995, the population was 120 million in Bangladesh and 193 million in Indonesia, while the per capita GNP was US$ 240 for Bangladesh and US$ 980 for Indonesia. Both BRI unit banks and Grameen began their present banking activities in the mid-1980s, and by the end of 1995 the number of loans outstanding was roughly comparable at 2.1 million for Grameen and 2.3 million for BRI (Table 4.2). Grameen lends to groups of borrowers while BRI's unit banking system offers individual loans directly.

Both banks serve poor borrowers, although Grameen reaches the poorest borrowers directly, while BRI reaches them primarily through the BKDs. The BKDs and Grameen require compulsory savings from all borrowers. However, Grameen deposits much of its savings in fixed and short-term accounts in other banks and uses subsidized funds to finance it loan portfolio. In contrast, BRI uses its deposits to finance its entire KUPEDES loan portfolio.

Since Bangladesh is poorer than Indonesia, the average loan balance at Grameen (US$ 140) was considerably smaller than at BRI (US$ 617). However, the average loan balance as a percentage of GNP per capita was similar: 59.3% for Grameen and 62.9% for BRI. BRI's local banking system and the Grameen Bank both serve large numbers of low-income borrowers, although in different ways. There are, however, some major differences between their microfinance activities.

Institutional purpose and performance

Grameen Bank[3] maintains an integrated approach providing social services and credit to members (Khandker, 1993, p. 1; Khandker, Khalily and Khan, 1995, p. 12). Grameen Bank trains members in health, nutrition, family planning, livestock and poultry care; promotes seedling distribution, tree planting, and kitchen gardens; and operates schools and day care centers. BRI's services are limited to financial intermediation.

Grameen's 1995 annual effective interest rate for loans was about 20%, while at BRI's local banking system the rate was about 32%. According to a 1994 study, salary costs for lending operations as a percentage of average annual loan portfolio at BRI (5.0%) were less than half those of Grameen (11.2%). Other administrative costs as a percentage of portfolio at BRI (2.1%) were below the Grameen figure of 5.7% (Rhyne and Rotblatt, 1994, Table 7). The operating costs of the two banks reflect the different services provided to customers.

Table 4.2   Indicators of outreach and sustainability: BRI unit banks and the Grameen Bank (1995)[1]

	Grameen Bank	BRI Unit Banks
Country population	119.8 million	193.3 million
Country GNP/capita	US $ 240	US$ 980
Average inflation (GDP deflator)	8.8%	8.7%
Number of branches	1,056	3,512 (plus 423 village posts)
Number of staff	12,268	17,174
Annual effective interest rate	20%	26%–32%
Real effective interest rate	10.3%	15.9%–21.2%
Average loan balance	US$ 140	US$ 617
Average loan balance as a % of GNP/capita	59.3%	62.9%
Number of loans outstanding	2.1 million	2.3 million
Default rate (arrears as a % of total loan portfolio)	3.6%[2]	3.5%
Value of loans outstanding	US$ 289 million	US$ 1,419 million
Number of savings accounts	2.1 million	14.5 million
Value of deposits	US$133.2 million[3]	US$ 2,675 million
Average value of savings accounts	US$ 65	US$ 185
Total savings as a % of outstanding loans	46.1%	188.5%
Return on assets (ROA)	0.14%[4]	6.5%

Sources:

1   Country data are from World Bank (1997). Data for the Grameen Bank are from Yaron, Benjamin and Piprek (1997) and the Grameen Bank Data for BRI are from Bank Rakyat Indonesia (1997). *All data represent 1995 end-of-year figures except where otherwise noted.*

2   After 1995, Grameen's repayment rate declined sharply. For 1996, Grameen's default rate (defined as amounts overdue after at least one year) jumped to 13.85% (Grameen Bank, December 1996); the BRI unit bank de-

fault rate for 1996 (defined as amounts remaining unpaid after one week) was 3.65%.

3   Data on the value of Grameen's savings are difficult to interpret. The figure above is an estimate based on a comparison of multiple sources (see Yaron, Benjamin and Piprek (1997); Khandker, Khalily and Khan (1995); World Bank (1997); and Christen, Rhyne and Vogel (1995)).

4   Grameen's 1995 reported ROA of 0.14% was positive only because of the substantial subsidies the bank received.

Grameen serves its members; BRI serves the public. Grameen calls its customers 'beneficiaries'; BRI calls its customers 'clients'. In 1995 Grameen had 2.1 million members who were both borrowers and savers; BRI's unit banks had 2.3 million borrowers and 14.5 million savings and deposit accounts. Fixed deposit accounts constituted 10.1% of total unit bank deposits and 6.5% of the total number of accounts as of December 31, 1995. The rest of the funds are held in various types of savings instruments. (The terms deposit and savings are used synonymously in this chapter.) The BRI local banking system maintains more than three times the number of branch offices operated by Grameen. BRI and the BKDs together have about eight times as many local offices as Grameen.

The philosophies of the two banks concerning savings mobilization are very different. The Grameen Bank uses the slogan: 'Savings is an integral part of lending' (Khandker, p. 4). Believing that its members must be taught to save, Grameen requires compulsory savings from its members. This is thought to 'promote the financial discipline of the poor' (Khandker, 1993, p. 5). Grameen reportedly accepts savings from non-members, but the number of such savers and the value of their deposits are not known (Rhyne and Rotblatt, 1994, p. 13).

In contrast, BRI does not assume that savings is part of lending, but believes rather that lending and savings are both integral parts of financial intermediation. BRI assumes that the working poor save, and that if a bank offers savings instruments and services appropriate for their demand, many poor clients will save in the bank voluntarily. BRI understands also that the microfinance market is large, and that at any given time, savings services will be demanded by more people than credit services. Accordingly, BRI's local banks provide savings services to the public.

The approaches of the two institutions are reflected in their respective performances and degrees of sustainability. At Grameen, the value of outstanding loans at the end of 1995 was US$ 289 million; at BRI it was US$ 1.4 billion. As of December 31, 1995, Grameen had about US$ 133 million in savings compared with US$

2.7 billion for BRI's local banking division. BRI's 6.1 ratio of savings accounts to numbers of loans, in comparison with Grameen's 1:1 ratio highlights the difference between requiring compulsory savings from members and mobilizing voluntary savings from the public.

Sustainability

BRI's local banking system is not subsidized; it has been profitable since 1986 and has operated without subsidy since 1988 (Yaron et al., 1997). All the loans in the system are financed by its deposits. At Grameen (compulsory) savings do not finance most of the loans and the bank is unable to leverage commercial funds. The institution remains dependent on low-cost funds and it is not self-sufficient.

The primary subsidies Grameen receives are in the form of interest-free loans or concessional interest rates on loans obtained from donors and the government. Of Grameen's nearly US$ 74 million in foreign funding in 1994, most was received interest-free with the remainder provided at an interest rate of 2% per year (Morduch, 1997). Moreover, a study of the Grameen Bank conducted by the World Bank and the Bangladesh Institute of Development Studies estimates that in 1993, foreign funds represented nearly 75% of total resources available for Grameen (Khandker, Khalily and Khan, 1995). However, more recently, 'The Grameen Bank has seen steady increases in the amount of subsidized capital obtained, but with a recent shift toward borrowing from the Central Bank' (Morduch, 1997).

Thus, in contrast to BRI's unit banking system, where there are no subsidies and where the 1995 return on assets (ROA) of 6.5% is calculated on a commercial banking basis, Grameen's 1995 ROA of 0.14% was positive only because of the substantial subsidies that the bank received (Table 4.2).

A USAID study of 11 successful microfinance programs (Christen, Rhyne and Vogel, 1995) analyzed the levels of sustainability of each institution.[4] The Grameen Bank was classified as Level 2: operationally self-sufficient. but not covering the commercial costs of loanable funds. BRI's unit banking system was classified as Level 3: fully self-sufficient, with revenues covering all costs and risks. Another measure is the Subsidy Dependence Index (SDI) developed by Jacob Yaron (1992). The SDI measures the percentage increase in the financial institution's average on-lending interest rate that would be needed to compensate for the elimination of all subsidies. SDI calculations for the two institutions in 1994 indicate that Grameen would have had to increase its on-lending interest rate by 21% (i.e., 1.21 times its lending rate in 1996) in order to break even in the absence of subsidies (Hashemi, 1997), while BRI's unit banking system is fully self-sufficient without subsidy (Yaron, personal communication).

Developing sustainable microfinance: policy implications

The new commercial microfinance model challenges the widespread assumption that subsidies are required for microfinance in developing countries and demonstrates that formal institutions can deliver services profitably at the local level. Since government and donor funds can supply only a small fraction of global microfinance demand, financial intermediation by self-sufficient institutions is the only way that financial services can be provided to lower-income people worldwide.

While Grameen Bank has helped large numbers of poor people, it currently depends on continuing donor and government injections of low-cost funds. The microfinance model developed in Indonesia, however, is sustainable and does not require infusions of government subsidy or foreign aid. Also unlike Grameen, BRI does not promote replicators or 'clones' of itself. BRI's approach is to explain the underlying principles of sustainable microfinance to its many international visitors, demonstrate its methods, and show its results. Many institutions in the developing world are in various stages of adapting the principles of the Indonesian approach to the circumstances in their countries.

The World Bank's Operations Evaluation Department identifies the reasons for the success of BRI's local banking system:

> The program succeeded because the banks loaned at market rates, used income to finance their operations, kept operating costs low and devised appropriate savings instruments to attract depositors. By mobilizing rural savings, ... [the local banking system] was not only provided ... with a stable source of funds, it also kept financial savings in rural areas, thus helping development growth in the countryside. Other reasons for success included: the simplicity of loan designs, which enabled the banks to keep costs down; effective management at the unit level, backed by close supervision and monitoring by the center; and appropriate staff training and performance incentives (*World Bank News*, April 4, 1996, p. 6).

Implications for governments

Microfinance made widely available is an effective and crucial tool for poverty alleviation; it is appropriately provided by commercial institutions. Credit subsidies, which are capital constrained, in fact prevent widespread access to credit by the working poor who could make good use of commercial loans. However, other tools are required for the 'poorest of the poor' who have prior needs. The provision of food, employment, health services and other basic requirements needed for overcoming desperate poverty are appropriately financed by governments and donor subsidies and grants. These tools are properly the responsibility of ministries of social welfare, health, labor and others, as well as of private charities.

Can the commercial approach to microfinance be successful in poorer countries like Bangladesh, as well as in higher-income, faster-growing economies like Indonesia? The answer appears to be yes, for several reasons. First, a number of other financial institutions providing microcredit in Bangladesh have proved that there are many poor borrowers who can use credit productively and who repay loans promptly. Second, commercial microcredit is already working in Bangladesh. Thus, the Association for Social Advancement (ASA), a highly successful NGO, provides microcredit in Bangladesh at commercial interest rates. Until August 1995, ASA's annual effective interest rate was 31.8%, as of December 1995 ASA reported 326,244 active borrowers with loans from US$ 50 to US$ 175. In August 1995, the rate was reduced to 24.4% (Rutherford, 1995, pp. 95–99). ASA's 1995 default rate defined as the value of loans over one month past due as a percentage of the loan portfolio was 1.10% (ASA, 1997, p. 4). ASA's approach to setting interest rates is similar to that of BRI which reduced its KUPEDES interest rates in 1995. Start-up costs and early mistakes can be expensive for institutions starting commercial microfinance. Therefore, pricing loans higher at the beginning, improving efficiency, and then decreasing interest rates later is a sensible strategy.

Third, other very poor countries, such as Tanzania (1995 per capita GNP: US$ 120) and India (1994 per capita GNP: US$ 340), have been able to mobilize large amounts of savings in their rural banks and are presently involved in large rural banking reforms designed to move them towards the commercial microfinance model. It appears that there is similar potential in Bangladesh (Rutherford, 1995, Epilogue).

Can borrowers in poor countries pay the interest rates needed for the lending institution to become sustainable? There is substantial evidence that poor borrowers around the world already pay higher interest rates to moneylenders than the rates needed for institutional viability. In addition, financial institutions using the group lending approach in poor countries tend to allow the group to lend its money to its members at a rate fixed by the particular group. Frequently these loans are provided at a substantially higher interest rate than that received by the group: thus the end borrower is already paying a non-subsidized interest rate.

The demand for commercial credit and savings services among the working poor is massive in developing countries generally, and meeting this demand through commercial microfinance is one of the most powerful tools in the poverty alleviation toolbox.

For commercial microfinance to be successful, however, government must undertake an enabling and supportive role. This includes regulation, supervision, education of the public, as well as recognizing and rectifying earlier mistakes. In Indonesia, the Minister of Finance played a crucial role in developing BIU's unit banking system. He commented:

> By the early 1980s we began to realize that year after year, the subsidies and the arrears of our subsidized rural credit programs were large, the programs were inefficient, and the loans generally did not reach the intended borrowers. In brief, our approach to local finance was ineffective and unsustainable. Not only were our subsidized credit programs not a driving force for rural development, they were actually slowing it down! Having recognized the severe deficiencies of these programs, we decided, in 1983, to begin a new program for rural finance that would be based on principles of commercial finance (Wardhana, forthcoming).

Many governments and institutions are becoming increasingly aware that while there are important lessons to be learned from Grameen's success in credit delivery to the poor, the model is not affordable on a global scale. For large countries, it is particularly important that their governments be well-informed about the crucial differences between institutional commercial microfinance and donor-driven credit delivery systems. For example, in India the central bank has taken the lead in identifying the problems in its subsidized credit programs and the losses that have occurred over decades in rural banks. In 1996 India deregulated interest rates, allowing commercial banks and regional banks to set their own interest rates. Consideration is now being given to restructuring the regional rural banks into sustainable financial intermediaries.

Implications for donors

Donors can help the emergence of commercial microfinance in a variety of ways. First, donors should not provide funds for onlending at subsidized interest rates. Microcredit programs that offer subsidized loans to borrowers undercut the institutions that provide commercial microfinance, thus harming the effort to meet microfinance demand on a large scale. Second, donors should insist that financial and social services be funded separately and differently. The former should be financed commercially. Third, donors can help to identify institutions that are potentially qualified for commercial microfinance and are committed to attaining self-sufficiency. These institutions can be provided with grants and concessional loans—not for their loan portfolios—but rather for their institutional development. Fourth, when necessary and feasible, donors should use their influence with governments to assist the latter in introducing appropriate regulations, or deregulations, and in developing supervisory bodies that can provide suitable oversight for institutions offering commercial microfinance. Fifth, donors can disseminate 'best practices' in microfinance through workshops, training courses, and study tours. In recent years there has been a shift in these directions by many donors.

Implications for social and economic development

Only institutional commercial microfinance can combine relatively low-cost credit with sustainability and wide outreach in the provision of financial services to the working poor. Therefore, the shift from donor-assisted credit delivery programs to sustainable financial intermediation is essential if microfinance demand is to be met on the global scale. Meeting this demand matters for several reasons.

Clients of institutions that offer microcredit at commercial rates and provide returns on deposits can improve the management of their financial affairs, raise productivity, and achieve enterprise growth and diversification. Financial institutions providing commercial microfinance can become fully self-sufficient without subsidy, enabling wide outreach to lower-income clients. Governments benefit from reduced subsidies and losses and from the increased social and economic development that results from sustainable microfinance. The economy benefits from increased production and from the new resources made available for investment. Overall, the widespread availability of financial services to the working poor could stimulate economic growth, increase equity, and improve the quality of life for hundreds of millions of people.

Acknowledgments

This chapter is reprinted (with some revisions) from Eichner and Staatz (eds.) (1998). The work discussed here has been supported by the Indonesian Ministry of Finance, the United States Agency for International Development, the Consultative Group to Assist the Poorest, the World Bank, the United Nations Development Program, the Ford Foundation, the Calmeadow Foundation, and others. The author is grateful to Peter Fidler for his assistance in the research and preparation of this chapter. An early version of this chapter was presented at a meeting on 'Financial Services and the Poor: U.S. and Developing Country Experiences,' sponsored by USAID and held at the Brookings Institution on September 28–30, 1994. Parts of the Introduction are adapted from Robinson (1997a), and parts of the section on policy implications are adapted from Robinson (1996).

Notes

1   See also, Ladman and Torico (1981); and Siamwalla et al. (1993) for Thailand; Aleem (1993) for Pakistan; and Carstens (1995) for Mexico. See also Bell and Srinivasan (1985); Von Pischke (1991); and Floro and Yotopoulos (1991).

2   For the development of BRI's local banking system see Sugianto (1989); Patten and Rosengard (1991); Robinson (1992, 1994a, 1994b, 1995a, 1995c, 1997) and Sugianto and Robinson (forthcoming). For comparative studies that include BRI, see Yaron (1992), Otero and Rhyne (1994); Rhyne and Rotblatt (1994); and Christen, Rhyne and Vogel (1994).

3   Sources for Grameen bank data are drawn from: Hossain (1988); Fogelsang and Chandler (1988); Yaron (1992); Khandker (1993); Hubbard (1994); Rhyne and Rotblatt (1994); Christen, Rhyne and Vogel (1994); Khandker, Khalily and Khan (1995); and Yaron, Benjamin and Piprek (1997); and others.

4   A USAID study of sustainability in 11 microfinance programs in developing countries (Christen, Rhyne and Vogel, 1994), found a continuum ranging from one new institution in which revenues did not yet cover operating costs to institutions that were fully self-sufficient without subsidy. The USAID study divided the continuum into three levels: (1) institutions in which revenues from interest and fees do not cover operating costs; (2) institutions in which revenues cover operating costs but not the commercial costs of loanable funds; and (3) fully self-sufficient institutions that cover all costs and risks. 'Sustainable' therefore refers to level 3 institutions;

revenues cover both non-financial and financial costs calculated on a commercial basis. Such institutions are profitable without subsidy, and a return on equity can be expected that is equivalent to those obtained in the private sector.

References

Adams, D.W and Graham, D.H. (1981), 'A Critique of Traditional Agricultural Credit Projects and Policies,' *Journal of Development Economics*, Vol. 8, No. 3, pp. 347–366.

Adams, D.W, Graham, D.H. and Von Pischke, J.D. (eds.) (1984), *Undermining Rural Development with Cheap Credit*, Westview Press: Boulder, CO.

Adams, D.W and Vogel, R.C. (1986), 'Rural Financial Markets in Low Income Countries: Recent Controversies and Lessons,' *World Development*, Vol. 14, No. 4, pp. 477–487.

Aleem, I. (1993), 'The Rural Credit Market in Pakistan: The Costs of Screening,' in Hoff, K., Braverman, A. and Stiglitz, J.E. (eds.), *The Economics of Rural Organization: Theory, Practice and Policy*, Oxford University Press: New York.

Association for Social Advancement (January 1997), *New Vision: A House Journal of ASA* (Dhaka), Vol. 15.

Bell, C. and Srinivasan, T.N. (1985), 'An Anatomy of Transactions in Rural Credit Markets in Andhra Pradesh, Bihar, and Punjab,' World Bank, Washington, DC: Mimeograph.

Bottomley, A. (1983), 'Interest Rate Determination in Undeveloped Rural Areas,' in Von Pischke, J.D., Adams, D.W and Donald, G. (eds.), *Rural Financial Markets in Developing Countries: Their Use and Abuse*, The Johns Hopkins University Press: Baltimore, MD, Extracted from *American Journal of Agricultural Economics*, Vol. 57, No. 2 (1975), pp. 279–291.

Bouman, F.J.A. (1984), 'Informal Saving and Credit Arrangements in Developing Countries: Observations from Sri Lanka,' in Adams, D.W, Graham, D.H. and Von Pischke, J.D. (eds.), *Undermining Rural Development with Cheap Credit*, Westview Press: Boulder, CO, pp. 232–247.

Bouman, F.J.A. (1989), *Small, Short and Unsecured: Informal Finance in Rural India*, Oxford University Press: Delhi.

Carstens, C.M. (1995), *Las Finanzas Populares en Mexico: El Redescubriniento de un Sistema Financiero Olvidado*, Institute Technologico Autonome de Mexico: Mexico City.

Christen, R., Rhyne, E. and Vogel, R. (1995), 'Maximizing the Outreach of Microenterprise Finance: The Emerging Lessons of Successful Programs,' USAID Program and Operations Assessment Report No. 10, USAID: Washington, DC.

Costello, C., Stearns, K. and Christen, R. (1994), 'Exploring Interest Rates: Their True Significance for Microentrepreneurs and Credit Programs,' Discussion Paper 6, ACCION International: Cambridge, MA.

Darling, M. L. [1925] (1978), *The Punjab Peasant in Prosperity and Debt*, South Asia Books: Columbia, MO.

Donald, G. (1976), *Credit for Small Farmers in Developing Countries*, Westview Press: Boulder, CO.

Eicher, C.K. and Staatz, J.M. (eds.) (1998), *Agricultural Development in the Third World* (3rd ed.), The Johns Hopkins University Press: Baltimore, MD.

Floro, S.L. and Yotopoulos, P.A. (1991), *Informal Credit Markets and the New Institutional Economics: The Case of Philippine Agriculture*, Westview Press: Boulder, CO.

Fogelsang, A. and Chandler, D. (1988), *Participation as Process—What We Learned From Grameen Bank*, Bangladesh, Grameen Bank: Dhaka.

Ghate, P., Das-Gupta, A., Lamberte, M., Poapongaskorn, M., Prabowo, D. and Rahman, A. (1992), *Informal Finance: Some Findings From Asia*, Published for the Asian Development Bank, Oxford University Press: Hong Kong.

Germidis, D., Kessler, D. and Meghir, R. (1991), *Financial Systems and Development: What Role for the Formal and Informal Financial Sectors?* Development Center of the Organization for Economic Co-operation and Development: Paris.

Gonzalez-Vega, C. (1993), 'From Policies to Technologies, to Organizations: The Evolution of the Ohio State University Vision of Rural Financial Markets,' Economics and Sociology Occasional Paper No. 2062, Rural Finance Program, Ohio State University: Columbus, OH.

Harriss, B. (1983), 'Money and Commodities: Their Interaction in a Rural Indian Setting,' in Von Pischke, J.D., Adams, D.W and Donald, G. (eds.), *Rural Financial Markets in Developing Countries: Their Use and Abuse*, The Johns Hopkins University Press: Baltimore, MD, pp. 233–241.

Hashemi, S. (1997), 'Building Up Capacity for Banking with the Poor: The Grameen Bank in Bangladesh,' in Schneider, H. (ed.), *Microfinance for the Poor?*, Development Centre of the Organization for Economic Cooperation and Development: Paris, pp. 109–126.

Hoff, K., Braverman, A. and Stiglitz, J.E. (eds.) (1993), *The Economics of Rural Organization: Theory, Practice and Policy*, Oxford University Press: New York.

Hossain, M. (1988), 'Credit for Alleviation of Rural Poverty: The Grameen Bank in Bangladesh,' Research Report No. 65, International Food Policy Research Institute: Washington, DC.

Hubbard, J. (1994), Paper delivered at a meeting on 'Financial Services and the Poor: U.S. and Developing Country Experiences,' Sponsored by USAID and held at the Brookings Institution, Sept. 28–30.

Indian School of Social Sciences, Calcutta (1976), *Bonded Labour in India*, India Book Exchange: Calcutta.

Kamble, N.D. (1982), *Bonded Labour in India*, Uppal Publishing House: New Delhi.

Khandker, S., Khalily, B. and Khan, Z. (1995), 'Grameen Bank: Performance and Sustainability,' World Bank Discussion Paper No. 206. Washington, DC.

Ladman, J. and Torrico, J. (1981), 'Informal Credit Markets in the Valle Alto of Cochabamba, Bolivia,' in Brasch, J. and Rouch, S. (eds.), *Proceedings of the Rocky Mountain Council on Latin American Studies Conference*, University of Nebraska: Lincoln, NE, pp. 83–89.

Long, M. (1968), 'Interest Rates and the Structure of Agricultural Credit Markets,' *Oxford Economic Papers*, Vol. 20, No. 1, pp. 276–287.

Marla, S. (1981), *Bonded Labour in India: National Survey on the Incidence of Bonded Labour*, Biblia Impex Private Ltd: New Delhi.

Morduch, J. (1997), 'The Microfinance Revolution,' Harvard University and Harvard Institute for International Development: Cambridge, MA, Draft.

Otero, M. and Rhyne, E. (eds.) (1994), *The New World of Microenterprise Finance: Building Healthy Financial Institutions for the Poor*, Kumarian Press: Hartford, CT.

Patten, R.H. and Rosengard, J.K. (1991), *Progress with Profits: The Development of Rural Banking in Indonesia*, International Center for Economic Growth and Harvard Institute for International Development: San Francisco, CA.

Rao, G. (1977), *Caste and Poverty: A Case Study of Scheduled Castes in a Delta Village*, Savithri Publications: Malikpuram, India.

Rhyne, E. and Rotblatt, L.S. (1994), *What Makes Them Tick? Exploring the Anatomy of Major Microenterprise Finance Organizations*, Monograph Series No. 9, ACCION International: Cambridge, MA.

Robinson M.S. (1988), *Local Politics: The Law of the Fishes*, Oxford University Press: New Delhi.

Robinson, M.S. (1992), 'Rural Financial Intermediation: Lessons from Indonesia,' Part One: 'The Bank Rakyat Indonesia: Rural Banking 1970–1991,' Harvard Institute for International Development: Discussion Paper No. 434, Cambridge, MA.

Robinson, M.S. (1994a), 'Financial Intermediation at the Local Level: Lessons from Indonesia,' Part Two: 'The Theoretical Perspective,' Harvard Institute for International Development: Discussion Paper No. 482, Cambridge, MA.

Robinson, M.S. (1994b), 'Savings Mobilization and Microenterprise Finance: The Indonesian Experience,' in Otero, M. and Rhyne, E. (eds.), *The New World of Microenterprise Finance: Building Healthy Financial Institutions for the Poor*, Kumarian Press: Hartford, CT, pp. 27–54.

Robinson, M.S. (1995a), 'Indonesia: The Role of Savings in Developing Sustainable Commercial Financing of Small and Microenterprises,' in Brugger, E.A. and Rajapatirana, S. (eds.), *New Perspectives on Financing Small Businesses in Developing Countries*, a joint publication of the International Center for Economic Growth (ICEG) and Fundacion para el Desarrollo Sostenible (FUNDES): San Francisco, CA, pp. 147–174.

Robinson, M.S. (1995b), 'Where the Microfinance Revolution Began: The First 25 Years of the Bank Dagang Bali,' GEMINI Working Paper No. 53, Development Alternatives Inc. and USAID: Bethesda, MD.

Robinson, M.S. (1995c), 'Leading the World in Sustainable Microfinance: The 25th Anniversary of BRI's Unit Desa System,' Bank Rakyat Indonesia: Jakarta.

Robinson, M.S. (1995d), 'The Paradigm Shift in Microfinance: A Perspective from HIID,' Harvard Institute for International Development: Discussion Paper No. 510, Cambridge, MA.

Robinson, M.S. (1996), 'Addressing Some Key Questions on Finance and Poverty,' *Journal of International Development*, Vol. 8, No. 2, pp. 153–161.

Robinson, M.S. (1997a), 'Microfinance in Indonesia,' *The UNESCO Courier* (Paris) (January), pp. 24–27.

Robinson, M.S. (1997b), 'Introducing Savings in Microcredit Institutions: When and How?' CGAP Focus Note No. 8, CGAP: Washington, DC.

Robinson, M.S. (forthcoming), 'The Microfinance Revolution: Sustainable Finance for the Poor,' Manuscript.

Rosenberg, R. (1984), 'Beyond Self-Sufficiency: Licensed Leverage and Microfinance Strategy' (draft), USAID: Washington, DC.

Roth, H.D. (1983), *Indian Moneylenders at Work: Case Studies of the Traditional Rural Credit Markets in Dhanbad District, Bihar*, Manohar: New Delhi.

Rutherford, S. (1995), *ASA: The Biography of an NGO*, Association for Social Advancement: Dhaka.

Sharma, M. (1978), *The Politics of Inequality: Competition and Control in an Indian Village*, Asian Studies at Hawaii, No. 22, University Press of Hawaii: Honolulu.

Siamwalla, A. et al. (1993), 'The Thai Rural Credit Systems and Elements of a Theory: Public Subsidies, Private Information, and Segmented Markets,' in Hoff, K., Braverman, A. and Stiglitz, J.E. (eds.), *The Economics of Rural Organization: Theory, Practice and Policy*, Oxford University Press: New York.

Singh, K. (1983), 'Structure of Interest Rates on Consumption Loans in an Indian Village,' in Von Pischke, J.D., Adams, D.W and Donald, G. (eds.), *Rural Financial Markets in Developing Countries: Their Use and Abuse*, The Johns Hopkins University Press: Baltimore, MD, pp. 251–254, Extracted from *Asian Economic Review*, Vol. 10, No. 4 (1968), pp. 471–475.

Sugianto (1989), 'KUPEDES and SIMPEDES,' *Asia Pacific Rural Finance*, July-September, pp. 12–14.

Sugianto and Robinson, M.S. (forthcoming), 'Commercial Banks as Microfinance Providers,' APRACA: Bangkok.

Tun Wai, U (1980), 'The Role of Unorganized Financial Markets in Economic Development and in the Formulation of Monetary Policy,' *Savings and Development*, Vol. 4, No. 4.

Vogel, R.C. (1984), 'The Effect of Subsidized Agricultural Credit on Income Distribution in Costa Rica,' in Adams, D.W, Graham, D.H. and Von Pischke, J.D. (eds.), *Undermining Rural Development with Cheap Credit*, Westview Press: Boulder, CO, pp. 133–145.

Von Pischke, J.D. (1991), *Finance at the Frontier: Debt Capacity and the Role of Credit in the Private Economy*, The World Bank (EDI Development Series), World Bank: Washington, DC.

Von Pischke, J.D., Adams. D.W and Donald, G. (eds.) (1983), *Rural Financial Markets in Developing Countries: Their Use and Abuse*, The Johns Hopkins University Press: Baltimore, MD.

Vyas, N.N. (1980), *Bondage and Exploitation in Tribal India*, Rawat Publications: Jaipur.

Wardhana, A. (forthcoming), Introduction to Robinson (forthcoming).

World Bank News (1996), 'KUPEDES: Indonesia's Model Small Credit Program,' World Bank, Operations Evaluations Department, Washington, DC.

World Bank (1997), *World Development Report, 1997*, Oxford University Press: New York.

World Bank (1997), 'An Inventory of Selected Microfinance Institutions in South Asia,' World Bank: Washington, DC.

Yaron, J. (1992), *Assessing Successful Rural Financial Institutions: A Public Interest Analysis*, World Bank Discussion Papers 174, World Bank: Washington, DC.

Yaron, J., Benjamin, M. and Piprek, G. (1997), *Rural Finance: Issues, Design, and Best Practices*, Agricultural and Natural Resources Department, World Bank: Washington, DC, Draft.

5 Altruistic or production finance? a donor's dilemma

DALE W ADAMS

Several years ago, a jaded bank official in Bangladesh told me it was time to give up on cajoling banks to lend to poor people, especially in rural areas. He was discouraged by chronic loan recovery problems— the specialized agricultural bank in the country at the time was collecting less than 20% of its loans—and by periodic government announcements of loan forgiveness. Since several large non-governmental organizations (NGOs) in the country had been relatively successful in providing loans to poor people, he argued that all rural lending should be transferred to them.[1] De facto, this transfer has been underway in dozens of countries where traditional development banks and cooperatives have collapsed and where thousands of NGOs are now used increasingly by donors as channels for loans to poor people. Although not announced as such, this is resulting in a shift in donor support from production credit to altruistic lending.

Given this sharp change it may be useful to briefly review why previous approaches often failed to provide sustained financial services to poor people and then go on to speculate on the strengths and limitations of using NGOs instead.

Production credit

For more than four decades donors employed credit programs in low-income countries to stimulate production, investment, and use of modern inputs. Many of these efforts involved cooperatives, super-vised credit programs, private rural banks, and specialized development banks. Government-sponsored loan guarantees, concessionary funds from central banks, and bank lending quotas were also elements of many programs. Donors commonly supported these efforts by placing funds in central banks that were on-lent through concessionary credit lines. Although production considerations were the primary objective, altruism was often a secondary objective; numerous credit programs targeted small farmers, for example (Donald, 1976; Sacay et al., 1986). Unfortunately, many of the cooperatives that once provided loans to farmers have disappeared, most of the supervised credit programs for farmers have evaporated, numerous rural private banks have collapsed, many specialized agricultural development banks have imploded, and most efforts to force commercial banks to lend in rural areas yielded only transitory results. A number of factors combined to undermine these production-credit efforts, the following being the most important:

(a) Hostile macroeconomic environments often dampened loan demand, lessened the creditworthiness of potential borrowers, weakened the ability of borrowers to repay loans, and lessened the capacity of many people to save. The weight of this bore most heavily on poor people.

(b) Repressive macrofinancial policies also constrained the expansion of formal financial markets. Interest rate controls, hefty bank reserve requirements, and extensive loan targeting lowered the revenues of formal financial intermediaries and boosted their costs. This discouraged them from seeking new clients and from handling small transactions.

(c) Numerous governments operated centrally planned economies. These severely limited the opportunities for small private enterprises which are typically operated by people of modest means, thus limiting their demand for formal loans. Central planning was accompanied by an inflexible banking system that performed mostly fiscal functions, rather than financial intermediation, thereby constraining the supply of loans for poor people.[2]

(d) In many cases loans were part of a package of inputs and little attention was given to the effect credit projects had on the performance of financial intermediaries. Even less attention was given to how credit projects affected the ability and willingness of financial systems to offer deposit services. These projects were typically evaluated on the basis of changes in the income of borrowers, in production, in use of inputs, in the pace of technological change, in employment, or in investments.[3] In many cases donors and governments used financial markets as a commons and there was little explicit concern given to enhancing their durability.

(e) Donors and governments inadvertently warped formal financial markets by providing concessionary lines of credit (Vogel, 1984). It was often cheaper for banks and cooperatives to obtain funds from a central lending source than it was to mobilize private deposits. This resulted in relatively few poor people having attractive places to deposit their savings; in numerous cases donor-nurtured development banks and cooperatives ignored potential depositors, most of whom were relatively poor.

(f) Many governments used financial markets to allocate grants by imposing negative real rates of interest on both loans and deposits, by occasionally forgiving loans, and by tolerating hefty loan defaults. This attracted rent seekers who colonized credit programs to the exclusion of poor people.[4] These rents attracted bank employees, the military, the politically influential, and government officials.[5]

(g) Because governments and donors provided most of the funds for lending, political influence permeated the operations of many of these lenders. Bank managers were often political appointees rather than bankers, the organizations were usually overstaffed, and political considerations commonly overrode prudent lending decisions. This resulted in excessive lending costs and in flawed screening of loan applicants for creditworthiness.

The net results of many of these efforts were institutions that could not endure without continual subsidies and financial systems that were allergic to poor people. When donors and governments grew weary of continual calls for more subsidies and withdrew their support, many donor-addicted organizations imploded.[6] Using Von Pischke's metaphor, the formal financial frontier expanded too little, despite massive efforts by donors to extend these frontiers. Many of the credit initiatives were unsustainable and became transient salients in these frontiers. This led major donors such as the World Bank, the Agency for International Development, and the Inter-American Development Bank to reduce substantially their funding for production credit projects in the late 1980s and to increasingly court NGOs.[7] These activities now include much more emphasis on expanding financial services for women and for operators of microenterprises through semi-formal lenders. It is still an open question, however, whether or not these more explicitly altruistic credit programs will be any more effective in reaching poor people than were earlier production-credit efforts.

Recent changes

In an increasing number of countries economic environments have become more hospitable to financial markets, largely due to recognition of the failure of previous strategies, reinforced by donor and International Monetary Fund proddings. Exchange rates are less distorted, interest rates are closer to market rates, product and input prices are more liberated, central planning has been lessened, and private enterprise is allowed to play a larger role in most economies. This has resulted in less inflation, real rates of interest that are generally positive, more economic opportunities for small businesses, and less indirect taxing of agriculture and of other enterprises commonly populated by poor people.

Although history cannot be replayed, it would be interesting to see how the credit projects of the 1970s and 1980s would have fared in the more hospitable economic environments of the 1990s in countries such as Argentina, Chile, China, Egypt, Ghana, Mexico, Indonesia, and Uganda. One might argue that there would have been fewer credit projects; some of the problems that previous projects attempted to treat may have been less severe and merited less attention. Would loan recovery have been higher? Most certainly. Would a larger number of people and firms—particularly small firms—have qualified as creditworthy? Most likely. Would a much larger number of people have had the capacity and incentive to place more of their savings in financial institutions? With little doubt. Would rent seekers have had incentives to colonize subsidized credit programs that had no rents? Of course not. Would many of the financial institutions involved have been so seriously undermined? Probably not. Would most of the financial institutions involved in development efforts have become addicted to government or donor funding? Highly unlikely. Would the formal financial frontier in many low-income countries have enveloped a much larger number of poor people? Without a doubt.

Following this analysis, it should be clear that this observer, for one, believes that loans are weak instruments for prodding development. On the other hand, I am also convinced that durable financial systems are critical infrastructure in market-driven economies. How else can resources be efficiently reallocated? In this regard, donor policies that focus on strengthening financial markets instead of pushing targeted and subsidized credit should be welcomed. And, because of major changes in macroeconomic and macrofinance environments, the results of finance programs in the future will likely be more satisfactory than they were in the past. This gives pause, however, when one considers the current donor fad that involves abandoning production credit and focusing instead on altruistic lending through NGOs.

The altruistic approach

Most societies have norms that warn against incurring debt. It is jarring, therefore, to hear spokespersons for disadvantaged people arguing that credit (debt) is an entitlement for poor individuals. The metamorphosis of the negative word 'debt' into the positive term 'credit' puzzles me, much as does the conversion of an ugly caterpillar into a lovely butterfly. Evil moneylenders are thought to impose debt on their supposed victims by issuing loans, but when laced with altruism and done with tender loving care by NGOs this act is transformed into granting credit to beneficiaries. Strangely, the morality of the act is defined by the intentions of the lender. If lenders are concerned about recovering the funds they lend and make a living from doing so, it is termed evil. If the lender is using someone else's money, doesn't worry much about recovering loans, and must continually seek outside subsidies, it is termed good. The fact that moneylenders usually provide sustained financial services to their clients, while some altruistic credit activities are transitory—depending on the depths of the patron's pockets—seldom enters the discussion. Also ignored is the fact that managers of most NGOs sustain a much higher standard of living than does the average, much maligned moneylender. Capturing some of the subsidy that passed through an NGO via attractive salaries, superior transportation, plush offices, and foreign travel is seen as part of doing good.

The term NGO covers a variety of organizations whose objectives range from social to developmental (Bowden, 1990). Here, I focus only on the increasing number of NGOs that are involved in extending loans or mobilizing deposits, often at the behest of donors. Many of the NGOs that currently provide semi-formal financial services were established with altruistic objectives. In some cases, financial services were added to existing altruistic NGOs, while in other cases NGOs were set up initially to be retail outlets for donor or government funds. Some of the best NGOs are indigenous while many of the weakest were spawned by donor or government funding. Most credit activities in these organizations rest on similar assumptions: that credit is a powerful antidote for poverty, that most poor people have a credit need, and that NGO managers are the only ones who care enough to lend to poor people.

While the work and dedication of a few NGOs that provide financial services is admirable and worthy of emulation, a much larger number of NGOs, in my opinion, have low prospects for growing into efficient organizations. Many pseudo-NGOs are managed by displaced government officials, are connected to life-support systems irrigated by government or donor funds, have only a few hundred beneficiaries, and are high-cost operations in terms of services rendered. In trying to winnow the wheat from the chaff in NGOs, it may be useful to summarize briefly their main strengths and limitations in providing financial services.

Strengths

The main strength of NGOs is that they are generally grassroots organizations which are working with poor people. The fact that these organizations are private operations, that they harness the energy of local people, and that some of them are indigenous further enhances their attractiveness. Clearly, a few NGOs have been able to fill important niches in financial markets: credit unions effectively mobilize deposits in many countries, the Grameen Bank provides loans to poor women in Bangladesh, ACCION International helps operators of small businesses access loans in Latin America, and ACORD provides financial services under adverse conditions in several African countries (Abugre, 1994). The fact that many NGOs are driven by altruistic motives further enhances their attractiveness in the eyes of donors.

Limitations

In providing financial services, NGOs have several inherent limitations. Because of their hands-on approach to development, many of them are high-cost lenders. Numerous NGOs lend to fewer than a thousand beneficiaries and therefore it will be difficult for most of them to realize scale economies.

Even more importantly, because NGOs operate mostly outside the formal financial system, prudential regulation and supervision are almost totally absent. This is particularly a problem once NGOs begin to mobilize deposits—although careless lending of donor funds is not insignificant, either. Allowing deposit mobilization without effective prudential regulation is unconscionable. Poor depositors are unable to assemble the information needed to assess the financial operations of NGOs and thus individually protect their deposits from malfeasance, let alone imprudence. In this light, donors should be more interested in protecting the interests of depositors through prudential regulation and deposit guarantees than about filling the supposed credit needs of a much smaller number of people.[8] Without proper supervision and regulation NGOs will be unable to realize economies of scope where the same facilities can be used to produce two financial services—loans and deposits—more efficiently than if it produced only one. This deposit-mobilizing handicap will also cripple the ability of NGOs to expand lending and largely restrict them to the largess of donors and government, thus further crimping their ability to realize economies of scale.

This handicap will further cripple the ability of NGOs to screen loan applicants for creditworthiness based on their saving record and also constrict the outreach of NGOs' financial services. The altruistic culture of many NGOs, and the fact that they are largely using donor funds compounds the problems of screening applicants for creditworthiness. If the distinction between a loan and a grant is fuzzy in the minds of the altruistic lender, 'loans' will likely be more clearly seen by beneficiaries as grants. Beneficiaries may be willing to repay as long as the volume of lending is expanding and additional loans continue to be available. Loan recovery problems tend to become more severe when the volume of loans stagnates, possibly due to donor fatigue.

Chaves (1994) has also stressed the limitations of NGOs regarding internal incentives. Many of these organizations, particularly cooperatives, have ill-defined ownership. Altruistic institutions may also have vague standards of performance that are incompatible with procedures that screen loans on the basis of creditworthiness. Organizations that are not disciplined by market forces and profits may act in ways that are in the best interest of their employees and managers, rather than in the best interests of the donor or the so-called beneficiaries.

Because of their size, most NGOs find it difficult to diversify their loan portfolio to manage risk. Many of them are also highly dependent on surges of external funding that compounds management difficulties. Loan recovery problems and relatively high costs, combined with altruism, make it difficult for NGOs to cover their costs of operation from loan revenues. This will subject them to the whims and fads of donors and force them continually to seek subsidies. Many NGOs also lack standard connections to other financial intermediaries and are, therefore, unable to borrow or lend funds systematically through broader financial networks. This will limit their ability to mature into more comprehensive financial markets that can intermediate over large geographic areas.

Particular concern is warranted for the ultra-altruistic NGOs operating in countries such as Bangladesh, Bolivia, Gambia and

Uganda. These organizations are typically small, depend entirely on the beneficence of donors, and compete aggressively for new clients by offering soft loans at low or no interest. Their activities undermine the efforts of more serious NGOs. Their corporate cultures make it virtually impossible to avoid dispensing grants (Boulding, 1981).

Conclusions

Providing formal or semi-formal financial services to poor people, especially in rural areas, is expensive. It is not surprising, therefore, that expanding the formal financial frontier to encompass these individuals has been difficult. Nor is it surprising that many fledgling financial institutions have disintegrated while temporarily providing these services. NGOs face the same harsh economic realities.

Although performance of production-credit projects has been disappointing, and, given the doubtless value of extending more financial services to poor people, altruistic lending through NGOs is not an effective response. Most poor people want better opportunities to save and ways to enhance their creditworthiness; a much smaller number of poor people are creditworthy. Specious claims about filling credit needs obscures these important facts. Because of their non-regulated nature, NGOs are usually ill equipped to provide secure deposit services. It is one thing to allow NGOs to do good with other peoples' money through unremunerative lending, but it is something quite different to promote unsafe deposit mobilization by such organizations. Instead of stressing altruistic lending through NGOs, or going back to production credit, donors should emphasize rebuilding and expanding formal financial infrastructure; the economic environment for doing so is much improved in many countries.

A much larger number of poor people might be reached relatively quickly through reformed formal financial institutions instead of NGOs—especially on the deposit side. In Egypt, for example, a large agricultural development bank has about 1000 offices in rural towns and villages. In a relatively short period of time, and with only modest changes in its corporate culture, the bank could provide deposit services to millions of additional poor people, particularly women. With a slightly revised mission statement and modified employee incentives it could find hundreds of thousands of creditworthy small borrowers who are increasingly involved in rural non-farm businesses. Buttressed by appropriate donor and government support, these activities could be both profitable and durable.[9]

To develop durable formal financial systems that are friendly to poor people, donors must alter their traditional money-driven approach. They must focus far less on moving large amounts of money which often gets in the way of deposit mobilization and concentrate more on reforming financial institutions into more efficient organizations. Major donors must play an important role in these reforms. Many of the financial institutions that might issue more financial services to poor people are hostages of special interest groups or continue to operate under mission statements that are out of step with new economic conditions. Many of the traditional agricultural development banks, for example, behave like a division of a ministry of agriculture, rather than as a bank. They are often managed by agricultural technicians rather than bankers, have weak ties to the rest of the banking community, and have directors who know little about banking. In other cases, extremely high reserve requirements and other banking regulations provide strong disincentives for banks to mobilize deposits, especially from poor people. Donors can be instrumental in encouraging appropriate changes in these areas.

In assisting with these reforms, donors face a dilemma. Credit projects that pursue either production or altruistic objectives directly—something that is politically popular—will yield disappointing results for basically the same reasons: both approaches cause financial markets to function less efficiently and to reach fewer poor people. Financial market development projects that pursue neither objective directly—something that is politically unpopular—will likely go much further in achieving both production and altruistic objectives.

Notes

1   In the early 1990s there were more than 800 registered NGOs in Bangladesh with about 140 of them pursuing development objectives. Many of the development NGOs offered financial services. Even small countries such as Bolivia and Gambia typically have a hundred or more developmental NGOs.

2   Centrally planned economies such as the former Soviet Union and the Peoples Republic of China, however, generally provided small savers attractive deposit opportunities until inflation increased in the late 1980s and early 1990s.

3   A recent example is World Bank, 1993.

4   Financial markets have a high propensity to distribute subsidies and grants regressively. Interest rate subsidies and the grants realized by absconding with loans are both proportional to loan size: large loan, large subsidy; small loan, small subsidy; and no loan, no subsidy. Tilting these subsidies in favor of the poor further discourages financial intermediaries from lending to poor people by adding to the high costs per unit of money lent asso-

ciated with making small loans. Ubiquitous low interest rates on loans resulted in even lower interest rates being paid on deposits. This penalized poor people because they had relatively few alternatives for holding their savings.

5   A blatant example of this occurred in inflation-racked Sudan several years ago when employees of the agricultural bank received most of the zero-interest-rate loans made by the bank, ostensibly for charity purposes.

6   Illustrative examples are the Agricultural Development Bank in Bolivia, the Jamaican Development Bank, many of the CNCAs in West Africa, the Co-operative Bank of Uganda, the FIRA system in Mexico, the directed credit programs of credit unions in Latin America, hundreds of rural private banks in the Philippines, the BIMAS program in Indonesia, credit activities in the Comilla project in Bangladesh, and lending through many agricultural co-operatives in India.

7   An Operational Directive (No. 8.30) issued in the early 1990s sharply reduced the World Bank's traditional agricultural credit activities. It mandated that credit projects must stress improving the performance of financial markets.

8   The highly successful village unit program of Bank Rakyat Indonesia has about six depositors for each borrower.

9   The Bank Rakyat's experience with reforming traditional production/altruistic lending in Indonesia reinforces this conclusion (Patten and Rosengard, 1991). Earlier experience in Japan, Korea, and Taiwan showed that relatively poor people desire deposit services, that many of them can become creditworthy, and that serving these clients can be profitable for financial institutions (Kato, 1985; Saeki, 1947).

References

Abugre, C. (1994), 'When Credit Is Not Due: A Critical Evaluation of Donor NGO Experience with Credit,' in Bouman, F.J.A and Hospes, O. (eds.), *Financial Landscapes Reconstructed: The Fine Art of Mapping Development*, West-view Press: Boulder, CO, pp. 157–175.

Boulding, K.E. (1981), *A Preface to Grants Economics: The Economy of Love and Fear*, Praeger: New York.

Bowden, P. (1990), 'NGOs in Asia: Issues in Development,' *Public Administration and Development*, Vol. 10, pp. 141–152.

Chaves, R.A. (1994), 'The Behavior and Performance of Credit Cooperatives: An Analysis of Cooperative Governance Rules,' Unpublished Ph.D. dissertation, Department of Agricultural Economics, The Ohio State University: Columbus, OH.

Donald, G. (1976), *Credit for Small Farmers in Developing Countries*, Westview Press: Boulder, CO.

Kato, Y. (1985), *Development of Agriculture and Political Finance*, Rakuyu-shyobou: Tokyo (in Japanese).

Patten, R.H. and Rosengard, J.K. (1991), *Progress with Profits: The Development of Rural Banking in Indonesia*, ICS Press: San Francisco, CA.

Sacay, O.J., Agabin, M.H. and Tanchoco, C.I.E. (1985), *Small Farmer Credit Dilemma*, Technical Board for Agricultural Credit: Manila, Philippines.

Saeki, N. (1947), *History of Agricultural Finance in Japan*, Tokyo University Press: Tokyo (in Japanese).

Vogel, R.C. (1984), 'Savings Mobilization: The Forgotten Half of Rural Finance,' in Adams, D.W, Graham, D.H. and Von Pischke, J.D. (eds.), *Undermining Rural Development With Cheap Credit*, Westview Press: Boulder, Colorado, pp. 248–265.

Von Pischke, J.D. (1991), *Finance at The Frontier: Debt Capacity and the Role of Credit in The Private Economy*, Economic Development Institute, World Bank: Washington, DC.

World Bank (1993), 'A Review of Bank Lending for Agricultural Credit and Rural Finance (1948–1992),' Operations Evaluations Department Report No. 12143, World Bank: Washington, DC.

6 Combining social and financial intermediation to reach the poor: the necessity and dangers

LYNN BENNETT

Participation and the financial sector

The World Bank *Participation Sourcebook* has given a reasonably clear definition of participation as 'a process through which stakeholders influence and share control over development initiatives, decisions and resources that affect them' (World Bank, 1995). But precisely how can a typical Bank lending operation be designed and implemented to ensure participation? The term must be placed in a sectoral context to have operational meaning. What would participation look like in financial sector operations—specifically in operations intended to build financial service systems that reach women and the poor?

The growing number of *group-based financial service systems* appear to be the perfect embodiment of participation in finance. The most well known, of course, is Grameen Bank in Bangladesh, which works through hundreds of thousands of groups to deliver cost-effective financial services to very poor men and women who would almost certainly not have access to such services through ordinary banks. There are many more examples of group-based systems all over the world (World Bank, 1996).

Admittedly, not all group-based have done as well as Grameen at combining *outreach* to the poor with *sound financial management*. A later paper in this collection describes two group-based programs studied by the author and others in Nepal. As with so many group-based projects, that effort did an impressive job with outreach to women and small farmers, but failed utterly in building a financially sustainable system.

While such failures are common, we know that Grameen is not the only success story for group-based lending. There is much we can learn from both the positive and the negative experiences of the thousands of group-based lending programs. There is much we can learn about what participation really means in finance, how it can work to increase outreach and sustainability—and how to make it happen. This paper outlines a conceptual approach to the subject, highlighting some key findings from an empirical study of five different group-based programs in South Asia.

Levels of participation

Participation in the financial sector can take place at different levels of intensity. At the most basic level, effort is placed on simply finding out what constraints the clients face and what products and services they want and are willing to pay for. This is really nothing more than good market research. Use of this knowledge about client constraints and preferences to guide the design of both products and delivery mechanisms is the starting point for client participation.

Group-based systems however, permit much higher levels of client participation. Figure 6.1 sets out the possible roles that group members can play as beneficiaries, clients, investors-shareholders, and managers.[1] These four major roles form a kind of *participation continuum*, moving from the beneficiary who receives free services to the manager who makes strategic and operational decisions about how services are designed and delivered. Most successful systems have moved along the continuum to the point where they view participants as clients: these systems invest in setting up timely feedback mechanisms to make sure they stay in touch with what their clients want. They also make sure that there is a clear contract that lets the client know what she or he must do in return to keep the services coming. Other projects have moved further along this continuum and devolve decision-making power to participants as shareholders or even as managers. In geographic settings where long distances cause isolation, such as rural areas of Nepal and Bolivia, these more intensive forms of participation may be the only way that the costs and risks of serving difficult-to-reach groups can be reduced sufficiently to enable the service to continue.

One of the premises of a group-based approach is that, with sufficient training and experience, group members can become effective owners and managers. Projects can be designed to prepare

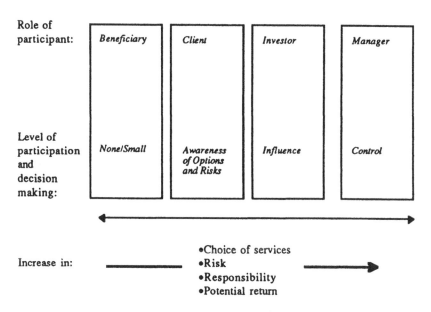

Figure 6.1 The participation continuum: the different roles

clients to advance along the continuum of increased responsibility by including significant investment in building up local institutions and training clients in accounting and other skills they need to manage their own institutions. From this perspective, probably the most important thing that donors can support is this kind of human resource development and local institution building in the context of microfinance projects.

However, not all people are equally willing to take on the increased risks associated with higher degrees of self management. The poorer the client and the lower her level of human capital endowment, the less able she may be to accept the risk and devote the time required for the higher levels of participation. Many of the most vulnerable may prefer the role of client to that of manager. While there is no necessary 'evolution' toward the full group ownership and management end of the continuum, it does appear that projects where group members remain in the passive 'beneficiary' role are almost guaranteed *not* to achieve financial self-sustainability. These are the ones that stay forever at Level One of the Otero/Rhyne model (Otero and Rhyne, 1994).

The nature or intensity of participation may change as group members gain experience, as their ventures mature, and as the range

of financial services they require expands. But wherever they are on
the continuum, the critical success elements seem to boil down to two
R's. The system must be *responsive* so that group members have an
opportunity to take part in defining the services and the delivery
mechanism and it must clearly define and enforce *responsibilities* so
that members understand the contract and their part in it.

Barriers to financial intermediation

Von Pischke's concept of the 'frontier' is very useful in considering
how to integrate marginalized groups into formal systems of financial
intermediation (Von Pischke, 1991). To move the boundaries of the
frontier outward toward women and the poor, it is important to know
something about the nature of the barriers that currently block this
group from participation in formal financial markets. These well
documented barriers seem to operate at three distinct levels, as shown
in Figure 6.2.

   *At the most aggregate level the constraints to successful interme-
diation with the poor include environmental, economic, and sociocultural factors.* Several of these conditions are endemic to the low-
income situations faced by the target groups and therefore pose
difficult problems in identifying and implementing effective policy
interventions. For example, in sparsely populated, remote rural areas,
poor households may be engaged in low-return, subsistence agricultural activities that tend to have high levels of production risk and,
where there is a subsistence surplus, market risk. A second example
from this category is found in the sociocultural barriers faced by
women, ethnic minorities, and castes. Gender-based barriers are
particularly difficult to overcome as they operate at both the societal
and intra-household level.

   Variations between sociocultural systems can profoundly affect
design options for projects and the likelihood that high levels of
participation will be possible. One important variable is the degree to
which a given society encourages cooperative efforts through local
clubs, temple associations, work groups, etc. These structures depend
on traditions of collaboration and on a certain level of trust among
members. Putnam (1993) has given this phenomenon a very apt
name. He calls it 'social capital', by which he means:

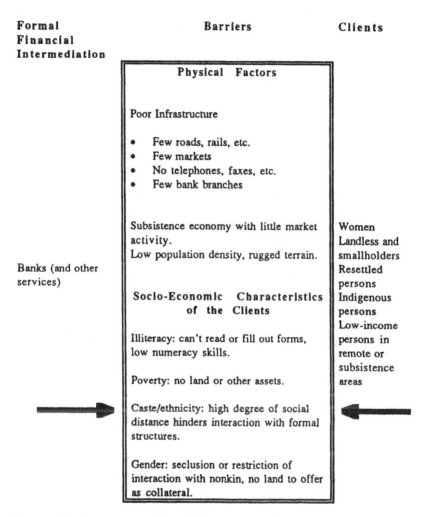

Figure 6.2 Barriers to financial intermediation

those features of social organization such as *networks, norms, and trust* that facilitate coordination and cooperation for mutual benefit. Social capital enhances the benefits of investment in physical and human capital (p. 36).

Some communities are rich in social capital, with a multitude of interconnecting formal and informal groups and networks and very strong expectations of reciprocity and incentives for cooperation. In others, such systems are less well-developed or have been undermined by economic and political stresses. Putnam gives the strong church-based networks of traditional African-American communities as an example of high levels of social capital; but also points to the erosion of these networks in inner-city slums.

For Asia two contrasting examples can be suggested. One is Bali, where people seem to form groups for almost everything and mechanisms that encourage trust and cooperation are so widely prevalent that one development expert[2] said the island is hardly a valid test for any development effort since 'everything works in Bali!' Focusing just on financial interactions, the Balinese have layers and layers of systems for intermediation ranging from traditional rotating credit societies (*arisang*) which abound in every village and market, to local community grain banks, to formal financial institutions run by villages, to a plethora of branches of national and even international commercial banks offering their services. As the same expert observed, Bali is, in fact 'over-banked.' Networks and systems to build social capital are so abundant that every possible niche for social and financial intermediation seems to be occupied.

Afghanistan offers a stark contrast. Although it has strong traditions of group cooperation along clan lines, the rugged terrain, sparse population, and harsh conditions have bred a tradition of strong individualism with a focus on the maintenance of the 'honor' or *izat* of one's family or group. Trust and cooperation is not easy to establish beyond family and clan boundaries. Prolonged conflict has intensified the situation. War has frayed traditional networks and eroded social capital. Experienced development workers involved in Afghanistan believe that it will be very difficult to launch community programs there.

Social capital is a particularly relevant concept for those working in finance because it has to do with the establishment of *trust*, which is essential to financial intermediation. Financial transactions involve promises about future actions, and such interaction simply will not take place unless there is some degree of trust between the borrower and the lender. Social networks are important because they are the basis upon which trust, based on mutual knowledge and expectations of reciprocity, can be built. However, to avoid over-romantic notions of cooperation and altruism in traditional societies, it is important to note that there are also numerous characteristics of social relations which may be conflictual.

At the next level, the barriers or constraints to financial interme-diation with the poor can be visualized in terms of macroeconomic and/or financial sector policy variables. These economic and financial policies represent opportunities for intervention which can either create or ameliorate problems such as poor repayment behavior on the part of clients or lack of interest in increasing outreach to the poor on the part of the financial intermediaries. Macroeconomic policy considerations include: inflation rates, tax and expenditure policies (particularly urban-biased policies or policies which skimp on education and other social sector investments in the poor), and targets for growth of money and incomes.

Many of these issues will generally be beyond the purview of a specific project but it is important to factor them into program design.

At the level of the overall economy it is also important to be aware of local production systems and technologies as well as marketing opportunities and constraints. One important variable is the degree to which the local economy is oriented toward subsistence or commercial production and the degree of monetization. Project designers also need to understand the existing local demand/supply network for financial services as well as the history of both successful and failed government initiatives. These factors directly affect the responsiveness of potential clients, especially those from low-income households.

Also of direct relevance are financial sector policy considerations, which include:
(a) interest rates,
(b) regulation of financial intermediaries,
(c) imposition of reserve requirements,
(d) incentives to mobilize savings, and
(e) equity and capital required of new bank entrants.

In addition, a legal system which does not permit collateral foreclosure or which does not otherwise enforce contracts may undermine the sense of trust necessary for financial intermediation. Harassment by local police and complex, expensive registration requirements may also make it difficult for individual microentrepreneurs to gain access to formal financial and enterprise development services. These variables jointly influence the likelihood of successful intermediation generally, and among the poor in particular.

Finally, a number of factors operate at the institutional level. These are generally much more responsive to the kind of interventions that are possible at the project level. They involve all the institutions concerned in the 'system' of financial and social intermediation to be established and relate to each of these institution's approach to the business and clients. Consequently, these factors are related to processes and policies internal to the institutions as well as to the mechanisms used to reach and interact with the clients and the products and services offered. Examples include *attitudinal factors* such as welfare orientation versus performance orientation for financial services provided to low-income individuals and groups. Other examples include *institutional practices* such as the use of staff incentives in the form of raises, bonuses, promotions;[3] decentralized decision-making authority and streamlined branch-level loan review and processing procedures; responsive design of savings and credit products to suit clients' situations, etc.

From the point of view of most formal lending institutions, people without tangible assets, those who live in difficult-to-reach areas or who are illiterate and unfamiliar with bureaucratic systems and procedures are not viewed as 'good risks.' Agriculture in particular, especially in marginal, unirrigated areas, is considered a risky investment because of its dependence on weather and other vagaries of nature. But more broadly, to most formal financial institutions nearly all of the tiny, informal businesses run by the poor are not attractive investments. The amounts these businesses require are too small. It is too difficult to get information from the clients, who may be illiterate or communicate in local dialects that the banker does not know. They are too far away, and it takes too long to visit their farms or their businesses in the slum. The costs per dollar lent will be very high, there is no real security for the loan, and so on.

Social intermediation: bridging the gap

A wide gap separates most low-income men and women from the formal financial system. To reach these people with financial services, ordinary financial intermediation is not sufficient. New mechanisms are required to bridge the gaps created by poverty, illiteracy, gender, and remoteness. Local institutions must be built and nurtured, and the skills and confidence of the new clients must be developed through a process of *social intermediation*. For those whose social and economic disadvantages have placed them 'beyond the frontier' of formal finance, successful financial intermediation requires social intermediation.

Reaching those beyond the frontier tends to require more than a single institution. Hence, in most cases, understanding how the process of social and financial intermediation takes place demands a systems analysis rather than a simple institutional analysis. Figure 6.3 presents a *systems framework* illustrating the various social intermediation options. The two major components to be linked are: (1) the formal financial, enterprise-development and social-service institutions on the

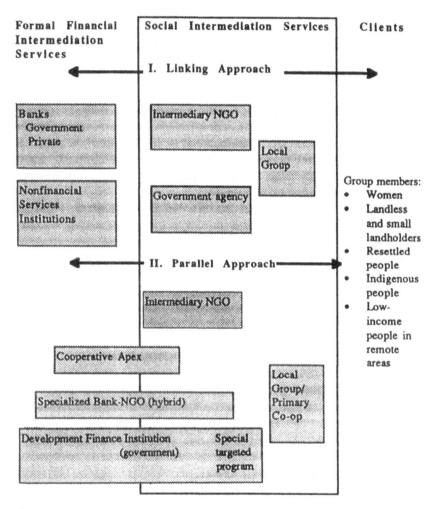

Figure 6.3 Approaches to social intermediation

left side of the diagram, and (2) the potential clients on the right.

The shaded area in the middle of the diagram includes the important actors who undertake social intermediation between the formal institutions and the individual clients. Although social intermediation takes place in many ways through many mechanisms,[4] one of the most effective is through fostering the development of *local savings and credit groups.*

The role of groups in social and financial intermediation

Social intermediation has two objectives or dimensions. Both have to be realized to pave the way for sustainable financial intermediation. The first objective is *increased target-group access to services and inputs*. The second objective is more difficult to measure: *the development of self-confidence and management skills by group members*. Ultimately, it is the cohesiveness and self-management capacity of the groups that enable them to bring down the costs of financial intermediation by: (1) reducing default through peer pressure and (2) lowering the transaction costs to banks in dealing with many small borrowers and savers.

Significant additional costs are incurred at the start in building the skills and systems that permit the target group eventually to take over most of the management of their own financial transactions. Thus, if they are to achieve sustainability, financial services projects for the poor may require substantial up-front investments in human resources and local institution building. In fact, these costs can be expected to be a larger part of the project funding than the actual 'credit' disbursed to the group members, especially in the early years of the system's establishment.

Evidence from five South Asian case studies undertaken by World Bank researchers (Bennett et al., 1996) points to certain features of program and institutional design that seem to promote success in combining social and financial intermediation. For example, although none of these cases has reached the impressive saving performance of Bank Rakyat Indonesia (BRI), the two systems which have made greatest progress toward financial sustainability depend wholly or largely on member savings as a source of lending capital. This may conflict with donor institutions' imperative to 'move money,' but it may be the most important lesson that we bring from our study of group-based systems.

There are many institutional alternatives for group-based social intermediation. In many countries the task of social intermediation has been most successfully carried out by nongovernment organizations (NGOs) rather than government institutions. However, as indicated in Figure 6.3, government agencies have also played this role—sometimes with unexpected success.

Approaches to social intermediation: linking systems and parallel systems

There are two main approaches to social intermediation. Development of participatory groups is common to both.[5] The linking model, shown in the top panel of Figure 6.3, seeks to integrate disadvantaged clients into the formal financial system through building up self-reliant groups that can reduce the costs and risks to banks in dealing with small savers and borrowers. The most common institutional arrangement for the linking model is for an NGO to mobilize groups and then link them to services from state-owned banks and other government agencies.

The advantages of linking to existing, experienced financial service providers include:

(a) an existing network of branches and other infrastructure,
(b) a system to maintain records and enforce loan repayment,
(c) reliable savings deposit services, and
(d) an experienced staff.

However, there may also be serious disadvantages. For example, linking systems may have to overcome gender, language, and ethnic barriers which existing formal-sector institutions present to target clients. In addition, in some cases the formal institutions may themselves be inefficient and poorly managed.

The second approach to social intermediation, shown on the lower panel of Figure 6.3, does not attempt of bring clients into the existing formal sector institutions. Instead, it develops groups into parallel financial institutions focused on the group members' opportunities and constraints. The development of cooperative banking systems federated from primary cooperative savings and credit groups is a familiar example of this approach. ROSCAs (rotating savings and credit associations) are another well-known parallel financial system for their members, essentially replacing or competing with formal institutions that typically have little interest in the poor.

Parallel systems must develop their own sources of loan capital, which is often in the form of members' savings. As they grow, cooperatives face the daunting task of federating with other coopera-tives to expand their pool of loanable funds and spread risk beyond the local group.

However, another parallel model that is less common but well known because of Grameen Bank is the bank-NGO hybrid, where the bank performs both social and financial intermediation. There are several cases where government-owned development finance institutions (DFIs) have attempted to take on the task of social intermediation through special programs. The Small Farmer Development Program (SFDP) of the Agricultural Development Bank of Nepal is one example, although high costs and loan defaults made it dependent on continuous government subsidy. The village units of BRI in Indonesia are one of the few cases where a DFI has successfully reached the unserved. However, as Robinson has pointed out elsewhere in this collection, the village unit program does not work through groups, and it does not claim to reach the very low end of the rural market in Indonesia.

The dangers of social intermediation

The *necessity* of social intermediation is clear, but it is also important to stress the *dangers* inherent in it, or in any attempt at 'social business' that tries to bring commercial and welfare goals and approaches together. In many instances there has been a 'muddling of the mission.' That is one of the difficulties that occur when different institutions must work together to do different parts of the task of social and financial intermediation. They often have different institutional attitudes and practices, and quite often one places much greater weight on financial sustainability as a goal while the other is more concerned with social access. Even more difficult, but quite common, is a muddling of goals within a *single* institution.

Three of the five case studies on group-based financial systems from Asia mentioned earlier provide ample evidence of what happens when the business and welfare aspects of a program are not kept distinct. The results of the studies (Bennett et al., 1996) are summarized here in Tables 6.1–6.4. Tables 6.1 and 6.2 provide background data on five programs and Table 6.3 presents the primary barriers faced by each and the services that were offered to overcome these barriers.

Clearly, on the outreach dimension, all five programs have been successful in reaching the rural poor, often in very remote and difficult areas. They have also done well in reaching non-literate women— even in such areas as northern Pakistan where strict female seclusion is practiced. However, Table 6.4 shows that only two (CDF in India and SANASA in Sri Lanka) have made solid progress towards financial sustainability and are well on their way to covering the full costs of their operations. Interestingly, these two are the ones that did not offer health, literacy or production support services (Table 6.3).

Table 6.1 Summary profile of five group-based financial intermediation systems in South Asia

Lead NGO	CDF	MYRADA (Dharmapuri Project)	SANASA	RSDC	SRSC
Full Name	Cooperative Development Foundation	Mysore Resettlement and Development Agency	Thrift and Credit Cooperative Society	Rural Self Reliance Development Center	Sarhad Rural Support Corporation
Country	India	India	Sri Lanka	Nepal	Pakistan
Year Established • NGO • Group Based Finance Program	• 1982 • 1991	• 1968 • 1984	• 1906 • 1991	• 1984 • 1991	• 1989
Institutions involved in 'System' for Financial and Social Intermediation ● = major role ◆ = minor role	◆ Sub-group ● Primary Co-op ◆ Cluster ◆ Advisory Council ● Apex Federation — ● NGO (CDF)	● Credit Management Group (CMG) ● Cluster — ● MYRADA & other NGOs ● Tamil Nadu Women's Development Corporation (DEW)	● Primary Society ● District Socials ● Apex Society — ● Ag & Training University ● Local Banks	● Income Generation Group (IGG) — ● NGO (RSDC)	● Male Community-Based Organization (MCBO) ● Female Community-Based Organization (FCBO) ● NGO (SRSC) ● Local Banks
Major Donors	◆ Neumann Fd. ◆ Oxfam ◆ Ford Fd.	◆ IFAD ◆ PLAN International ◆ GOI/GOT ◆ CAPART	◆ USAID ◆ WOCCU ◆ CCA ◆ SIDA ◆ HIVOS ◆ CIDA	◆ GTZ ◆ Helvetas ◆ CIDA	◆ USAID ◆ NOVIB ◆ IFAD ◆ ADB ◆ CIDA
Ownership	Members	No Equity	Members	No Equity	No Equity
Approach to Financial/Social Intermediation	Parallel	Sequential Parallel & Linking	Parallel (with links between primary societies & local banks)	Limited parallel (no federation of groups)	Parallel & Linking (but banks mainly used as place for group deposits and NGO's loan disbursement account)

Key: ● = Major Role
◆ = Minor Role
[- - -] = Membership Organization

Source: Bennett, L., Goldberg, M. and Hunte, P. (1996), 'Ownership and Sustainability: Lessons on Group-based Financial Services from Asia,' Journal of International Development, Vol. 8, No. 2, pp. 271–288.

Nor did they offer grants for community works, etc. as an 'entry point' into the community to help stimulate group formation. Both of the programs are membership organizations or cooperatives and apparently did not need to offer 'freebees' to attract members. The focus was on financial services and that appears to have been enough.

Both of the financially successful programs in this study followed the *parallel approach* described earlier where the NGO helped groups to form their own parallel financial institution (e.g., a cooperative or village bank) rather than *linking* the group to an existing formal financial institution. But the main factor behind the success of these two parallel systems is really the concept of *client ownership*. Both programs rely on members' savings rather than donor money as a source of loan capital. As can been seen in row 3 of Table 6.4, CDF's loans are nearly 100% backed by member savings, and SANASA's are completely backed by the deposits of members and others. Not only is this high savings mobilization a reliable and affordable source of loan capital that reduces dependency on external sources, but it directly affects members' repayment performance. Annual repayment rates for both CDF and SANASA were 95%, compared with around 50% for the others.

If it is the members' own savings that are being lent, they have a keen interest in seeing that these funds are paid back. Such internally generated funds (known in financial circles as 'hot' money) tend to instill a sense of ownership and respect for loan contract enforcement by all group members. External funds from the government or donors channeled through the NGO ('cold money') may be called loans, but are often perceived as grants by borrowers—especially if they are given by the same NGO that gives other services and inputs for free.

Another reason for success is that both CDF and SANASA are focused on financial sustainability as a goal and convey the message that loans are offered on a business basis rather than as a charitable activity. The other three programs, by contrast, appeared to be internally ambivalent about financial services, seeing them as adjuncts of other, more welfare-oriented services. This confused their message— for staff as well as clients and prospective clients. When NGO staff members are clear about their mission as they are in CDF and SANASA, they are better able to establish clarity of contracts with their clients. Members of CDF groups understand the terms of their contracts and are well informed concerning their repayment schedules and interest expenses. For SANASA, the high levels of literacy in Sri Lanka allow written rules and descriptions of loan and deposit terms

Table 6.2 Scale and depth of outreach of five South Asian NGO systems (1994)

Lead NGO (Country)	CDF (India)	MYRADA (India)	SANASA (Sri Lanka)	RSDC (Nepal)	SRSC (Pakistan)
Number of groups	81	696	6,843	445	154
Number of members	12,000	19,763	711,948	12,558	5,388
Average loan size					
• Internal*	$15	$12	$45	$8	$60
• External*	na	$158	na	$20	na
Average Internal loan as % per cap. GNP	5%	4%	8%	5%	na
Average External loan as % per cap. GNP	na	51%	na	12.5%	14%
Value of Average Savings Account	$9	$10 (1993)	$43	$4	$17 (1993)
Average Savings Account as % per cap. GNP	2.8%	3%	8%	2.4%	4%

Notes: *Internal loans are funded by members' savings. External loans are funded by resources obtained by or for a group from government programs, donor accounts or similar sources.

which also contribute to transparent contracts. In the other three programs, participants were often unaware of when repayment was due, the amount they had repaid or even, in some cases, of the interest rate that they were paying These were also the programs with poor management information systems so that even staff members were often unaware of how specific individuals—or the portfolio as a whole—were performing.

The fact that three of the five group-based programs were not performing well financially is clear evidence of dangers inherent in trying to combine social and financial intermediation. Yet the findings also suggest that, if great care is taken to be clear that participants are involved in a business rather than a welfare transaction, the contradictions can be overcome. If they are truly participatory in the sense of building ownership and mutual accountability, the mechanisms for social outreach in microfinance can enhance financial sustainability instead of undermining it.

Table 6.3 Socio-economic context and range of services for five South Asian NGO systems

Lead NGO (Country)	CDF (India)	MYRADA (India)	SANASA (Sri Lanka)	RSDC (Nepal)	SRSC (Pakistan)
Major and minor barriers to financial intermediation	• Gender • Poverty • Caste • Illiteracy • Rural	• Gender • Poverty • Caste • Illiteracy • Rural	• Gender • Poverty • Caste/ethnicity • Rural	• Gender • Poverty • Caste/ethnicity • Illiteracy • Remote/rural • Subsistence economy	• Gender • Poverty • Ethnicity • Rural
Financial intermediation services offered	• Savings (limited access) • Small, short-term loans	• Savings (limited access) • Small, short-term loans • Larger, longer-term production loans (up to 10 years)	• Savings (various types) • Loans (various types) • Insurance	• 'Savings' (No access) • Small, short-term loans • Larger production loans	• Savings (limited access) • Loans (various types)
Social intermediation services offered: • Access to service • Social Welfare • Production support	• Health • Literacy • Agric. extension • Local infrastructure (grants)			• Health • Agric. extension • Local infrastructure (grants)	• Health • Agric. extension • Income generation • Local infrastructure (grants) • Literacy • Initial group building
Self-reliance • Group capacity building	• Initial awareness raising • Training in organizational and cooperative management • Exposure tours for leaders • Advice and oversight CDF	• Initial group building • Advice and oversight by MYRADA	• Training in group management and accounting provided in response to group request for SANASA membership	• Initial group building advice and oversight by RSDC	

Source: Bennett, L., Goldberg, M. and Hunte, P. (1996). 'Ownership and Sustainability: Lessons on Group-based Financial Services from Asia,' *Journal of International Development*, Vol. 8, No. 2, pp. 271–288.

Table 6.4   Financial performance of five South Asian NGO systems (1993)

Lead NGO Country	CDF (India)	MYRADA (India)	SANASA (Sri Lanka)	RSDC (Nepal)	SRSC (Pakistan)
1. Outstanding loan portfolio	$57,800	$199,000	$22.6 m.	$37,000	$124,000
2. Savings deposits	$57,100	$97,000	$29.6 m.	$25,000	$92,000
3. Percentage of loan portfolio backed by savings	99%	49%	130%	70%	77%
4. Estimated annual repayment rate	95%	54%	95%	55%	52%
5. Administrative cost per $ lent	24%	31%	14%	115%	>400%

Notes

1   The concept of the continuum of participation was developed with Mike Goldberg, a World Bank colleague.

2   Gloria Davis of the World Bank, personal communication.

3   These incentives might be tied to overall disbursement, sector/client targeted disbursement, savings mobilization, loan recovery, or overall profits—with very different results.

4   One example of a nongroup-based mechanism for reaching poor and marginal groups is the technique of 'mobile banking' in which the loan officer from a formal sector bank provides financial services to clients in their workshops and market stalls. This delivery mechanism has been successfully used in Latin America by ACCION's microenterprise programs, in India by SEWA in its work with self-employed women (whose savings are collected door to door by bank staff) and by CARE/Niger in its MARADI credit initiative. The MARADI project used mobile banking techniques to provide working capital loans to thousands of microenterprise operators in rural Niger. Administrative costs are monitored regularly, a positive interest rate is used and loan officers offer financial services in the village to individual clients. Originally, a group based approach was tried, but this did not match the preferences of rural low-income households in Niger. The Niger example illustrates the importance of listening and responding to clients and being willing to tailor the delivery system to the local culture and economic system.

5   The classification used here is similar to the one developed by Otero and Rhyne (1994, pp. 21–22), which mentions three approaches: (1) linking

nongovernmental programs to sources of finance, (2) transforming programs into specialized financial institutions and, (3) specialized operations within commercial financial institutions. However, Otero and Rhyne's classification does not focus on the role of groups in the social intermediation process, but instead covers all the institutional models that are usually used to deliver financial services to the poor.

References

Bennett, L., Goldberg, M. and Hunte, P. (1996), 'Ownership and Sustainability: Lessons on Group-based Financial Services from South Asia,' *Journal of International Development* (Special Issue on Banking with the Poor), Vol. 8, No. 2, pp. 271–288.

Otero, M. and Rhyne, E. (eds.) (1994), *The New World of Microfinance: Building Healthy Financial Institutions for the Poor*, Kumarian Press: West Hartford, CT.

Putnam, R. (1993), 'The Prosperous Community: Social Capital and Public Life,' *The American Prospect*, No. 13 (Spring), p. 38.

Von Pischke, J.D. (1991), *Finance at the Frontier: Debt Capacity and the Role of Credit in the Private Economy*, EDI Development Studies, World Bank: Washington, DC.

Webster, L., Riopella, R. and Chidzero, A. (1996), 'World Bank Lending for Small Enterprises 1989–1993,' World Bank Technical Paper Number 311, World Bank: Washington, DC.

World Bank (1995), *Participation Sourcebook*, Environmental Department, World Bank: Washington, DC.

World Bank (1996), 'A Worldwide Inventory of Microfinance Institutions,' Sustainable Banking With the Poor Project, World Bank: Washington, DC.

7 Balancing perspectives on informal finance

OTTO HOSPES

Increasingly, the importance of tailor-made financial services is being recognized in the microfinance arena. These services are characterized by their practitioners' tendency to take into account in their loan appraisal operations the borrower's scale of operations, competing claims on borrowers' resources, their savings practices, and the socio-economic environment within which loans are being provided and deposits taken (Abugre, 1994). Although such activity has been researched over recent years, it is still not widely known that millions of agents and mutual societies offer tailor-made financial services to poor people in low-income countries.

Informal financial agents and traditional savings and lending societies have often been stereotyped as usurious moneylenders or as remnants of traditional culture. Indeed, many of the programs and, in particular, financial sector operations aimed at assisting poor and rural people in developing countries have been legitimized, in part, by their perceived prospects for moving economies beyond this sort of usurious and ineffective finance. However, recent research has shown that many moneylenders are less usurious than was assumed.

Several researchers (cf. Adams, 1992; Ghate, 1992) have shown that opportunity cost and risk premia are the main determinants of interest rates on informal loans—not monopoly profit. It has also been recognized that there is much more 'occurring outside the regulation of a central monetary or financial market authority' (Adams, 1992, p. 2) than the practices of moneylenders only. Financial and quasi-financial services in low-income countries that are used by poor people on a large scale include those provided by merchants, pawnbrokers, loan brokers, landlords, friends and relatives, money guards, ROSCAs (rotating savings and credit associations) and ASCRAs (accumulating savings and credit associations).

From sustained failure to balanced perspectives

The increased recognition of informal finance as a positive force should be seen against the wider backdrop of consistent failure among state-regulated suppliers of targeted, cheap credit. (A more general assessment of the phenomenon of the over-development and crisis of the Third World state can be seen in Holmen, 1990). The recognition of informal finance and the role that it plays as a non-state activity has led to a re-assessment of private initiatives aimed at fostering financial sector development. In particular, NGOs have become widely perceived as an attractive organizational form for implementing and organizing financial technologies which emulate informal finance.

The widespread perception that poor people can neither save nor organize themselves has undermined innovation in programs aimed at providing assistance to the poor. In particular, it has helped to sustain failure in directed credit programs and activities. One corollary to this perception has been the belief that what the poor need is cheap credit and some cooperative education. Another is that high default rates indicate that people are too poor to repay loans and do not understand how to use a loan productively. These perceptions have not been conducive to progress in microfinance sustainability.

The aim of this chapter is to examine questions and approaches that might lead to a more balanced view of informal finance. Traditionally, such research has not received the attention it deserves. While expensive, empirical research is not as expensive as massive losses through ineffective credit projects. Much of the research on informal finance has entailed short-term work which assesses or examines informal mechanisms as a peripheral element of some wider effort. And, while casual investigations or snapshot research is cheaper and less time-consuming, it cannot grasp the complexity and dynamics of informal finance. Finally, it is should be emphasized that informal finance is a more important and rewarding subject of investigation than such issues as credit demand or sub-project internal rates of return achieved by the ultimate borrower which are traditional research subjects in financial sector operations.

Balanced perspectives on informal finance take into account its diversity and flexibility. This requires care in applying acronyms or models extracted from the rich world of informal finance. A cautionary example is the ROSCA. Much research on financial self-help has focused on ROSCAs and this has generated a self-perpetuating process wherein, because there is an increasing amount of literature available on the topic, new students of finance tend to concentrate on this form and ignore other types of associations such as the ASCRA or one of the many 'hybrid' associations with both a rotating and accumulating element (Bouman, 1994a, pp. 375–394). Focused expectations (along with language barriers) have sometimes led researchers to overlook the fact that the local idiom for ROSCA might also include the ASCRA and/or intertwined forms (contrast Maters, 1993; Hoeben, 1994).

For a better understanding of the complexity of informal finance, it is necessary to develop integrated approaches, analyzing savings and credit transactions of both individuals and institutions in relation to changing contexts (cf. Hospes 1994, p. 229). Inherent in such approaches is a comparative look at 'informal' and 'formal' institutions through the eyes of the individuals who are looking for ways to borrow, to save and/or to guarantee social security. Because 'the poor' in low-income countries are such a heterogeneous group, it is quite difficult to generalize about their savings and credit decisions. Under many different circumstances and for different reasons 'informal finance' still seems to be a first choice within this group.

The first choice

Schmidt and Kropp (1987) maintain that the complexity and diversity of informal financial contracts mirror decisions by poor people about financing consumption and investment and managing scarce money resources. Following this approach, it would be worthwhile to explore these decisions and the conditions under which various choices are made.[1] Three key methodological issues that lead to balanced insights on informal finance are discussed below.

Financing options: Rather than beginning analysis with target groups in the abstract, their presumed credit needs, and how finance institutions ought to be managed in order to deal with them, I suggest to start the other way around. That is, to take an individual in search of money as the starting point and to analyze his or her changing financing options. Such an approach can lead to unexpected findings (cf. Wagenaar, 1991) for those who assume that lack of capital or lack of access to credit (further narrowed down as formal finance) is the major bottleneck of the target group. As McLeod (1980, 1992) demonstrates through his extensive study of small firms in Jogjakarta, Indonesia: 'Many of the firms interviewed relied heavily on self-finance for their expansion, and they often did so by choice—not because they were denied outside finance' (McLeod, 1992, p. 255).

Both McLeod (1992) and Liedholm (1992) found that the external sources of finance that are first accessed by evolving microenterprises are informal ones. Only, '[A]t a later stage in their evolution, [do] microenterprises begin to have access to the formal financial market' (Liedholm, 1992, p. 275). The lack of interest from commercial banks for financing microenterprises may indicate those bankers' awareness of the risky and insecure environments in which microenterprises operate. Informal financial agents seem best equipped to operate under such conditions and environments.

Savings practices: Financing options presume savings practices, as evolutionary patterns of microenterprises illustrate. Regarding savings practices, economists often assume liquidity preferences to be the guiding principle, calling for money guards or savings accounts that are safe and can be quickly mobilized in case of unexpected but highly rewarding investment opportunities. However, the significance of illiquidity preferences that lead to savings forms other than money, such as 'jewelry, livestock, farm machinery, individually and collectively stored crops, household furniture, and radios' (Shipton, 1992) should not be overlooked. Such forms of savings are common strategies of many rural-based African microentrepreneurs, as Shipton found in The Gambia. These agents face enormous pressure on scarce money resources and probably struggle on an evolutionary path different from that of their 'colleagues' in urbanized areas of Indonesia, Thailand or the Philippines (Liedholm, 1992, pp. 268–269).

In low-income countries the pressure on scarce money resources comes from many sides. First, monetary instability and lack of dependability in the banking system might very well explain illiquidity preferences. A balanced perspective on informal finance would explore the background and motives for non-monetary transactions and the conversion of cash to kind and vice versa. It would take into account the impact of uneven monetization and financial deepening on the emergence and scope of informal finance.

Another pressure on scarce money resources comes from 'inside,' that is, kin and neighbors who have a social claim on some share of an individual's wealth. Illiquidity preferences (in a social sense) refer to savings practices that constitute a socially acceptable argument to deny claims for financial assistance from people belonging to the same social or socio-spatial unit (household, clan, lineage, neighborhood). The most sophisticated and widespread examples of such a savings practice are the ROSCA and ASCRA (Bouman, 1994a, pp.

375–394) that often evolve as new social phenomena in developing economies (Hospes, 1992). Illiquidity preferences can, under these arrangements, be described as senior claims—with illiquidity preferences putting more emphasis on savings practices, and senior claims on repayment strategies.

Senior claims: Another element for assessing informal finance from the perspective of the (potential) client is to explore obligations that the borrower considers more important than repaying the lender. These types of obligations are, effectively, senior claims (Von Pischke, 1994, p. 63). Inquiries about senior claims will demonstrate that individuals have their own 'personal hierarchies of creditors and that the newest, most distant, and least familiar lenders rank at the bottom' (Shipton, 1992, p. 28).

Senior claims do not only refer to competing claims of informal and formal suppliers of finance but also include paying school fees, buying house construction material, medicines, food and making contributions to social events (Von Pischke, 1994, p. 63). Heidhues (1994) argues that informal loans in Cameroon and Benin show high repayment rates exactly because they are mainly used for these popular purposes. A balanced perspective on informal finance not only recognizes the role of informal finance in helping microenterprises to evolve and to seize exceptional opportunities, but should also explore the popularity and persistence of informal financial arrangements which provide social security services. This is made all the more important by macroeconomic reform programs which seek to reduce government obligations in this area.

Informal finance in context

Banks within banks: Because informal finance is precisely dependent on local conditions, it is important to analyze it in context (Baas, 1994; Bouman and Hospes, 1994). Failure to seriously apply a contextual approach can lead to generalizations that do not travel well outside a specific context. To the extent that informal finance is 'organic,' growing out of a specific set of circumstances, generalizations that do not account for the roots of the informal arrangements under study will be neither dependable nor useful. A more contextual look at informal finance leads one to unexpected places and critical questions.

It is not exceptional to find ROSCAs or ASCRAs flourishing behind bank windows in developing countries. Employees of banks and credit cooperatives privately design these associations within their own organization. Frustration with the inefficiency of these institutions and the lack of deposit services, in particular, undoubtedly figure high in the list of users' motives (Adams, 1993). But ROSCAs and ASCRAs are also organized among staff of schools, the police, the military and local units of the state administration. In some countries these associations are used by local government extension services as a tool to mobilize women to attend meetings (Hospes, 1992).

Structural adjustment impacts on financial self-help organizations

The study of informal financial arrangements requires a significant investment in research in order to describe in full detail the multitude of nuances found across countries in just a single structural pattern such as ROSCAs (Adams and Ghate, 1992, p. 355). In addition, placing research findings about structural forms and variations into their wider context is essential to explain this 'multitude of nuances.' The context for informal financial arrangements includes elements of macroeconomic, political-administrative and agro-ecological conditions. In many developing countries dramatic reform of political, administrative and economic organization has taken place. This reform is generally aimed at generating better economic opportunities for individuals and groups. Under many macro reform efforts, government agencies redefine their administrative responsibilities by emphasizing facilitative interventions. The goal is to create favorable conditions for private enterprise and self-help initiatives. The reduction of state controlled enterprises, subsidies and civil servants is typically a major element of structural adjustment programs. At the same time, it is hoped that leading politicians and their followers will further the development of public-private relations in such a way that the political system develops proper checks and balances to create a broader and more legitimate power base.

Implementation of some of these measures and policies have weakened rather than strengthened the economic position of poor people in some countries. Sometimes, policy reform has increased social and economic insecurity and even led to social and political turmoil. It is argued here that these negative, unintended consequences could be limited if self-help initiatives at the local level are facilitated by policies improving pre-conditions for membership-based financial self-help organizations (SHOs).

Although recent macroeconomic reform measures aim to allow greater scope for private self-help and self-regulation, little research has been done on either the impact of reform on financial self-help groups and their clients or impacts of these groups on the reform process. An initial attempt is made here to address these issues by outlining the questions that are likely to be relevant.

- What are the impacts on the form of savings, length of cycle (ROSCA) or savings period (ASCRA) of adjustment policies that increase (temporarily or otherwise) monetary instability? Is the absence or decline of ASCRAs (with permanent funds) and shortening of cycles of ROSCAs an expression of monetary instability such as inflation? Are contributions in kind another expression of this instability?

- What are the changes in the nature, location, geographical distribution and number of participants of SHOs in the presence of dependable as opposed to non-dependable banking systems? Does a breakdown of the banking system result in an increase of the number of financial SHOs? Does stability and expansion of the banking system result in transformation of ROSCAs and AS-CRAs to deposit-taking arrangements in partnership with rural banks? Do reduced government subsidies to development banks result in an increase in the number of savings and credit groups supported by NGOs?

- How do relations with other forms of financial intermediation (at the individual and organizational level) change when banking services become more or less dependable?

- Does the normative-institutional framework (registration, conflict resolution, enforcement of bye-laws) change when perceptions of members of SHOs regarding local-traditional leadership and the organization of public services change? A comparison of the rural and urban environments might be very revealing here, since tradition and conservatism lose much of their value in the shift from rural to urban environments (Bouman, 1994a, pp. 375–394).

- Are there changes in the use of funds (for agricultural inputs, working capital, food, medicines, education, housing, etc.) in times of increasing insecurity of food provision and income flows? A comparison between areas or times of economic expansion and decline might be very revealing (Crow, 1994).

- What other changes might generate shifts in the importance of financial SHOs as part of livelihood strategies of urban and rural people?

Further study of the uses of SHOs by their clients would provide insights into illiquidity preferences and restricted mobility of funds[2] as a function of financial sector liberalization and other macro-economic reform measures. Strategies by which the rural and urban poor seek to achieve their financial objectives through SHOs would be especially relevant in periods of economic reform and social insecurity. If adjustment programs entail cuts in government budgets and if this leads to worsening living conditions in rural areas in terms of housing, health and education, one result might be to increase the mobilization of own funds. Financial SHOs often have been perfect tools for accumulating local funds to finance expenditures for housing, health and education.

Alternatively, people often resort to family help and traders' credit in times of social-economic insecurity. It would be particularly revealing to analyze how women—with both productive and repro- ductive responsibilities—cope with such insecurity (Verstralen, 1995). It is largely ignored that many women select suppliers of financial services with the aim to start and consolidate their social security network—realizing that a greater emphasis on income-generating activities cannot take place when social security has not been guaranteed.

Processes of social disintegration and integration[3]

Structural adjustment programs are based on the view that the choices of buyers and sellers in markets should be the main allocation mechanism for scarce resources. Such views imply monetization of local economies and can accelerate rural out-migration.

Monetization and migration strongly affect the social organization of local communities. Traditional, non-monetary forms of coopera- tion in housing, agriculture and community works seem to make less sense in monetized economies, though it is not clear why this is the case. But, on the evidence, monetary exchanges typically come to dominate other forms of culturally defined social security networks and tend to disrupt social cohesion. The relevance of this tendency to the current discussion is how to retain the social underpinnings of financial SHOs so that they evolve and help to offset processes of social disintegration.[4]

Countries that are overcoming the effects of an oppressive regime that undermined bonds of mutual trust offer an example. Not surprisingly, Nagarajan notes that ROSCAs have re-emerged in

Uganda in the 1990s[5] with small group size and short periods of rotation, expressing more positive but yet insecure feelings about the future.

Over-development and centralization of the Third World state are characterized by lack of community and effective political institutions, by the absence of agreed procedures, the fragility of institutions and the lack of widespread sentiment of their legitimacy (Holmen, 1990). Not surprisingly, decentralization of state powers has either failed or sparked conflict between ethnic mini-societies about territory, management of natural resources and the revenues that they produce and labor 'markets', explaining the paradoxical emergence of new boundaries and patterns of exclusion in an era of globalization.

How will these new boundaries and patterns affect the distribution and functions of financial SHOs? Financial SHOs might very well mirror ethnic conflict and be re-organized accordingly. Maybe they will not drastically change at all in this connection because many SHOs are already organized along ethnic lines.[6] It is also possible that financial SHOs increasingly adopt political and social functions or are incorporated into new socio-political units.

In any case, a minimum of social-political stability and social cohesion is a pre-condition for people, even from a common origin, to be able to organize financial SHOs at all. For a better understanding of the significance and structural adjustment patterns of financial SHOs, and other types of informal finance, one needs to develop analytical frameworks or contextual perspectives of which insecurity is an integral part.

Notes

1   An actor analysis implies the use of terms such as 'decisions' or 'preferences' to denote financial behavior rather than donor-driven words like 'credit needs' or 'wants.'

2   Preferences for limited mobility of funds refer to practices of SHOs to limit the circulation of funds to prevent scarce financial means from leaking away.

3   This final part draws partly on a position paper entitled 'Social Change in Africa: Some Themes on Development Strategies,' (June 1994) by Dr. Cyprian Fisiy, former researcher at the Department of Agrarian Law, Wageningen Agricultural University, The Netherlands, who is currently a social scientist at the World Bank.

4   Processes of social disintegration—with other backgrounds and ugly expressions, of course—do not only occur in Third World countries but also take place in highly industrialized countries, such as the USA. Instead of bluntly embarking on credit programs directed at the poor in industrialized

countries, it would be useful to describe how their urban poor and bankrupt farmers cope with insecurity and what role informal financial arrangements play in this connection.

5   Geetha Nagarajan of Ohio State University (e-mail communication, May 12, 1994) reports that, 'While these groups were performing several functions including social, financial and political ones in the 1960s, they were largely inactive during the 1970s and 1980s.'

6   This certainly applies to (new) migrant populations among which financial SHOs will be used as an (alternative) social safety network and, if economic and social-political stability increase, as a way to accumulate capital for investment purposes.

References

Abugre, C. (1994), 'When Credit Is Not Due: A Critical Evaluation of Donor-NGO Experiences with Credit,' in Bouman, F.J.A. and Hospes, O. (eds.), *Financial Landscapes Reconstructed: The Fine Art of Mapping Development*, Westview Press: Boulder, CO, pp. 157–175.

Adams, D.W (1992), 'Taking a Fresh Look at Informal Finance,' in Adams, D.W and Fitchett, F.A. (eds.), *Informal Finance in Low-Income Countries*, Westview Press: Boulder, CO, pp. 5–23.

Adams, D.W and Fitchett, D.A. (eds.) (1992), *Informal Finance in Low-Income Countries*, Westview Press: Boulder, CO.

Adams, D.W and Ghate, P. (1992), 'Where to From Here in Informal Finance,' in Adams, D.W and Fitchett, F.A. (eds.), *Informal Finance in Low-Income Countries*, Westview Press: Boulder, CO, pp. 349–359.

Adams, D.W and Von Pischke, J.D. (1994), 'Micro-Enterprise Credit Programs: Deja Vu,' in Bouman, F.J.A. and Hospes, O. (eds.), *Financial Landscapes Reconstructed: The Fine Art of Mapping Development*, Westview Press: Boulder, CO, pp. 143–156.

Baas, W.F. (1994), *Le dynamisme des associations feminines d'epargne et de credit dans quatre villages de la Region du Gorgol en Mauretanie*, M.Sc. These, Departement Droit Rural, Universite Agronome Wageningen, Pays Bas.

Baydas, M.M., Bahloul, Z. and Adams, D.W (1993), 'Informal Finance and Women in Egypt: "Banks" Within Banks,' Economics and Sociology Occasional Paper No. 2078, Rural Finance Program, Department of Agricultural Economics and Rural Sociology, The Ohio State University: Columbus, OH, and The Economic Research Department of the Principal Bank for Development and Agricultural Credit: Cairo, Egypt.

Bouman, F.J.A. (1994), 'Informal Rural Finance: An Aladdin's Lamp of Information,' in Bouman, F.J.A. and Hospes, O. (eds.), *Financial Landscapes Reconstructed: The Fine Art of Mapping Development*, Westview Press: Boulder, CO, pp. 105–122.

Bouman, F.J.A. (1994a), 'ROSCA and ASCRA: Beyond the Financial Landscape,' in Bouman, F.J.A. and Hospes, O. (eds.), *Financial Landscapes Reconstructed: The Fine Art of Mapping Development*, Westview Press: Boulder, CO, pp. 375–394.

Bouman, F.J.A. and Hospes, O. (eds.) (1994), *Financial Landscapes Reconstructed: The Fine Art of Mapping Development*, Westview Press: Boulder, CO.

Crow, B. (1994), 'Finance in the Context of Exploring Diverse Exchange Conditions,' in Bouman, F.J.A. and Hospes, O. (eds.), *Financial Landscapes Reconstructed: The Fine Art of Mapping Development*, Westview Press: Boulder, CO, pp. 271–291.

Ghate, P., Das-Gupta, A., Lamberte, M., Poapongaskorn, M., Prabowo, D. and Rahman, A. (1992), *Informal Finance: Some Findings From Asia*, Oxford University Press: Hong Kong.

Heidhues, F. (1994), 'Consumption Credit in Rural Financial Market Development,' in Bouman, F.J.A. and Hospes, O. (eds.), *Financial Landscapes Reconstructed: The Fine Art of Mapping Development*, Westview Press: Boulder, CO, pp. 33–48.

Hoeben, C. (1994), *Beyond the ROSCA and ASCRA Model: Insights from Local Financial Self-Help Groups of Uganda*, M.Sc. Thesis, Department of Agrarian Law, Wageningen Agricultural University, The Netherlands.

Holmen, H. (1990), 'State, Cooperatives and Development in Africa,' Research report No. 86, The Scandinavian Institute of African Studies, Uppsala.

Hospes, O. (1992), 'People That Count: The Forgotten Faces of Rotating Savings and Credit Associations in Indonesia,' *Savings and Development*, Vol. 4, No. 16, pp. 371–400.

Liedholm, C. (1992), 'Small-Scale Enterprise Dynamics and the Evolving Role of Informal Finance,' in Adams, D.W and Fitchett, F.A. (eds.), *Informal Finance in Low-Income Countries*, Westview Press: Boulder, CO, pp. 265–280.

Maters, E. (1993), *Avec cet argent tu peux acheter un elephant: accumulation et organisations locales de Batseng'la, une Chefferie Bamileke au Cameroun*, M.Sc. These, Departement Droit Rural, Universite Agronome Wageningen, Pays Bas.

McLeod, R.H. (1980), 'Finance and Entrepreneurship in the Small-Business Sector in Indonesia,' Ph.D. dissertation, The Australian National University: Canberra, Australia.

McLeod, R.H. (1992), 'The Financial Evolution of Small Businesses in Indonesia,' in Adams, D.W and Fitchett, F.A. (eds.), *Informal Finance in Low-Income Countries*, Westview Press: Boulder, CO, pp. 249–264.

Schmidt, R.H. and Kropp, E. (1987), *Rural Finance: Guiding Principles*, Rural Development Series, BMZ/GTZ/DSE, TZ-Verlagsgesellschaft: Rossdorf, Germany.

Shipton, P. (1992), 'The Rope and the Box: Group Savings in The Gambia,' in Adams, D.W and Fitchett, F.A. (eds.), *Informal Finance in Low-Income Countries*, Westview Press: Boulder, CO, pp. 25–41.

Verstralen, K. (1995), *On Whose Account: A Study of Structural Adjustment Policies on Financial Self-Help Activities Among Women in Mamobi, A Low Income Area in Accra, Ghana*, M.Sc. Thesis, Department of Agrarian Law, Wageningen Agricultural University, The Netherlands.

Von Pischke, J.D. (1983), 'The Pitfalls of Specialized Farm Credit Institutions in Low-Income Countries,' in Von Pischke, J.D., Adams, D.W and Donald, G. (eds.), *Rural Financial Markets in Developing Countries: Their Use and Abuse*, The Johns Hopkins University Press: Baltimore, MD, pp.175–182.

Von Pischke, J.D. (1994), 'Structuring Credit to Manage Real Risks,' in Bouman, F.J.A. and Hospes, O. (eds.), *Financial Landscapes Reconstructed: The Fine Art of Mapping Development*, Westview Press: Boulder, CO, pp. 49–70.

Wagenaar, C. (1991), *On se debrouille: une etude sur l'importance de credit et d'epargne pour des femmes Mossi et Nuni dans le Sud de Burkina Faso*, M.Sc. These, Departement Droit Rural, Universite Agronome Wageningen, Pays Bas.

8 Developing alternatives to informal finance and finding market niches

CARLOS E. CUEVAS

Efforts to expand the 'frontier of formal finance' to reach the poor have given rise to an eclectic set of institutions, organizations and programs during the last decade or so. These efforts were commonly articulated and justified as 'alternatives' to stereotypical informal financial arrangements, deemed 'inferior, exploitative, and anti-developmental' (Von Pischke, 1991, p. 174). Although the myths and misconceptions about informal finance have been overturned for the most part, questions remain as to whether the emerging institutions have truly introduced alternatives to informal finance and, if so, whether there is a set of identifiable pre-conditions for these options to develop.[1]

I will argue in this chapter that what has been observed over the last ten or fifteen years is the emergence of a variety of institutions, in the general sense of the term, offering financial products and contracts which bear little resemblance to those found in informal markets. Further, these institutions are organized under structures and governance rules much different from those prevailing in informal finance. Thus, they can hardly be considered as true alternatives, although they share some of the limitations observed in informal finance. I will conclude that innovative institutions currently recognized as successful have indeed created market niches, complementing rather than substituting for informal financial arrangements.

The chapter presents first a brief overview of the issues that are most relevant when considering alternatives to informal finance, and a summary of the key features of informal financial transactions and institutions. In *lieu* of pre-conditions, I subsequently review a number of observed regularities in the development of relatively successful 'alternative' institutions, to conclude with an assessment of what these institutions have accomplished in diversifying the supply of financial products to the poor, and serving specific market segments. A final note on the key obstacles to further expansion of the frontier concludes the chapter.

Informal finance: contracts and institutions

Among the diversity of informal financial arrangements, three are worth special mention when discussing what the so called alternative institutions may have attempted to either replace or to replicate. Two of these, frequently documented and analyzed in recent literature, are the moneylender and the rotating savings and credit association (ROSCA).

Moneylenders, private individuals lending their own funds or funds obtained from other formal or informal sources, are the most commonly blamed for allegedly exploitative interest charges and widespread abuse. However, empirical evidence has shown that moneylender rates, although relatively higher than those charged in formal markets, contain little or no extraordinary profits (Von Pischke, 1991). Moneylender transactions are typically short term, impose low transaction costs on the borrower and are secured by strong tangible or intangible collateral.

ROSCAs, on the other hand, voluntary associations based on mutual trust and regulated by entry rules and strict social sanctions, tend to remain small as the quality of information about other members diminishes with increases in group size. This limits the size of the fund to be allocated among members, while still providing a valuable means of accumulating regular voluntary savings. As a form of association, the ROSCA has been considered a benchmark for the analysis of financial services strategies (Baulier et al., 1988; Von Pischke, 1991). Their expansion in size and types of instruments, however, is constrained by the very nature of their risk management mechanisms, and their future and potential as financial markets integrate is unclear (Callier, 1990; Krahnen and Schmidt, 1991; Slover, 1991).

The third type of informal arrangement, trade finance, particularly relevant to the poor entrepreneur, has often been overlooked in the informal finance debate. Recent evidence indicates that supplier and/or customer credit constitute the most significant, reliable and stable source of finance for micro and small entrepreneurs. According to a survey carried out in 1991 in El Salvador (Cuevas et al., 1991), between 50% and 65% of enterprises of different size categories relied upon supplier credit for working capital. In The Gambia, 81% to 85%

of bakeries were funded primarily by suppliers, while customer advances represented a primary source of funding for 92% of the tailors and 97% of the metal shops (Baydas, 1993). Similar results have been reported by studies at the World Bank on African manufacturing enterprises.

Among the key features of informal financial arrangements, I distinguish two categories for the purposes of this chapter: the characteristics of the contracts, explicit or implicit, that predominate in informal loans; and the supervision and regulation mechanisms governing these informal contracts. Both of these categories offer points of comparison with and contrast to the contracts and institutional arrangements observed.

Informal loans are typically small, payable in short maturities, and low in transaction-costs. For the most part, informal loans involve individual liability for the borrower. Even within groups (e.g., ROSCAs), joint liability is rarely observed in specific transactions, although the information and trust associated with joint liability contracts play a role when first accepting a member into the group. In addition, informal loans are almost always unrestricted with respect to the end-use of funds. This makes informal borrowing an important way of stabilizing consumption, reducing a primary risk for low-income households and, perhaps, favoring the undertaking of relatively risky ventures in production and trade (Eswaran and Kotwal, 1989).

Perhaps the most distinctive feature of informal loan contracts is their role as insurance. Loan transactions between partners who know each other well allow the spreading of the risks of unforeseen shocks among the partners. Evidence reported by Udry (1991) shows that terms and conditions of informal loans were adjusted to mitigate unexpected shocks suffered by either the borrower or the lender, a finding that defies conventional models of loan contracting. These state-contingent loans, made possible by near perfect and symmetric information between the contracting parties, thus represent true risk pooling arrangements for both sides of the contract.

Direct supervisory mechanisms characterize informal finance. With no end-use requirements, agency problems do not exist for individual lending contracts between a moneylender and a borrower or between a supplier and a customer. Even in ROSCAs, all members of the group are likely to know exactly who are net borrowers from the group at any given time. Not surprisingly, the few reported failures of African *tontines* are associated with 'excessive' trust in the group leader, who then deviates from the agreed rotation in the allocation of the group fund (Cuevas et al., 1991). This observation highlights another distinctive feature of informal group governance: they are essentially non-democratic, and leadership is determined by relative wealth, prestige, or seniority.

The absence of indirect regulatory and supervisory mechanisms in informal finance, while helping to minimize transaction costs in the system, limits its ability to expand and grow. This limitation, however, does not render informal finance 'inefficient' as some may argue. Instead, it creates favorable conditions for innovation and penetration by new institutions, and generates potential gains for market integration.

Alternative institutions and programs

The institutions and programs I refer to here are primarily those deemed relatively 'successful,' such as the BRI Village Unit system in Indonesia, Grameen Bank in Bangladesh, and BancoSol in Bolivia. These also include 'high-level,' or serious 'financial' non-governmental organizations (NGOs), at or near self-sustainability, as distinct from the large population of NGOs with a primary emphasis of non-financial services. The discussion that follows is not a comprehensive review of these institutions and programs, which can be found elsewhere.[2] Instead, I highlight some patterns in the development of these institutions that seem to be associated with their success, and emphasize the features of their financial products, and their governance structures that distinguish them from informal finance.

Gestation and evolution

Curiously, and not surprisingly, no 'alternative' institution has evolved from an informal financial entity. On the contrary, they seem to develop in parallel to, or as a complement to existing informal arrangements. Such is the evidence reported, for example, for credit unions in Togo, Cameroon, and Zaire, where credit union members maintain their affiliation with tontines, and continue their relationships with informal moneylenders and trader-creditors (Cuevas et al., 1991). Likewise, well-known efforts to reach the poor with credit and deposit services such as those represented by Grameen and BRI do not seem to have displaced existing informal providers of financial services. In Von Pischke's terminology, the so-called alternative institutions appear to have found or created 'market niches' by introducing efficiency, innovation and quality of service into previously unserved or underserved market segments (Von Pischke, 1991, Chapter 10).

All successful cases of institution building have developed under some kind of partnership between a donor (or several donors) and counterparts of diverse types. Governments, NGOs, and credit unions are among these different partners. Donor partnerships with NGOs of different origins and motivation include some of the best known success stories. The business community in association with ACCION International created PRODEM, the precursor of BancoSol in Bolivia, and Actuar Bogota in Colombia. On the other hand, micro and small entrepreneurs organized in the association AMPES in El Salvador— after successfully establishing a highly effective credit service as an NGO—created a new non-bank regulated financial institution with donor equity participation.

Finally, a few credit union networks entering carefully designed partnerships with donors (primarily USAID) have succeeded in developing sustainable movements, or in creating the bases for sustainability. Such has been the case of the Cameroon Credit Union League, the Togo Credit Union Movement, and more recently the Guatemala Credit Union Federation.

In addition to donor support, most of these successful institutions appear associated with a crucial catalytic agent, individual or institutional, which has been instrumental in their gestation and/or growth. Grameen was initiated as an experimental project at Chittagong University by Dr. Mohammed Yunus. ACCION International and Women's World Banking have been especially important in Latin America. The GTZ in Peru and El Salvador, and the World Council of Credit Unions in Africa, further exemplify the diversity of the catalytic agents associated with institution building.

Financial products

Information reported for successful programs indicates that these 'alternative' institutions have succeeded in producing loan instruments sharing some, though not all, of the characteristics of informal loans. Of course, a rigorous analysis would require a simultaneous assessment of all dimensions of loan contracts before drawing any conclusions. Leaving this rigorous treatment as a topic deserving further research, I review and compare below some of the main components of loan transactions. Similarities arise in features such as loan size, loan maturities, and interest charges, but striking differences exist in other respects.

Loan-sizes reported for alternative institutions clearly overlap with average loan amounts observed in informal finance. Christen, Rhyne and Vogel (1994) cite a range for average loans outstanding in successful programs from US$ 38 to US$ 1,016, or from 6% to 136% of the corresponding GNP per capita.[3] Loan maturity, however, although relatively short in most niche programs and hence comparable to informal transactions, does not seem to reach the extremely short loan turn around observed among market vendors, or short-cycle manufacturing activities such as food processing. This type of lending, it seems, will always be done more efficiently by informal agents.

Successful programs appear to keep borrower transaction costs low, although empirical evidence of this is lacking. However, interest rates charged on loans by programs aiming at self-sustainability do not seem to be much lower than those observed in informal transactions for loans of comparable maturity and security. Again, a multidimensional analysis would be more conclusive, but the sketchy evidence suggests that market pricing of loans to disadvantaged clienteles results in relatively high rates compared to those that banks charge to their established clients, regardless of who is doing the lending.

Financial products offered by alternative institutions differ from informal loans in at least three aspects: (1) they have introduced joint liability and group lending, certainly an innovation in markets where informal finance prevails; (2) they have not totally eliminated end-use requirements; and (3) they are still highly imperfect as insurance substitutes.

Although reviews of group lending and joint liability are mixed, this is clearly a market niche worth developing and improving. It may provide the only feasible way of reaching the poor in remote, isolated areas, while still pursuing the goals of cost-effectiveness and sustainability (Bennett et al., 1994).

Doing away with end-use requirements is particularly important to improve the value of loan services as consumption-smoothing and risk-reducing mechanisms. This, combined with flexible contracts, and the supply of reliable portfolio management options, would enhance the value of new institutions as providers of insurance substitutes. It is unlikely, however, that any single contract devised by alternative institutions will bear the state-contingent nature described above for informal loans (i.e., contracts that are shaped by accurate information about the client and his or her condition). Even locally based intermediaries such as credit unions or village banks do not enjoy the near perfect information required by state-contingent contracts.

The potential market niches may be even wider for savings mobilization among the poor than they are for loan services. Although banks have penetrated this niche much more than they have the loan market, especially in Latin America, (Cuevas et al., 1991; and Almeyda, 1997) many new (alternative) institutions have successfully introduced deposit mobilization services, the best example being the BRI village unit system (Robinson, 1994, and chapter 4 in this book). More broadly, while banks, i.e., regulated financial intermediaries (including BRI) offer improved savings instruments compared to those available informally, with comparable safety and higher return, the same is not true for non-bank institutions such as NGOs and credit unions, where regulation and supervision remain as problems.

Regulation, supervision and governance

Non-bank 'alternative' institutions have not found, and governments and donors have not helped create, adequate substitutes for the direct supervision and regulation exercised in informal finance. While several credit unions networks have established relatively effective monitoring and supervisory mechanisms that offer reasonable confidence to depositors. (e.g., in Colombia and Guatemala), there remains room for improvement. Governance conflicts emerge between the democratic rule of credit unions, and the need for supervision to reflect the concerns and interests of the owners of the funds. Self-regulation has its limits.

As long as independent prudential regulation and supervision are not implemented for alternative institutions, these programs face constraints to expansion and growth not unlike those associated with informal finance. One could not advocate aggressive savings mobilization programs without adequate mechanisms that ensure financial discipline and safety. Furthermore, even donor funded lending programs need to ensure that loan portfolios are properly managed and funds are not wasted. Donors, governments, and institutions have a major challenge in this area.

Conclusion and summary

My conclusions can be summarized in three statements: (1) the emergence and growth of 'alternative' institutions has resulted in a much more diverse array of financial products available to the poor—clearly a positive result; (2) these institutions have introduced complements to rather than substitutes for informal financial arrangements, thus effectively expanding the frontier of formal finance—also a good outcome; and (3) the new institutions share with informal finance the limitations to growth and deepening associated with the absence of adequate prudential regulation and supervision.

Innovative institutions currently recognized as successful have indeed created 'market niches,' introducing efficient and reliable services where these were previously absent. The same institutions now face the challenge of expanding those niches to reach a larger share of the poor.

Notes

1   For a 'demythification' of informal finance, see Von Pischke (1991), chapter 8, and Adams and Fitchett (1992).
2   Insightful reviews are found in Christen et al. (1994), and in Rhyne and Rotblatt (1994). See also Robinson (1994), for a thorough description and analysis of the BRI experience.
3   Christen et al. (1994) and Schmidt and Zeitinger (1994), report average outstanding loan sizes between US$ 60 and US$ 1404, albeit for 'not-so-successful' programs in Latin America.

References

Adams, D.W and Fitchett, D.A. (1992), *Informal Finance in Low-Income Countries*, Westview Press: Boulder, CO.
Almeyda, G. (1996), *Money Matters: Reaching Women Microentrepreneurs with Financial Services*, Inter-American Development Bank: Washington, DC.
Barham, B.L., Boucher, S. and Carter, M. (1994), 'Credit Constraints, Credit Unions, and Small-Scale Producers in Guatemala,' Unpublished, University of Wisconsin: Madison, WI (July).
Baulier, F. et al. (1988), 'Les tontines en Afrique,' Caisse centrale de cooperation economique, *Notes et Etudes No. 12* (Septembre).
Baydas, M.M. (1993), 'Capital Structure and Asset Portfolio Choice among Manufacturing Enterprises in The Gambia,' Ph.D. Dissertation, Ohio State University: Columbus, OH.

Bennett, L., Goldberg, M. and Von Pischke, J.D., 'Basing Access on Performance to Create Sustainable Financial Services for the Poor in Nepal,' Chapter 9 in this volume.

Callier, P. (1990), 'Informal Finance: The Rotating Savings and Credit Association—An Interpretation,' *Kyklos*, Vol. 43, pp. 273–276.

Christen, R.P., Rhyne, E. and Vogel, R.C. (1994), 'Maximizing the Outreach of Microenterprise Finance: The Emerging Lessons of Successful Programs,' IMCC, Arlington VA (September).

Cuevas, C.E., Schrieder, G., Slover, C. and Viganò, L. (1991), 'Financial Markets in Rural Zaire: An Assessment of the Bandundu and Shaba Region,' Report to USAID Kinshasa, Ohio State University: Columbus, OH (March).

Cuevas, C.E., Graham, D.H. and Paxton, J.A. (1991), 'The Informal Financial Sector in El Salvador,' The Ohio State University, Report to USAID San Salvador (November).

Eswaran, M. and Kotwal, A. (1989), 'Credit as Insurance in Agrarian Economies,' *Journal of Development Economics*, Vol. 31, No. 1, pp. 37–53.

Krahnen, J.P. and Schmidt, R.H. (1991), 'Informal and Formal Financial Systems in Developing Countries,' Interdiziplinare Projekt Consult GmbH, Frankfurt am Main, Germany (September).

Rhyne, E. and Rotblatt, L. (1994), 'What Makes them Tick? Exploring the Anatomy of Major Microenterprise Finance Organizations,' ACCION International Monograph Series No. 9, Somerville, MA.

Robinson, M.S. (1994), 'Savings Mobilization and Micro-enterprise Finance: The Indonesian Experience,' in Otero, M. and Rhyne, E. (eds.), *The New World of Microenterprise Finance: Building Healthy Financial Institutions for the Poor*, Kumarian Press: West Hartford, CT, pp. 27–54.

Schmidt, R.H. and Zeitinger, C.-P. (1996), 'The Efficiency of Credit-Granting NGOs in Latin America,' *Savings and Development*, Vol. 20, No. 3, pp. 353–384.

Slover, C.H. (1991), 'Informal Financial Groups in Rural Zaire: A Club Theory Approach,' Ph.D. Dissertation, The Ohio State University: Columbus, OH.

Udry, C. (1990), 'Credit Markets in Northern Nigeria: Credit as Insurance in a Rural Economy,' *World Bank Economic Review*, Vol. 4, No. 3, pp. 251–269.

Von Pischke, J.D. (1991), *Finance at the Frontier: Debt Capacity and the Role of Credit in the Private Economy*, The World Bank: Washington, DC.

Von Pischke, J.D. (1992), 'ROSCAs: State-of-the-Art Financial Intermediation,' in Adams, D.W and Fitchett, D.A. (eds.), *Informal Finance in Low-Income Countries*, Westview Press: Boulder, CO, pp. 325–335.

9 Basing access on performance to create sustainable financial services for the poor in Nepal

LYNN BENNETT, MIKE GOLDBERG & J.D. VON PISCHKE

The Government of Nepal (GON) has for 20 years used rural banking networks to provide credit and other services to low income households through 'priority sector' lending programs. These programs target credit to farmers, low income families, rural women and cottage industries. In 1992 about 5.5% of total domestic credit outstanding was priority sector lending.

Since 1974, the Intensive Banking Program (IBP) has required commercial banks to lend to target groups or to specific activities in order to meet portfolio composition targets. Production Credit for Rural Women (PCRW), begun in 1982, is part of IBP. It brings commercial banks together with the Ministry of Local Development to provide finance and other services to more than 15,000 women organized into groups. In addition to its borrowers, PCRW has reached more than 250,000 rural men, women and children with a wide range of production and community development activities and training (International Fund for Agricultural Development, 1987, 1991).

The Small Farmer Development Program (SFDP) of the Agricultural Development Bank of Nepal (ADBN), also initiated in 1974, operates through groups of farmers and now has approximately 200,000 low-income borrowers. SFDP has improved participant access to basic veterinary and agricultural extension services, health and family planning, drinking water and other community infrastructure (Agricultural Projects Services Center, 1989 and International Fund for Agricultural Development, 1992, 1988, 1989).

As these programs have expanded, their financial performance has deteriorated. Through loan losses and overstaffing these programs have eroded the capital of the financial institutions implementing them. Using data collected in 1992 we estimated the net costs to the

banks for annual IBP lending to be 28% of the amount disbursed
each year. This comprises 23% in estimated bad debt costs and 5% in
funding and operating expenses. SFDP is estimated from these data to
cost ADBN about 37% of the amounts disbursed each year. This
method of viewing losses brings out costs clearly and suggests the size
of the provision that should reasonably be made at the time loans are
issued. Sustainability requires realistic costing of loan losses and this
requires that banks make annual provisions equal to approximately
one-quarter of the amounts of IBP loans they disburse each year.

The cost of priority sector lending is also high in institutional
terms: Subsidies obtained by borrowers who default are not a neutral
transfer to disadvantaged sections of society. They undermine the
efficiency and credibility of the financial sector and perpetuate
dependency on an overextended government and donors whose
priorities may change. Moreover, they inhibit development of local
institutions that are accountable to the target group and capable of
becoming sustainable. The 'default subsidy' offers the opposite of
empowerment to the poor and disadvantaged groups it purports to
help.

Poor and deteriorating repayment performance for priority
lending programs is a result of too rapid and externally funded (in the
cases of PCRW and SFDP) expansion. Lending that is driven by
administratively established disbursement targets and that is unrelated
to absorptive capacity often results in poor repayment performance.
In Nepal's priority sector lending, this problem is reinforced by a lack
of credible sanctions against defaulters and low levels of group
cohesion. At their worst, these systems combine over-financing (in the
form of loans equal to high proportions of borrowers' costs for new
activities) with unclear credit contracts, poor record-keeping, targeting
very poor households in remote areas, sporadic monitoring and little
or no technical back-stopping by banks or government agencies.

Moving beyond priority sector lending

Priority sector programs appear to present an unpalatable choice
between *outreach* and financial *sustainability*. The government can
continue to lose money by using the banking system to reach out to
poor men and women in remote areas; or it can free the banks to
concentrate on soundness, which only indirectly helps reduce rural
poverty. Sustainability and political economy require an approach to
rural finance that:

(a) develops the financial sector and builds sound, market-responsive financial institutions;

(b) reduces government subsidies over time and makes transparent those that remain; and

(c) increases access to viable financial services for poor men and women in all parts of Nepal.

This chapter suggests that group-based programs that systematically move their beneficiaries toward sustainable financial performance can minimize the conflict between outreach and sustainability and the market distortions inherent in directed credit. *Social intermediation* is a means of directing such movement.

Social intermediation consists of special efforts to integrate poor men and women into formal financial markets and to link them to government services that may help them to become more productive and to generate higher incomes. A principal vehicle for social intermediation is group formation, which involves economies in outreach and initial measures of empowerment. Cohesiveness and self-management capacity of groups enable them to bring down the costs of financial intermediation by reducing default through peer pressure and by lowering banks' transaction costs in dealing with small borrowers and savers.

Social intermediation is, potentially, a cost-effective means for expanding formal credit and savings facilities for the poor in Nepal. While group-based priority sector lending programs appear to have been a great success in widening access to formal sector credit and providing a channel for the delivery of social and production support services, progress toward genuine, self-reliant groups has been slow (although there are some notable successes). Savings mobilization has been irregular and has not become an accepted means of capitalization for groups or members. Declining loan recovery rates indicate that group development has not consistently established systems that weed out bad credit risks and motivate borrowers to repay.

Financial and social intermediation are closely linked; success of the former greatly depends on success of the latter in engaging the poor. Social intermediation, in the form of group formation, training of members and related support services, can improve loan repayment performance through the formation of cohesive groups that provide reliable joint guarantees of loans. It can also remove from banks some of the costs of lending and deposit-taking through collective savings deposits, and through subproject vetting and support by group members and extension staff.

Social intermediation is niche marketing, attempting to create systems and products for people who do not normally interact with formal financial institutions because of illiteracy, lack of assets, gender or ethnic background. It seeks to create new attitudes and self-perceptions as well as new systems and institutions for the poor. By engendering self-reliance and building self-confidence, these systems and institutions will help to empower their clientele as they gain the financial means for investing capital. These qualities are subjective and difficult to measure but, as they constitute part of the welfare benefit from expanded access to finance, they are important.

Cost recovery issues

Cost recovery objectives for social intermediation and for financial intermediation differ greatly (Bennett, 1993). Subsidies appear to be warranted for social intermediation which seeks to increase access to social and community development services such as adult literacy, family planning and immunization. For the start-up costs in developing self-reliant local institutions, a time-bound subsidy would be appropriate as an 'infant industry' investment in human resources and institutional capacity necessary to interface effectively with formal financial institutions.

Once such systems are in place, there would be no need to subsidize financial services. The challenge is to maintain clarity about these distinct dimensions of delivering integrated financial and other services to the poor. It is also very important for lenders and outreach programs to maintain good accounts and management-oriented information systems that distinguish between initial investments in delivery mechanisms and the unsubsidized financial products used by the target population.

An important element with ramifications for subsidy costs is the competitiveness and cost structures of formal financial intermediaries. Commercial banks in rural Nepal have been social service providers, as suggested by the government's policy of having one bank branch for every 30,000 people. This has created many remote branches that are quite sleepy most of the time. In the study on which this chapter is based, it was found that some branches, not terribly remote by local standards, had on average about as many transactions in a day with clients as they had employees at the branch.

Rural commercial banks are government-owned. They are not challenged by competition, and have little incentive to pay close attention to costs or to reduce them through innovation (Yadav et al., 1992). (Cost control currently involves shunning small savers and borrowers because of the workload they impose on bank staff.) The higher the costs of the banks in dealing with small clients, the greater the subsidies required to assist small savers and borrowers to reach the banks' thresholds at which they become attractive business prospects. High intermediation costs keep the frontier of formal finance closed for most of Nepal's population of 20 million.

Consideration of costs and competitiveness should lead to searches for forms of financial intermediation that are less costly than commercial banks or similar government-owned specialized intermediaries such as ADBN and regional rural banks. Viable alternatives would use simple systems, operate in modest quarters without head offices in Kathmandu, enlist volunteer or member participation and leadership, and pay staff rural wages rather than relying on civil service or commercial bank scales.

While PCRW and SFDP are not sustainable in financial or institutional terms, parts of existing systems could possibly be adapted to create a sustainable, low-cost lending model for low income rural clients. This can be approached through reliance on and cultivation of local capacity as demonstrated by the best performing borrowers, groups, banking services and support activities in rural areas.

An example of promising social intermediation

Encouraging developments in social intermediation emerge from the GTZ-funded Dhading Development Program (DDP) (Dhading Development Project, 1991). This program, which began in 1987, seeks to make SFDP groups more self-reliant. DDP has used action research to explore ways to expand SFDP coverage while reducing ADBN's role in group formation and support. They have endeavored to build groups into a federated structure to capture two types of benefits: the accountability offered by small group size and economies of scale in community development and financial intermediation.

Training group leaders. In the first stage of DDP research, group members selected the 12 best group leaders to become Group Promoters (GPs), who were trained for 10 days to take over some group identification and organization work. To emphasize self-reliance, each Group Promoter was asked at the end of the training what he or she could do during the next year to benefit small farmers without outside help. These GPs were illiterate, but effective. It became clear that their credibility depended upon speedy SFDP recognition of the groups they organized, so that the members could get credit quickly.

Leveraging illiterate leaders and low status. The next stage of the research responded to GPs' low literacy levels by selecting young school leavers from local small farm families to become Youth Workers and Women Group Organizers (WGOs). They expressed a sense of accountability to the small farmers who have a say in their selection. Eventually they will depend on SFDP groups for their pay as GTZ support for their salary (Rs. 2000 per month in 1992, about US$ 45) is phased out. A Youth Worker in Bhumistan reported that small farmers convinced him to take the job instead of continuing his studies in Kathmandu. He reported that he had difficulty four years earlier when he took the job because the farmers viewed him as too young to have any authority. Nevertheless, he has effectively handled nearly 70 groups. While the GPs organize groups and weed out potentially bad credit risks, he assists with paper work required to get groups recognized by ADBN, loan applications, repayment and savings records, and collection of repayments.

In 1992 there were 18 Youth Workers and 10 Women Group Organizers in the District. DDP shows that in combination with Group Promoters, Youth Workers can greatly accelerate program expansion. From eight SFDP groups in two villages in mid-1984, the program served 439 groups in 18 villages in mid-1991.

Intergroups: lateral linking for vertical expansion. Another advance in social intermediation has been the development of 'intergroups' of between eight and 13 groups. About 85 group members are represented on an intergroup executive committee composed of their group leaders and the three or four GPs in their ward.[1] By July 1991, 47 intergroups had been formed by 280 SFDP groups. The intergroup committee meets monthly. It promotes economic and social activities and oversees community development projects selected by the intergroup. In Bhumistan these include renovation of a school and construction of a community hall and drinking water and sprinkler irrigation systems. Materials or a subsidy for their purchase are available through donor programs. The intergroup committee organizes community labor and raises up to 25% of cash costs.

In Bhumistan, intergroup members must contribute Rs. 1 to 2 per month (less than US$ 0.05) to the Intergroup Savings Fund in addition to contributions to their own group savings fund. Many intergroups start joint marketing enterprises or other ventures such as seedling production, agricultural input marketing or, in one case, electricity generation. Start-up capital is generally provided by the intergroup.

One intergroup in Bhumistan accumulated Rs. 35,000 (about US$ 8000) by 1992, of which Rs. 20,000 was loaned to group members at 20% annual interest. This is above the SFDP rate and the Intergroup Fund lends for a wider range of purposes including consumption and medical treatment. The fund makes loans to purchase local buffaloes which women prefer because they require less medical care and fodder than the expensive improved breeds for which SFDP lends. The rest of the fund earns 8.5% interest at a commercial bank. (In 1992 the rate of inflation in Nepal was about 17%.) GTZ reported that by mid-1991 the eight intergroups in Bhumistan had saved Rs. 175,000 (about US$ 4000); Rs. 80,000 had been relent to group members with reported repayment rates of 100%. The Bhumistan experience illustrates that a demand-driven orientation toward the interests of clients, regular savings, use of groups as credit managers, and realistic interest rates contribute to positive results.

Building on success. The project's next planned step is to create a federation of intergroups as a Small Farmers Association or 'main committee' that can link farmers with government and non-governmental agencies and provide expanded financial intermediation, marketing and technical support. Progress by main committees has appearantly been good. A DDP workshop in 1992 concluded that ADBN should begin handing over its small farmer savings and credit operations to selected main committees. ADBN would work out transfer arrangements, including legal registration, dealing with default, and allowable lending margins. DDP/GTZ plans to phase out support for these over three or four years and main committees will determine the terms and conditions of employment of Youth Workers and WGOs. DDP is moving toward the final stages of group self-reliance and institutional development envisaged in the joint action research program.

Resolving the cost vs. outreach dilemma: rationalizing access to financial services

Goals for reform of priority sector credit programs should be derived from the objectives of optimal outreach and sustainability for these programs. Under these objectives, large and growing numbers of people would use formal financial services provided by sustainable institutions. Priority sector lending would then be redundant because the day-to-day conduct of financial intermediation would satisfy the objectives of priority sector lending, not requiring special schemes. Institutions would be sustainable because they would normally make a profit on financial activities after making realistic loan loss provisions.

Against this standard, the test of any policy, program or intervention is two-fold: (1) Does it expand outreach and services to the poor? (2) Will the implementing financial institutions at least break even on their lending after making initial investments in outreach and local capacity building? Can they achieve a surplus to self-finance their expansion?

Existing financial outreach to poor people in Nepal contains two related flaws. First, the system does not accurately evaluate the probability of success in loan investments. An example of this is livestock loans for the purchase of large animals by poor women who are not experienced or trained in buffalo husbandry for the breeds obtained. Secondly, the system does not adequately value the past performance of borrowers. An example of this is PCRW groups who borrow repeatedly, repay satisfactorily and save systematically and still face the same procedures for obtaining new loans that they did when they first borrowed. In the first case too much is given too soon; in the second too little is offered too late. In each case potential is wasted and efforts are misdirected. Strategies that could prevent or diminish the costs of these flaws would permit more efficient outreach: the same volume of subsidies could underwrite services to more people.

Matching services to clients' capacities and widening access based on clients' performance appears to offer great scope for improvement in group-based programs. While increasing borrowing limits for good clients is commonplace in finance, the strategy proposed here derives from the idea that phasing—risk phasing and access phasing—is an effective organizing principle for the operation of the group-based portion of the rural credit system. Social intermediation would facilitate implementation.

A critical element of this strategy is ensuring scope for growth and development of relationships between clients and financial intermediaries. Social intermediation can accelerate this process significantly by preparing clients to articulate their concerns and preferences and take increasing responsibility for developing and maintaining the institutions that supply services to them. These ideas can be applied to existing programs and to new initiatives.

Categories of clients and services: linking contracts to performance

How can PCRW and SFDP's lending impact be made sustainable, and their coverage expanded? There are two threats to the sustainability of group-based financial intermediation. One consists of the high operating costs of group formation and continued outreach to groups. The second is the risk of default. These are related: more investment in social intermediation may reduce default because groups function more effectively, creating greater incentives for members to repay in full and on time so that the group's access to credit is maintained.

Willful default is relatively common in government-promoted credit operations in most countries, including Nepal. It undermines contracts between individuals or groups and financial intermediaries. But groups provide a means of managing this risk when they are cohesive, when incentives are provided to encourage timely debt service, and when an overwhelming majority of the group favor abiding by contract terms and conditions. Membership self-selection, peer pressure and internal monitoring systems can minimize willful default.

Inability to pay. Default is not always willful. Borrowers may obtain too much debt or choose projects with insufficient financial return. This is especially likely when subsidized credit is wed to disbursement targets. Some default results from bad investment decisions, independent of the type of financing provided, and adversity that could not reasonably be predicted. These risks also face groups, and may be a great burden.

For any approach to work, controllable causes of unwillful default must be contained. This is necessary because groups cannot survive more than small amounts of bad investment or bad luck. Unwillful default occurs when a borrower cannot repay due to: (1) misunderstandings arising from lack of clarity in the contract; (2) selection of a risky venture without adequate experience or technical support; or (3) inappropriately structured credit that makes timely payment difficult or that fails to provide incentives for businesslike behavior. The repayment schedule including grace periods, term of the loan to maturity, loan size, the borrower's equity stake, and the interest rate are key variables.

Inability to repay also occurs when bad luck strikes, such as the death of a borrower or a natural disaster. Group solidarity is an important source of repayment capacity in this situation as is the lender's willingness to provide continued support when this is likely to reduce bad debt loss.

Building on local capacity. Group-based finance in Nepal has created a basis, however limited, for reform and innovation. As shown by such examples as PCRW groups in Walling, this potential and its constraints are illustrated by the best performers. Some of these groups have existed for as long as eight years, during which they have saved regularly and taken a succession of loans, borrowing anew after clearing their previous debt. Group members, whose husbands spend most of the year in India as soldiers or security guards, are competent as farmers and managers. When these borrowers want to borrow again they must complete the same paperwork that was required for their first loan.

In one case a group's savings had been growing at a rate of Rs. 100 per month over an eight-year period, in another by Rs. 80 per month for a six-year period. These savings were accepted only grudgingly by the commercial bank serving PCRW in the area, whereas bankers in a competitive system would accept such deposits happily. There also was no apparent mechanism by which these clients' experience with saving, borrowing, investing and managing group dynamics could be shared with younger women or less experienced borrowers and savers.

Performance classification and risk phasing. The positive aspects of these experiences can be supported by stratifying groups based on their performance. This innovation permits more efficient targeting of social intermediation and the subsidies it requires, while providing incentives to lower bad debt losses. It also fosters good contracts by managing the risks faced by the borrowers and by the lender. In addition, its emphasis on savings mobilization creates a funding base for the lender and incentives for borrowers to perform according to their loan contracts.

Phasing will work only by offering greater benefits for better performance. This requires that groups gain more opportunities as their energies and skills develop: *hierarchies of access should complement hierarchies of performance.* New groups would have limited access and benefits, e.g., loans for chickens, not buffaloes. Experienced groups with good repayment records can obtain large loans. Their members can act as leaders in group formation and development, and in development and enforcement of credit and savings discipline beyond their own groups.

Household surveys conducted at the start of relationships with PCRW and SFDP provide the basis for marketing financial services and permit stratification of new borrowers. Potential lenders could rank households according to the amount of land under cultivation and cropping pattern, the type of enterprise, and production technology. These surveys provide reference and entry points for agencies that provide support services such as agricultural extension.

In general, groups should consist of homogeneous borrowers. This would contribute to group solidarity for joint liability, as each member would be eligible for loans of roughly equal size. Groups that were not homogeneous could still be accommodated, but at a level that would be more modest than their most sophisticated members could obtain in a group of their peers. However, heterogeneous groups that show signs of strong group cohesion should be encouraged. These may include existing groups engaged in activities other than credit.

Each group would have the opportunity to progress through stages of services based on performance. A staged approach enables clients to demonstrate creditworthiness under less risky conditions, while they accumulate financial assets and experience. Staging could also generate greater contract clarity by requiring that results be evaluated periodically, linking future access to repayment performance systematically and predictably. This approach deepens financial services for those who perform well, giving them more choices over their access to financial services.

Application of risk phasing to PCRW and SFDP

To provide clear incentives and contracts, and to focus managerial attention by group organizers, promoters and members, six stages of progression are proposed: (1) formation, (2) savings, (3) lending group funds, (4) seasonal credit, (5) term credit, and (6) transformation. The social intermediary helps groups advance through these stages. However, no targets should govern progression. Each group should move at its own speed. Some will remain happily at one level for a long time. Some will collapse. Some will lose members and accept new members. Others will progress steadily, increasing members' welfare and contributing to the economy and society with each upward step. Better risk management, reflected in lower bad debt losses, would be a material source of gains from the staged approach.

Stage 1: formation. At this initial stage the group is recruiting members, selecting its leadership and developing rules and procedures reflecting group and credit program objectives. Performance is measured by participation in group meetings and development of responsive 'rules of the game' and internal control systems. This stage permits the group to judge the commitment and reliability of individual members before including them in joint liability relationships. This stage addresses, before credit provision, the difficulties faced by both SFDP and PCRW in developing group solidarity and provides the time required to conduct household surveys. This stage could be relatively short, measured in weeks or months.

An interesting feature of group activities involving women in Nepal is the proliferation of special, prudential funds created by groups for their members' benefit. Periodic contributions are frequently put aside for purposes such as medical expenses for family members as well as for livestock. When group members spontaneously include such funds in their 'rules of the game' strong evidence is provided of group spirit and solidarity.

Stage 2: savings. In the second stage the group mobilizes and accumulates individual and joint savings through regular deposits by members under their own rules. Promoting savings first emphasizes the importance of internal financial management. It is also consistent with the progression and popularity of normal patterns of interaction with formal financial institutions. Most people want to save and do so, while many may not be creditworthy or within the reach of social intermediation. In virtually every country depositors outnumber borrowers and responsive, well-managed formal financial intermediaries generally find it easy to attract more deposits than they can profitably lend. The authors' work in Nepal found no evidence that would suggest that Nepal is an exception. Savings takes on added importance when it is the basis for group managed activities.

The role of the financial intermediary at this stage is to offer a secure, attractive savings facility. The amounts involved would often be extremely modest. Groups would maintain their own records and would participate in an evaluation of savings mobilization, participation and recordkeeping. Extension and production-oriented technical assistance might be provided in response to requests from groups. Groups should, however, be willing to pay a nominal fee for these services so that the system avoids the development of a subsidy-dependent mentality. Contacts between the group and the financial intermediary would be broadened to include credit, but as savings accumulate, self- and group-financing would begin to be seen as an alternative to credit.

Stage 3: lending group funds. Movement to stage 3, which begins when groups begin lending some portion of their own collective fixed fund to each other or to outsiders in whom they have confidence, should be spontaneous. This is customary among groups that save together or make other periodic contributions as part of their activities. This progression, involving only a group's own resources, would not require any involvement or changes in relationships between the group and its bank or other service providers.

Stages 2 and 3 would require months or years to demonstrate a commitment, a capacity to save at regular meetings of the group, and to shut down the default culture based on excessively easy access to credit. It is also quite possible that group members would establish their own rotating savings and credit association (ROSCA) in addition to the fixed fund that is the focus of the phased approach. A ROSCA or *dhikuti* is another symbol of group cohesiveness (Yadav and Pederson, 1992). It also creates credit relationships and credit histories that might make lending from the group's fixed fund seem less risky. However, it would probably not be unusual for a ROSCA to be formed at the same time as the fixed fund is established in phase 2.

Stage 4: seasonal credit. Groups in the seasonal credit stage obtain joint liability loans from the financial intermediary. Initial loans are short term, working capital (seasonal) loans for low risk ventures that (1) members felt capable of conducting profitably, and (2) the group is willing to support with a loan guarantee. Repayment problems would lead to a temporary halt in credit access and group savings would be held as a complementary form of collateral to reinforce the guarantee. Services provided at this stage would include savings, short term loans, further training in recordkeeping, and technical assistance requested by the group. Performance would be evaluated by repayment, deposit mobilization and enterprise results. This stage would last for several seasons in order to demonstrate the willingness and capacity to manage repeated cycles of borrowing and repayment.

Stage 5: term credit. The fifth stage provides 'full service rural banking' to groups that have proven organizationally sound and financially reliable. Long- as well as short-term credit could support livestock, wells or business development, for example. Repayment would be the main indicator of group creditworthiness. This stage would last for several years during which the group continues to build its debt capacity through savings and good repayment. Uses for savings would multiply. Funds might be loaned, possibly to outsiders, or invested in an activity performed or managed by the group. Measures to deal with risk and other concerns of members would also become more complex and far-reaching. Members of groups at this stage would increasingly be called upon to advise and assist new or aspiring groups of less-experienced, probably younger members.

Stage 6: transformation. At the final phase the group transforms itself because its members no longer are interested in borrowing or in doing so as part of a group or of their particular group. Some may perceive that they could now deal effectively with formal financial institutions as individuals at lower transaction costs based on their saving and credit histories. Some members may seek loans that are much larger than the group's policies permit. Transformation can also occur as a life-cycle phenomenon or when group members become 'fully invested.' In these cases either their time is fully employed operating their credit-supported investments or they have fully exploited all of their skills.

Transformation could take many other forms. One would be to dissolve, as group members would have saved material amounts. Another option would be to join an intergroup (as in Dhading) with others selected on the basis of some common bond. A group or intergroup might decide to become a registered credit union or adopt another legal form. Based on their experience as producers, savers and investors, the group should be able to enter contracts better informed, making it more likely that they comply with conditions and take full advantage of access to funds.

Transformation should mean that all group members generally set an example in the community. Those that choose to remain involved with group activities of any sort would be likely to be chosen as group leaders. Leadership would include running their own financial intermediary as board members, credit committee members and record-keepers; encouraging newer, less experienced groups; and giving specialized training in skills that they have mastered. Many would be innovators in addressing commercial opportunities and contributing to public welfare.

Phasing in existing groups. No new programs or institutions are required for implementation of the phased strategy. PCRW and SFDP groups would be phased into the staged approach based on their status and performance. Classification using household budgets would determine the types of credit facilities for which they could be eligible, and repayment performance to date would determine their actual eligibility. (Performance could be measured systematically using the Repayment Index.[2]) Past problems with repayment performance could be tempered to some extent by past savings performance.

All SFDP and PCRW groups could be phased into the new system over a five-year period, beginning with the oldest and ending with the youngest. All new groups should be formed under the staged approach, and new programs and institutions should be free to adopt phasing. Groups in arrears should not enter the system until they have cleared those arrears. If they refuse to do so they should be dissolved and their members blacklisted from further participation. Classification based on performance could then begin. Groups that have not performed well would be downgraded in terms of credit access, usually through reductions in the loan sizes for which they are eligible. They would be encouraged to concentrate on savings. Those that have performed moderately well would be held at their present level of access until they master the savings routine while servicing their debts on time.

Introduction of the staged approach should provide dramatic and immediate expansions of credit access for the very few that are the best performing. Also, members of the best performing groups should be trained very quickly in record-keeping and in the mechanics of staging. They should be used as primary promoters of the new system, demonstrating the rewards of good performance. These two features provide positive incentives for members of groups that have not performed particularly well, and set the tone for the new system.

With these proposed changes, priority sector lending programs would be far more likely to become sustainable and profitable while continuing to target services to low income groups. It is envisaged that the initial impetus for organizing groups would come from SFDP or PCRW field staff. Subsequent responsibility for expansion of coverage and services would be left to the groups themselves. Participating financial institutions would be responsible for offering reliable, appropriate services at a price that covers their expenses. This built-in form of continuing market research would enable the groups to clearly articulate their concerns to interested financial institutions, including existing programs and those which intend to enter rural markets.

Notes

1   The ward is the smallest unit of local government. There are nine wards in a
     Village Development Committee. Some active wards in Dhading had organ-
     ized two intergroups.
2   Von Pischke, J.D. (1991), 'The Repayment Index,' and 'Algebraic
     Treatment of the Repayment Index,' Annexes A and B, *Finance at the Fron-
     tier: Debt Capacity and the Role of Credit in the Private Economy*, pp. 383–
     394.

References

Agricultural Projects Services Centre (1989), *Mid-Term Evaluation of the Small
     Farmers Development Program: Phase II*, Draft Report, Kathmandu, Nepal.
Agricultural Projects Services Centre (1989), *Impact Evaluation Intensive Banking
     Program (IBP) Final Report*, Kathmandu, Nepal.
Bennett, L. (1993), 'Developing Sustainable Financial Systems for the Poor: Where
     Subsidies Can Help and Where They Can Hurt,' Gender and Poverty series of
     the Asia Region Gender and Poverty Team, October, 26, The World Bank:
     Washington, DC.
Bennett, L. (1990),'Rural Indebtedness in Nepal,' World Bank, Washington, DC.
Canadian Centre for International Studies and Cooperation (CECI/NEPAL) and Small
     Business Promotion Project (GTZ) (1992), *Workshop on Financing Micro-
     Enterprises*, Kathmandu, Nepal.
Dhading Development Project (DDP) (1991), *Small Farmer Development Programme:
     Programme Component Status Report*, Kathmandu, Nepal.
Institute for Integrated Development Studies (1992), *A Strategy for Rural Service
     Delivery*, Kathmandu, Nepal.
Integrated Development Systems (1989), *An Assessment of Poverty Alleviation
     Programmes of Selected NGOs*, Draft Report. Kathmandu, Nepal.
International Fund for Agricultural Development (1987), *Nepal: Production Credit for
     Rural Women Project: Appraisal Report* (Implementation Edition), Rome,
     Italy.
International Fund for Agricultural Development (1991), *Nepal: Production Credit for
     Rural Women Project: Report of Implementation Follow-up Mission*,
     Rome, Italy.
International Fund for Agricultural Development (1992), *Aide Memoire, Completion
     Evaluation: Nepal Second Small Farmer Development Project*, Draft, Rome,
     Italy.

International Fund for Agricultural Development (1988), *SFDP Completion Evaluation Report*, Rome, Italy.

International Fund for Agricultural Development (1989), *Project Completion Report of the Small Farmer Development Project*, Rome, Italy.

Khatri, N.N. (1992), *SFDP Joint Liability Group as Collateral Substitute*, Case Study Presented in the APRACA Regional Workshop on Collateral Substitutes: Manila, Philippines.

Nepal Rastra Bank, Agricultural Credit Division, Development Finance Department (1991), *Impact Evaluation of the Small Farmer's Development Programme of Nepal*, Kathmandu, Nepal.

Pal, M.S. (1991), *Nepal: Production Credit for Rural Women Case Study: Final Draft*, Montreal, Canada.

Production Credit for Rural Women (1989), *An Impact Evaluation Study, Centre for Women and Development*, UNICEF: Kathmandu, Nepal.

Production Credit for Rural Women (1989), *A Tripartite Review*, HMG of Nepal, Government of the Netherlands and UNICEF: Kathmandu, Nepal.

Production Credit for Rural Women (1989), *Conclusions and Recommendations of the Tripartite Review*, HMG of Nepal, Government of the Netherlands and UNICEF: Kathmandu, Nepal.

Von Pischke, J.D. (1991), *Finance at the Frontier: Debt Capacity and the Role of Credit in the Private Economy*, World Bank: Washington, DC.

Yadav, S., Otsuka, K. and David, C.C. (1992), 'Segmentation in Rural Finance Markets: The Case of Nepal,' *World Development*, Vol. 20, No. 3.

Yadav, S.N. and Pederson, G. (1992), *Determinants of Interest Rates in Informal Credit Markets of Nepal*, Unpublished manuscript.

Annex

Table 9.1   Summary and comparison of major lending programs
            targeting the poor in Nepal

Key Variable	IBP	PCRW	SFDP
General			
1. Year established	1981	1982	1975
2. Type of institution	Financial program through state-owned banks (RBB, NBL)	Program linked to IBP and operated by Women's Dev. Div. of Min. of Local Development	Program of ADBN (National Agric. Bank of Nepal)
3. Financial services provided	Credit, savings	Credit, savings and livestock insurance	Credit, savings and livestock insurance
4. Non-financial services provided	NA	Group organization, training, adult literacy, smokeless stoves, latrines, health and nutrition, community projects	Group organization, technical training, adult literacy, latrines, community projects
5. Target population	Urban and rural clients for wide range of activities	Low income rural women	Small farmers
6. Major donors	NA	UNICEF, IFAD, ILO, USAID, UNFPA, FINNIDA	IFAD, GTZ, UNICEF, ADB/Manila

Table 9.1   Summary and comparison of major lending programs targeting the poor in Nepal (continued)

Key Variable	IBP	PCRW	SFDP
Outreach Indicators: Clientele			
7. Number of borrowers receiving loans in 1991	NA but probably more than 200,000	10,830	186,971
8. Women as % of borrowers	Very low	100%	17%
9. Number of groups	Very few, except for PCRW groups	3539	4147 (women's groups) 20,334 (men's groups)
10. Percentage of loans to groups	9%	100%	100%
11. Number of clients for non-financial services	NA	Approximately 250,000	Approximately 135,000
Branches and staffing			
12. Branches/ offices	318	80	435
13. Central staff	83	54	NA
14. Field staff	504	439	NA
15. Total staff	587	493	903
16. Number of districts covered	NA	49	75

Table 9.1   Summary and comparison of major lending programs
            targeting the poor in Nepal (continued)

Key Variable	IBP	PCRW	SFDP
Financial outreach and performance			
17. Loan disbursements: • 1990 • 1991	Rs. 309 million Rs. 238 million	Rs. 5 million Rs. 34 million	Rs. 238 million Rs. 240 million
18. Volume of loans outstanding • 1990 • 1991	Rs. 806 million Rs. 1,135 million	Rs. 19 million Rs. 21 million	Rs. 537 million Rs. 625 million
19. Real growth rate of outstanding loan portfolio (1988-1991)	(-3%)	+34%	+6%
20. Estimated bad debt losses of principal incurred on annual disbursements (%)	23%	NA	33%
21. Average loan size	Rs. 12,470	Approximately Rs. 4,800	Approximately Rs. 4,500
22. Term of loan	Wide variation	Upto 5 years	Predominantly seasonal loans
23. Collateral required	Tends to be formal	Joint liability (but sometimes land certificate)	Joint liability (but land pledge taken where possible)
24. Repayment frequency	Various terms	Seasonal repayment and annual installments	Seasonal repayment
25. Loan arrears definition	Amount received/ Amount due	Overdue when final installment is overdue	Amount received/ Amount due
26. Main activities financed	43% agriculture 40% cottage industry 17% services	83% agriculture 5% cottage industry 12% services	82% agriculture 13% cottage industry 5% services

PART III

SUSTAINABILITY AND ACCOUNTABILITY IN MICROFINANCE

10 Credit scoring to predict loan repayment performance: an application to rural customers in Burkina Faso

LAURA VIGANÒ

Object of the research

This chapter investigates the scope for improving credit risk evaluation criteria and procedures in financial markets in less developed countries where common bank loan analysis techniques are not appropriate, due to borrowers' and environmental characteristics.

Many authors have focused their research on loan repayment problems in less developed countries (LDCs). The quality of loan portfolios has been related to weaknesses in the management of development banks and to the way that rural credit programs are implemented (Adams, Graham and Von Pischke, 1984; Masini, 1987 and 1989; Von Pischke, Adams and Donald, 1983; Von Pischke, 1991).

Studies that have focused on loan repayment and the different causes for defaults have found that these often correlate with borrower's characteristics, the financial institution's performance, conditions of loan contracts and government interventions (see, among others, Adera, 1987; Aguilera and Gonzalez-Vega, 1990; Aguilera, Gonzalez-Vega and Graham, 1990; Baker and Dia, 1987; Barry, Baker and Sanint, 1981; Khalily and Meyer, 1990; Nelson and Cruz-Letona, 1991; Njoku and Obasi, 1991; Njoku and Odii, 1991; Sanderatne, 1986 and 1989; Stickley and Tapsoba, 1980; Vogel, 1981; Yabile, 1987).

The results of these studies imply that loan portfolio quality could be improved through the analysis of creditworthiness that takes into account local conditions. Effective control of credit risk is a crucial aspect of bank management, increasing in importance as do loan loss and loan processing costs. This chapter discusses a credit scoring model that meets this objective successfully in Burkina Faso.

Two major problems concerning loan analysis are evident:
(a) the difficulty and the high cost of collecting dependable information on borrowers' businesses; and
(b) the absence of benchmark procedures by loan analysts, consistent with bank lending policy.

Loan evaluation procedures can be improved through more efficient use of the information necessary to estimate the probability of repayment. This chapter identifies the relevant information and defines the criteria by which it can be weighted in the loan evaluation process. This analysis is particularly relevant to rural customers, the agricultural, commercial, handicraft, and other microenterprises that are often the most difficult to evaluate.

Two hypotheses are offered. The first assumes there are some factors affecting the borrower's behavior that are likely to increase the probability of default. In certain situations the way the loan contract is presented to customers affects their perception of the loan obligation and their willingness to repay. This hypothesis relates to the classic principal-agent problem (Jensen and Meckling, 1976). Empirical results confirm this hypothesis. Second, the problem of the quality of information is explored. In this analysis, it is assumed that some of the error in credit risk evaluation is related to the difficulty of obtaining the commonly used information on customers' ability and willingness to repay.

To overcome the widespread absence of correct information, this article presents evaluation models that identify symptoms of the borrower's performance and behavior. For this purpose *symptomatic variables* are employed to create indicators of the *borrower-customers' ability and willingness to repay.*

With regard to the credit evaluation procedures, there is often a need for shared decision frameworks and coordination between the head office and bank branches in order to maintain consistent loan decisions. This is addressed through a relatively simple quantitative model for creditworthiness based on multivariate discriminant analysis. Quantitative models allow for the adoption of common evaluation criteria across bank branches so that branch lending policies will be more consistent with the general objectives of the bank. The quantification of the judgment in a score is also important because it provides a basis for evaluating loan officers' lending decisions. This last aspect is very important in development banks, where accountability of loan officers is often a problem.

The proposed model is also relevant for the theoretical interpretation of credit risk determinants offered in this chapter. This clear relationship between theory and the interpretation of results can be an important tool for improving the decision making and learning process and, therefore, the portfolio management in development banks.

Theoretical framework

Credit risk evaluation is a complex process involving careful analysis of borrower information in order to estimate the probability that the loan will be regularly repaid. The probability of regular repayment depends on the borrower's operating environment and personal attitude toward the obligation. Repayment performance also depends on the bank's ability to evaluate these two aspects through available information and on the bank's ability to control credit risk through specific contractual conditions.

In analyzing the borrower's characteristics, the unreliable information that is common in rural areas of LDCs confounds credit risk analysis by placing another element of uncertainty in the evaluation. In these cases risk depends not only on the borrower's actual performance but also on the ability to evaluate this performance through available information. This may occur due to the actual difficulty of interpreting the data or as a consequence of opportunistic reporting by the borrower, who may hide relevant information. The borrower might not be seriously motivated to establish a responsible relationship with the bank, especially if an eventual default is unlikely to cause serious consequences.

It is hypothesized here that banks can change such behavior by demanding contractual conditions that induce the borrower to respect the obligation. The introduction of various penalties or collateral guarantees in the form of liens on properties that the borrower considers important are examples of mechanisms that might improve the likelihood of responsible repayment.

Four groups of factors affecting credit risk can then be summarized:

(a) the customer's ability to repay, depending also on favorable external (economic and environmental) conditions,

(b) the customer's willingness to repay,

(c) the quality of the information upon which the analyst bases the judgment, and

(d) the bank's ability to insure the customer's willingness to repay through an incentive-compatible contract.[1]

The analytical framework applied to understanding these determinants of credit risk identifies several strong indicators for credit risk evaluation. The most important of these indicators directly relate to these four categories of factors.

Research implementation

The CNCA of Burkina Faso

The Caisse Nationale de Crédit Agricole du Burkina Faso—CNCA—is a rural development bank established in 1979. Field operations were initially performed by various existing public structures that the bank was not able to control effectively, distorting the bank-customer relationship. The CNCA has undergone several restructurings and effort has been applied to decentralize the institution through branch management of the lending process.

The bank was able to face these changes by instituting more effective control systems (L'Aot, 1989), permanent efforts to reduce costs, and a serious effort to improve creditworthiness evaluation and lending processes.

The present research was stimulated by a search for innovative and beneficial credit evaluation techniques. In contrast to many development banks where costly administrative and bureaucratic procedures still prevail, CNCA showed serious management commitment to the goal of improved efficiency. This fact is very important for model testing since bureaucratic and unmotivated bank personnel would invalidate the result, making the bank's internal problems more relevant than other elements of credit risk.

Sampling

For this first application, the analysis is limited to loans granted to individuals operating small and micro-firms. A sample of 118 loans to individuals was obtained. The sample was extracted from the population of all individual customers of the bank, targeted by population typologies and loan characteristics such as loan type, maturities, repayment performance and declared use of the loan.

The data were not complete for all sets of observations, requiring that the original sample of 118 observations be reduced to 100 complete observations. In order to limit the reduction of observations (Zmijewski, 1984) the following choice was made:

(a) estimating a model with 100 observations, dropping important variables with many missing values; and

(b) estimating a second model for 31 observations for which more complete data on the customer's profitability, financial situation and asset and liability composition were available and reliable.

Collection of information

Quantitative and qualitative information was collected through questionnaires and direct interviews with loan managers. In this LDC context, qualitative information is sometimes more relevant than quantitative data, given the absence or unreliability of bookkeeping by loan applicants. The satisfactory results of the model confirm the relevance of qualitative data or *symptomatic variables* as indicators of the borrower's financial performance (Viganò, 1992a and 1992b).

The questionnaire covered all the common fields of loan analysis:

(a) the customer's personal characteristics,

(b) data on the enterprise,

(c) profitability,

(d) asset and liability amount and composition,

(e) financial situation,

(f) investment plans,

(g) customer's relationship with the CNCA, and

(h) the bank's control of credit risk through contractual conditions.

In most of these areas, quantitative data were not reliable and *symptomatic information* was used. This was the case for profitability where information on technology, adaptability to changes, and revenue stability was more important than revenue estimations. Another example is the use of data on asset composition as *symptoms of the customer's self-financing and management abilities*. Again, notwithstanding money fungibility (Dell'Amore, 1965; Von Pischke and Adams, 1980), a well defined investment plan may be considered a *symptom of the customer's seriousness and professional skills*.

Historical data on the bank-customer relationship were collected, as well as information on the way contacts between the bank and the customer take place (at the bank, through projects, etc.). A clear understanding of the contractual obligation is easier if the two counterparties meet and discuss loan terms and conditions; the presence of a project might distort the customer's perception of the obligation. Variables reflecting this aspect were considered as *symptoms of the willingness to repay*.

Variable selection

A first selection of original variables was determined by the number of observations for which they were available. This elimination is also consistent with the theoretical framework since the lack of information is one area of credit risk that the bank has to address. The purpose of the research is to find a model that accounts for this lack of information and that allows the bank to evaluate credit risk given a limited amount of data on the customer. A second selection of the variables from the original data set was based on the relevant theory.[2]

The remaining sets of respectively 53 and 54 variables were retained for the total sample (100 observations for which symptomatic variables prevail due to incompleteness of data on the usual areas of investigation such as profitability) and the reduced one (31 observations).

The model

Factor analysis was applied to the final set of variables for both the total sample and the reduced sample. Eleven and 13 factors were respectively obtained. The first test used all the 11 factors. Four out of the 13 factors were selected through a stepwise forward method for the second test.[3]

Factor analysis was used for two principal reasons. First, the description of complex situations through relatively simple basic information leaves input variables over-dimensioned (i.e., too many variables relative to the number of observations). Factors allow a reduction in the number of input variables with no loss of relevant information. Second, these factors are related to crucial aspects of credit risk set forth in the theoretical introduction. It would be more difficult to find this correspondence between theory and the variables that, taken individually, reflect only partial aspects of a complex phenomenon.

The satisfactory discriminant power of the factors confirms the validity of the approach from both the theoretical and empirical points of view.[4] The loan analyst can perceive the relative weight of each factor on credit risk and take ad hoc measures to control the aspect that seems more significant.

The classification results

The following tables summarize the results of discrimination for the total sample and the reduced one. Results reflect respectively the reclassification of the original samples and the application of the jack-knife method, which classifies iteratively all the observations through a discriminant function estimated using all the observations except the one to be classified (Lachenbruch, 1975).

Table 10.1   Discrimination on 100 observations with 11 factors

Table 10.1a   Discrimination on 100 observations with 11 factors—Results of classification of the original sample (% values in brackets)

Sample actual composition	Model sample classification		Total
	Regular	Default	
Regular	32 (62.75)	19 (37.25)	51 (100.00)
Default	4 (8.16)	45 (91.84)	49 (100.00)
Total error		23.00%	
Priors weighted error		26.78%	
EC_{DE}		3.61%	
EC_{mat}		25.20%	
EC_{prop}		17.63%	
R^2		53.06%	

Table 10.1b   Discrimination on 100 observations with 11 factors—Results of jack-knife classification (% values in brackets)

Sample actual composition	Model sample classification		Total
	Regular	Default	
Regular	32 (62.75)	19 (37.25)	51 (100.00)
Default	10 (20.41)	39 (79.59)	49 (100.00)
Total error		29.00%	
Priors weighted error		31.19%	
EC_{DE}		6.69%	
EC_{mat}		25.20%	
EC_{prop}		17.63%	
R^2		41.00%	

The best classification was obtained when the same sample used to compute the discriminant functions (original sample) was classified. Jack-knife results, however, are also satisfactory, especially considering the experimental character of the application and the difficulty in obtaining reliable data.

The results of this first classification show better model accuracy in locating defaults. This follows, at least partially, from the computing of the cutoff point that penalized Type I errors through weighting misclassification cost C_{12}.

The original sample classification is particularly satisfactory for defaults as it correctly classifies 92% of the observations. The jack-knife method does not worsen the Type II reclassification error but shows a loss of quality for default loans that are correctly classified in 80% of the cases.

The comparison of the discrimination error costs[5]—EC_{DF}—with the benchmarks EC_{max} and EC_{prop} shows a superiority of the proposed model particularly compared with the 'Maximum Chance' model, given the basis of its computation.

The classification on the reduced sample, which only includes the observations for which most variables were available, gives the results presented in Tables 10.2a and 10.2b.

Table 10.2   Discrimination on 31 observations with 4 factors

Table 10.2a   Discrimination on 31 observations with 4 factors—Results of classification of the original sample (% values in brackets)

Sample actual composition	Model sample classification		Total
	Regular	Default	
Regular	13 (68.42)	6 (31.58)	19 (100.00)
Default	1 (8.33)	11 (91.67)	12 (100.00)
Total error	22.58%		
Priors weighted error	23.21%		
EC_{DF}	3.41%		
EC_{max}	25.20%		
EC_{prop}	17.63%		
R^2	51.72%		

Table 10.2b   Discrimination on 31 observations with 4 factors—Results of jack-knife classification (% values in brackets)

Sample actual composition	Model sample classification		Total
	Regular	Default	
Regular	12 (63.16)	7 (36.84)	19 (100.00)
Default	1 (8.33)	11 (91.67)	12 (100.00)
Total error			25.81%
Priors weighted error			26.58%
EC_{DP}			3.63%
EC_{max}			25.20%
EC_{prop}			17.63%
R^2			44.83%

The introduction of variables usually included in creditworthiness evaluation, such as revenue measures or total asset estimations, causes a slight improvement in the classification on the original sample for regular loans, as compared to the discrimination on 100 observations. The classification of defaults does not change significantly. The jack-knife method shows a good stability for default classification (92%) and a worsening for regular loans. Also in this second model the comparison of total error costs EC_{DP} with EC_{max} and EC_{prop} shows a superiority for the proposed model.

Conclusions

The two discriminant models applied respectively to the total sample and to the reduced one have quite good predictability, particularly as concerns the elimination of Type I errors. In spite of the limited available information, these results show that credit scoring techniques can be used even in very simple realities, very far from the typical credit scoring applications.

The major problem encountered—the absence of the usual profitability and financial measures on the customers—finds an interesting solution in the use of factor analysis. In rural areas of LDCs it is quite difficult and costly to collect reliable information on the customer's profitability. The small average loan size may not justify time and personnel investment for its estimation. In contrast, the model uses very simple information about the customer, which the analyst can get easily and quickly.

These data may not be very meaningful when considered individually, since they could play a minor role in credit risk determination. They are often symptoms of a more complex situation and need to be combined to become important indicators of repayment probability. Factor analysis is an easy way to combine these symptoms in a way that they become useful for both the theoretical interpretation and the practical application of the results.

Symptomatic variables are very important in both the analyses. Of course, the introduction of precise revenue measures for the reduced sample improves the models' performance. However the results of the analysis of the total sample are also quite satisfactory, particularly in relation to the low collection cost of symptomatic variables. The use of these models is consistent with a strategy of maximizing the loan's expected value, (as reported in Eisenbeis, 1981a; Masini, 1975) which suggests that lending decisions depend on the loan's expected value related to the interest rate, information and evaluation costs and the probability of default.

Even in cases where powerfully predictive factors are generated, discriminant models should be used to support loan decisions, the final judgment being the analyst's. In this respect, credit scoring models may become an important control tool *and* a means to devolve responsibility to loan analysts. Such an approach to credit evaluation would conform with the bank's goals of consistency (in lending decisions) and time and cost efficiency. Indeed, these models are relevant as they provide a way of conducting the loan analysis according to a logical and theoretical framework and reduce arbitrary decisions.

A new application of this analysis, taking advantage of this first experience, could give very interesting and useful results. For instance, GVs (village groups, another important category of CNCA's borrowers) are very peculiar entities for which it may be difficult to find a clear-cut correspondence with the theoretical framework presented here. Further research would be necessary to obtain a suitable model for GVs. However, the elaboration of a quantitative model for GVs would not be a problem, once the method first demonstrates its validity for individual loans.

The introduction of this method in the CNCA would be quite easy. The CNCA is well organized and uses computers. They are also aiming to expand their loan portfolio to include customers often rejected by commercial banks, and to control loan portfolio risk. The proposed evaluation method, based on a quantitative model and on *symptomatic information*, helps the bank to reach these two apparently conflicting objectives since it rationalizes the evaluation process and allows customers that cannot demonstrate creditworthiness by traditional standards to become eligible borrowers.

Technical appendix

Results interpretation: total sample

In factor analysis on the total sample of 100 observations 10 out of 11 factors are strictly related to the credit risk areas mentioned in the theoretical part. They can be classified and described as follows:

Area of the customer's performance

Factors related to profitability: # 2, 4, 5. The second factor has high loadings for variables reflecting profitability and revenue stability especially through symptoms of profitability such as the degree of productive flexibility, the dependence on weather conditions, the prevalence of monetary revenue, the sector of activity. The fourth factor stresses the variables related to the productive sector, still connected with profitability and its variability. The fifth factor reflects the stability of the customer's personal and economic situation.

Factor related to the financial situation: # 3. The third factor is weighted with variables related to the customer's financial exposure and the customer's ability to manage several borrowing contracts.

Factors related to assets/liabilities: # 6 and 7. Factor six is related to the customer's general economic conditions (with indicators on the dimensional and economic importance of the customer's activity). The seventh factor is related to the customer's financial situation and wealth (total debts, repaid debts, presence of a telephone).

Area of the customer's attitude

Factor related to the borrower's attitude toward the transaction: # 1. The first factor is weighted with variables related to the presence of a development project and to the quality of the bank-customer relationship and is interpretable as an indicator of the borrower's perception of the transaction.

Factor related to the borrower's morality and character: # 8. In factor eight, two important elements are the gender variable and a dummy variable indicating whether the borrower belongs to a village group or cooperative. These two aspects correlate with a borrower's seriousness toward the loan obligation. Women often have a historical record of more proper use of loan resources; and being a GV member, having received a group loan with a group guarantee and applying for an individual loan indicate a determination in contracting a real financial obligation.

Factor related to the borrower's behavior as the bank's customer: # 11. Factor eleven is weighted with past defaults and relates to the quality of the customer's banking behavior.

Area on available data and the quality of information: factor # 10

In factor ten, two dummy variables are relevant: one strictly related to the quality of information and the other indicating if the financing is invested for a specific purpose. These are symptoms of the adequacy of information. Knowledge about the destination of loan funds is not an effective means of controlling risk; however, it provides information that can improve lending decisions. The loadings for the dummy indicating whether the customer is a depositor and the age of the firm appear to confirm this interpretation of the factor.

Area of the bank's control of credit risk: factor # 9

The ninth factor is related to some variables reflecting the bank's ability to control credit risk. Interest rates and the ratio 'amount granted/amount solicited' are relevant contractual conditions for this purpose.

Most of the total variance is explained by factors related to the customer's attitude (see the tables in this appendix), i.e., *willingness to repay*. (Notwithstanding the positive restructuring that took place in the CNCA, the bank still bears the legacy of its past policies and of the time when it used the services provided by the public administration for appraisal and disbursement). The *customer's performance* is mainly estimated through symptomatic variables rather than by quantitative data. Several factors relate to this aspect. One factor clearly relates to the *control of credit risk* through contractual conditions. Another relates to the *quality of information*. The four areas of credit risk mentioned in the theoretical part are clearly covered by this analysis.

Results interpretation: reduced sample

The factors obtained on the reduced sample of 31 observations, for which reliable data on profitability were available, can be grouped as for the larger sample.

Area of the customer's performance

Factors related to profitability: # 3, 5, 10, 13. Factor 3 reflects complementary aspects. It shows high values for variables related to the customer's personal and economic stability and to profitability. Factors 5, 10 and 13 still reflect profitability through symptoms of revenue and its variability.

Factor related to the financial situation: # 8. Factor 8 reflects the customer's financial exposure and the customer's ability to manage several borrowing contracts (variables related to total borrowing with the CNCA).

Factors related to assets and liabilities: # 2 and 12. The second factor is related to the customer's wealth. The variables: total assets, total debt and annual debt have high values. The loading for the variable 'loan amount' confirms this interpretation. Indebtedness and loan amount should be viewed as indicators of the customer's economic size and creditworthiness. The meaning of the twelfth factor is still the customer's financial situation and wealth as it has high loadings for the variable total debt/total assets and land owned. In this case total debt loses its function as a dimensional indicator that it has when used in absolute values, and becomes an indicator of the customer's financial constraints.

Area of the customer's attitude

Factors related to the borrower's attitude towards the transaction: # 1 and 6. The first factor shows high loadings for previously mentioned variables indicating the customer's attitude. The sixth factor also contains some variables covering this aspect (those related to the presence of a development project).

Factor related to the borrower's morality and character: # 9. The ninth factor expresses the borrower's seriousness in the loan transaction as in the eighth factor of the total sample.

Factor related to the borrower's behavior as the bank's customer: # 7. While the seventh factor is difficult to interpret, one important variable is 'regular repayment of past debts'.

Area on available data and the quality of information: factor # 6

Factor number 6 reflects the quality of information through the variables on project intermediation which may reduce the bank's ability to control for data reliability; the variable on the loan destination confirms the factor meaning.

Area of the bank's control of credit risk: factors # 4, 10, 11

The fourth factor reflects the bank's ability to control credit risk through loan conditions since it shows high loadings for interest rates and the ratio revenue/amount granted. The already mentioned tenth factor is related to loan amount determination also through symptomatic variables such as 'loan destination' and the presence of mortgages. Factor 11 has high loadings for loan amount and maturity.

In contrast to the factor analysis run on the total sample, where each factor reflected a particular aspect of credit risk, in this case some factors are not very meaningful and others do not have an exclusive meaning. For this reason some of them were selected through a stepwise forward analysis and four factors were kept (3, 5, 6, 10). As previously described, factors 3 and 5 are indicators of the customer's *economic performance and of revenue variability*. Factor 10 is still related to profitability but also to *credit risk control* through the loan amount determination. The sixth factor relates to the *quality of information*. None of these is exclusively related to the borrower's attitude which proved to be important for the discrimination on the total sample. It might be inferred that those customers who can provide the bank with correct information on their revenue and assets can also correctly evaluate the bank-customer relationship and the importance of their financial obligation. However, the sixth factor includes the *customer's attitude*; in this case the bank-customer relationship mainly exerts its effects on the quality of information.

For this group of customers commonly used evaluation criteria prevail, even if supported by symptomatic variables. Profitability and revenue stability variables, as well as credit risk control measures linking loan amount to profitability, become more important than in the first discrimination.

Another interesting observation emerging from the comparison of results on the total sample and the reduced one concerns the role of total assets on credit risk. In the total sample variables related to total assets are symptoms of investment opportunities and ability to save and reinvest rather than indicators of the presence of real guarantees. These variables become *symptoms for the customer's economic performance.* Wealth variables lose their specific meaning in the reduced sample, since in this case quite accurate information on revenue is available. This confirms the theory stating that ability to repay depends on profitability and not on wealth.

Table 10.3   Credit scoring input factors

(Full Sample)

Factors	Explained variance (%)	Correlation with insolvency	Meaning			
			Ability to repay	Willing-ness to repay	Quality of infor-mation	Risk control (contract)
F1	26.3	0.18		x		
F2	19.0	-0.21	x			
F3	13.9	0.35	x			
F4	7.1	-0.14	x			
F5	6.9	-0.20	x			
F6	6.8	-0.22	x			
F7	4.8	-0.07	x			
F8	4.2	0.25		x		
F9	3.9	0.07				x
F10	3.6	0.05			x	
F11	3.5	0.01		x		

Table 10.3   Credit scoring input factors (continued)

(Reduced Sample)

Factors	Explained variance (%)	Correlation with insolvency	Meaning			
			Ability to repay	Willing-ness to repay	Quality of infor-mation	Risk control (contract)
F1	21.5	0.08		x		
F2	14.8	-0.11	x			
F3	9.3	-0.33	x			
F4	7.5	0.21				x
F5	7.5	-0.28	x			
F6	7.4	-0.26		x	x	
F7	6.5	-0.06		x		
F8	5.2	0.17	x			
F9	5.0	-0.20		x		
F10	4.8	0.26	x			x
F11	4.1	-0.03				x
F12	3.5	0.20	x			
F13	2.9	-0.14	x			

Acknowledgments

This chapter is a shortened version of an article published by *Savings and Development* (Viganò, 1993a) where the empirical part of this research is widely described. The researh was sponsored by the University of Bergamo and Finafrica Foundation (Milan). The author would like to thank professor Douglas Graham of The Ohio State University and professor Mario Masini of the University of Bergamo for their helpful comments. Full responsibility for the ideas contained in the chapter is the author's alone. The author is also grateful to the CNCA of Burkina Faso for the full cooperation received during the field work.

Notes

1   On the influence of contractual conditions on repayment probability see Viganò (1993b) and (1994).
2   Given that in multivariate discriminant analysis univariate correlation with insolvency is not a sufficient criteria to eliminate variables (see Eisenbeis, 1981b, pp. 144–148), variable correlation with insolvency was used as a supporting criteria in variable selection.
3   See Table 10.3 in the Appendix.
4   For methodological issues related to the model construction see Viganò (1993a).

5   EC_{DP}, EC_{max}, EC_{prop} are different measures of total classification costs. The first is the error cost of the proposed classification while the others are benchmark error costs computed according to the Maximum Chance Model and the Proportional Model (Joy and Tollefson, 1975).

References

Adams, D.W, Graham, D.H. and Von Pischke, J.D. (eds.) (1984), *Undermining Rural Development with Cheap Credit*, Westview Press: Boulder, CO.

Adera, A. (1987), 'Agricultural Credit and the Mobilization of Resources in Rural Africa,' *Savings and Development*, Vol. XI, No. 1, pp. 29–75.

Aguilera, N.A. and Gonzalez-Vega, C. (1990), 'Loan Repayment in Rural Financial Markets: A Multinomial Logit Analysis,' Economics and Sociology Occasional Paper No. 1776, The Ohio State University, Department of Agricultural Economics and Rural Sociology: Columbus, OH.

Aguilera, N.A., Gonzalez-Vega, C. and Graham, D.H. (1990), 'The Agricultural Development Bank of the Dominican Republic: A Loan Repayment Analysis,' Economics and Sociology Occasional Paper No. 1733, Ohio State University, Department of Agricultural Economics and Rural Sociology: Columbus, OH.

Altman, E.I. (1983), *Corporate Financial Distress*, John Wiley & Sons: New York.

Altman, E.I. (1984), 'The success of business failure prediction models: An international survey,' *Journal of Banking and Finance*, Vol. 8, No.2, pp. 171–198.

Altman, E.I., Avery, R.B., Eisenbeis, R.A. and Sinkey, J.F. (eds.)   (1981), *Application of Classification Techniques in Business, Banking and Finance*, JAI Press: Greenwich, CT.

Baker, C.B. and Dia, B. (1987), 'Default Management in an Agricultural Lending Program in Ivory Coast,' *Savings and Development*, Vol. XI, No. 2, pp. 161–180.

Barry, P.J., Baker, C.B. and Sanint, L.R. (1981), 'Farmers' Credit Risks and Liquidity Management,' *American Journal of Agricultural Economics*, Vol. 63, No. 2 (May), pp. 216–227.

Caisse Nationale de Crédit Agricole (1989), *Rapport d'Activité 1988/89*, CNCA: Ouagadougou, Burkina Faso.

Dell'Amore, G. (1965), *Economia delle aziende di credito*, Vol. I, I prestiti bancari, Giuffrè: Milano.

Eisenbeis, R.A. (1981a), 'Credit Scoring Applications,' in Altman, E.I., Avery, R.B., Eisenbeis, R.A. and Sinkey, J.F. (eds.), *Application of Classification Techniques in Business, Banking and Finance*, JAI Press: Greenwich, CT. pp. 167–198.

Eisenbeis, R.A. (1981b), 'Discriminant Analysis Application Problems,' in Altman, E.I., Avery, R.B., Eisenbeis, R.A. and Sinkey, J.G. (eds.), *Application of Classification Techniques in Business, Banking and Finance*, JAI Press: Greenwich, CT, pp. 119–166.

Howell, J. (ed.) (1980), *Borrowers and Lenders: Rural Financial Markets and Institutions in Developing Countries*, Overseas Development Institute: London.

Jensen, M.C. and Mackling, W.H. (1976), 'Theory of the Firm: Managerial Behavior, Agency Costs and Ownership Structure,' *Journal of Financial Economics*, Vol. 3, No. 4, pp. 305–360.

Joy, M. and Tollefson, J.O. (1975), 'On the Financial Applications of Discriminant Analysis,' *Journal of Financial and Quantitative Analysis*, Vol. 10, No. 5 (December), pp. 723–739.

Khalily, B.M.A. and Meyer, R.L. (1990), 'Political Economy and Rural Loan Recovery: an Example from Bangladesh,' Economics and Sociology Occasional Paper No. 1773, Department of Agricultural Economics and Rural Sociology, The Ohio State University, Columbus, OH.

Lachenbruch, P.A. (1975), *Discriminant Analysis*, Hafner Press: New York.

L'Aot, L. (1989), *Rapport d'évaluation du renforcement de la structure financière et des ressources de la Caisse Nationale de Crédit Agricole du Burkina Faso*, Caisse Centrale de Coopération Economique: Paris (juin).

Masini, M. (1987, 1989) (ed.), *Rural Finance Profiles in African Countries*, Vol. I and II, FAO-Finafrica Working Group: Milano.

Masini, M. (1985), 'Alcune relazioni tra tassi di interesse, propensione al rischio e valore della capacità di credito,' in *Studi in onore di Francesco Parrillo*, Volume Primo, Giuffrè: Milano, pp. 405–417.

Masini, M. (1975), 'Un'applicazione dell'analisi delle decisioni alle indagini svolte negli uffici fidi,' in *Scritti in onore di Ugo Caprara*, Vallardi: Milano, pp. 433–447.

Mauri, A. (ed.) (1989), *Problematiche finanziarie dello sviluppo rurale*, Finafrica, Giuffrè: Milano.

McLeod, R.H. (1991), 'Informal and Formal Sector Finance in Indonesia: The Financial Evolution of Small Business,' *Savings and Development*, Vol. XV, No. 2, pp. 187–209.

Nelson, G.C. and Cruz-Letona, R. (1991), 'The Importance of Default Risk to Agricultural Development Banks: An Example from El Salvador,' *Savings and Development*, Vol. XV, No. 1, pp. 19–38.

Njoku, J.E. and Obasi, P.C. (1991), 'Loan Repayment and its Determinants Under the Agricultural Credit Guarantee Scheme in Imo State, Nigeria,' *African Review of Money, Finance and Banking, Supplement of Savings and Development*, Vol. XV, No. 2, pp. 167–180.

Njoku, J.E. and Odii, M.A.C.A. (1991), 'Determinants of Loan Repayment under the Special Emergency Loan Scheme (SEALS) in Nigeria: A Case Study of Imo State,' *African Review of Money Finance and Banking*, Supplement of *Savings and Development*, Vol. XV, No. 1, pp. 39–52.

Orgler, Y.E. (1970), *Analytical Methods in Loan Evaluation*, Lexington Books, D. C. Heath and Company: Lexington, MA.

Ousseni, C.A. (1991), 'Expérience de la Caisse Nationale de Crédit Agricole du Burkina Faso (CNCA-B),' *Atelier sur les structures institutionnelles pour améliorer les services financier en milieu rural*, Abidjan, Côte d'Ivoire (février).

Sanderatne, N. (1989), 'La mancata restituzione dei prestiti da parte dei piccoli coltivatori: un approccio analitico,' in Mauri, A. (ed.), *Problematiche finanziarie dello sviluppo rurale*, Finafrica, Giuffrè: Milano, pp. 107–124.

Sanderatne, N. (1986), 'The Political Economy of Small Farmer Loan Delinquency,' *Savings and Development*, Vol. X, No. 4, pp. 343–354.

Stickley, T. and Tapsoba, E. (1980), 'Loan Repayment Delinquency in Upper Volta,' in Howell, J. (ed.), *Borrowers and Lenders. Rural Financial Markets and Institutions in Developing Countries*, Overseas Development Institute: London, pp. 273–285.

Viganò, L. (1992a), *African Banks' Funding Policies and Effective Lending*, Quaderni del Dipartimento di Economia Aziendale, No. 4: Università degli Studi di Bergamo, Italia.

Viganò, L. (1992b), *La capacità di credito: analisi delle determinanti e strumenti per la valutazione in un contesto di sottosviluppo*, Ph.D. Dissertation, Università degli Studi di Bergamo, Italia, Revised and published as *La capacità di credito: analisi delle determinanti e strumenti per la valutazione nelle economie in via di sviluppo*, Università degli Studi di Bergamo and Fondazione Giordano Dell'Amore (Collana 'Moneta e finanza nelle economie in sviluppo,' Vol. 4): Bergamo and Milano, 1996.

Viganò, L. (1992c), *The rural demand for financial services, the response of the informal financial market and the intervention of credit projects: Critical evaluation*, Quaderni del Dipartimento di Economia Aziendale, No. 5, Università degli Studi di Bergamo, Italia.

Viganò, L. (1993a), 'A Credit Scoring Model for Development Banks: an African Case Study,' *Savings and Development*, Vol. XVII, No. 4, pp. 441–482.

Viganò, L. (1993b), 'Un modello per la valutazione del rischio creditizio,' *Il Risparmio*, Vol. XLI, No. 4, pp. 845–864.

Viganò, L. (1994), 'Condizioni di prestito e controllo del rischio creditizio,' *Il Risparmio*, Vol. XLII, No. 5, pp. 1177–1210.

Vogel, R.C. (1981), 'Rural Financial Market Performance: Implications of Low Delinquency Rates,' *American Journal of Agricultural Economics*, Vol. 63, No. 1, pp. 58–65.

Von Pischke, J.D. (1991), *Finance at the Frontier: Debt Capacity and the Role of Credit in the Private Economy*, Economic Development Institute of The World Bank, World Bank: Washington, DC.

Von Pischke, J.D. (1989), 'Risk: the Neglected Dimension in Rural Credit Projects,' *Savings and Development*, Vol. XIII, No. 2, pp. 133–147.

Von Pischke, J.D. and Adams, D.W (1980), 'Fungibility and the Design and Evaluation of Agricultural Credit Projects,' *American Journal of Agricultural Economics*, Vol. 62, No. 4 (Nov.), pp. 719–726.

Von Pischke, J.D., Adams, D.W and Donald, G. (1983), *Rural Financial Markets in Developing Countries: Their Use and Abuse*, The Johns Hopkins University Press: Baltimore, MD.

Von Pischke, J.D., Vogel, R.C., Flath, P. and Mould, M.C. (1988), *Measurement of Loan Repayment Performance*, Economic Development Institute of The World Bank, EDI Catalog No. 030/085 (April), The World Bank: Washington, DC.

Yabile, K.R. (1987), 'Provision of Liquidity Management: An Incentive to Curb Loan Default in the Ivory Coast's Agricultural Credit Programs,' *Savings and Development*, Vol. XI, No. 4, pp. 403–422.

Zmijewski, M.E. (1984), 'Methodological Issues Related to the Estimation of Financial Distress Prediction Models,' *Journal of Accounting Research*, Vol. 22, Suppl., pp. 59–82.

11 Keys to financial sustainability

Introduction

Until recently, most microfinance institutions focused their attention almost exclusively on outreach. For many, financial sustainability meant meeting cash flow needs. Extrapolating from the fact that smaller clients are more costly to serve per dollar lent or mobilized, most practitioners have felt that reaching the poor with microfinance services is essentially an unprofitable endeavor and that imposing financial viability requirements on programs would be tantamount to forcing them to abandon their target group. As Jacob Yaron's work at the World Bank shows, most microfinance programs continue to depend on subsidies and could not operate on a commercially viable basis (Yaron, 1992).

A study for USAID (Christen, Rhyne and Vogel, 1994), however, demonstrates that 'most' should not be taken to mean all. A handful of highly specialized programs have developed during the past 15 years which are achieving both broad outreach and long-term financial viability. More important, the study concludes that institutions must achieve the financial goal of long-term sustainability first, as a precondition for achieving more broadly available financial services for the poor.

In that study, it was shown that several programs operating in widely varying economic contexts, utilizing different service delivery mechanisms, had achieved returns on earning assets comparable to private commercial banks in their respective countries even after taking account of explicit and implicit subsidies. Other institutions assessed in the study could easily reach this level of returns on assets if they imposed more adequate interest rates or increased the volume of their loan portfolios. All had adopted the financial and service technologies that would enable them to be financially viable in the long run.

Originally, much of the concern about financial sustainability came from the desire of donors to wean microfinance programs from the steady flow of subsidies. This was motivated both by a desire to derive more long term impact from donations and in anticipation of cutbacks in donor budgets. More recently we have realized that the key advantage of financial sustainability in microfinance institutions is the leverage social investors can obtain with their funds, multiplying many times over the final outreach impact of their initial capital contributions.

The following typology of microenterprise finance programs illustrates the manner in which strong financial performance provides programs the opportunity to leverage their initial investments into increasing levels of outreach with decreasing levels of new capital investments. This typology is based on one simple criterion: If a donor puts one dollar into a microenterprise finance program today, how much in microfinance assets will that dollar have generated after several years?[1]

The classification scheme that follows does not represent airtight categories but rather is illustrative of different outcomes possible given different levels of financial performance.

Level 1: subsidy-dependent programs

At this level, a microfinance program does not break even on a cash flow basis and requires constant injections of fresh funds to cover out-of-pocket expenses. This means that if these injections are not forthcoming, the program will quickly consume its equity to finance the operational costs of administering its assets, or, in the absence of these funds, let its portfolio quality deteriorate. Either way, without constant capital injections, the program will cease to exist within a brief period of time. A donor dollar invested at the beginning of the year is worth considerably less than a dollar at the end of the year (if it remains at all). Because of their prospects, these programs have virtually no ability to leverage their initial equity investment by 'borrowing' from third parties.

Level 2: self-sufficient programs

A program at the second level has achieved at least a break-even point on a cash basis. It completely covers the out-of-pocket expenses associated with the administration of its assets. Such programs may also cover most or all of their non-cash operating expenses such as fixed asset depreciation, impact of inflation on the program's equity, creation of reserves, and the opportunity cost of subsidized sources of funds. Over time, programs at this level show an ability to maintain themselves without continual injections of new capital. Under normal circumstances, a donor dollar invested into self-sufficient programs is still worth approximately a dollar in later years. In situations of high inflation, however, these programs are susceptible to having their portfolios eroded unless they implement aggressive interest rate policies. Programs at this level are usually managed by NGOs or specially created government financial intermediaries, generally with significant initial capital contributions.

Programs that are self-sufficient can usually leverage their equity by obtaining limited commercial or donor loans on the strength of their solvency. If the program is managed by an NGO, sustained solid financial performance will allow it to develop commercial financial relationships with banks. In several countries, banks have demonstrated that they are willing to lend up to two dollars for each dollar of program equity. At first these loans have typically been backed by additional guarantees (offered by donor or technical support agencies) but after a time, they have been issued on the basis of sustained high levels of portfolio quality and financial performance with no collateral guarantee. In these cases, the investment of one donor dollar yields several dollars of total microfinance resources for poor clients.

Level 3: profitable programs

Level three programs have demonstrated sustained profitability. Sustained profits have three basic and immediate effects: (1) they directly increase the program's equity base, (2) they can potentially attract additional outside equity participation, and (3) they can cause others to replicate the experience in the hope of attaining similar levels of profitability.

Ultimately, profitable programs may be allowed by regulators to incorporate as a formal financial intermediary. Once an institution is considered a formal financial institution, whatever its type (license), it immediately gains access to commercial sources of funding either through access to local capital or credit markets, or permission to capture savings directly from the general public. This transformation would allow them to fund their credit portfolio fully in commercial financial markets, either by capturing individual savings deposits or by attracting institutional investors through the issuance of bonds or securities.

It is here that one dollar of donor investment can really pay off, leveraging up to twelve dollars of microfinance assets after a few years (under the Basle standard capital-to-assets ratio of 8%). Even more so, using donor funds to establish a commercially successful program that provides models for them or motivated private entrepreneurs to replicate, the leveraged effect of a one dollar investment far exceeds even the twelve dollars in microfinance assets.

The following results from ten of the best microfinance programs demonstrate that we currently have the technology to generate microfinance services for a broad share of previously underserved borrowers and savers. The specific service delivery technology employed by these programs varies greatly among them, as do overall levels of expenditures. Nevertheless, all achieve the basic financial sustainability necessary for significant outreach.

The remainder of this chapter focuses on what these widely dispersed programs do to ensure good financial performance and on their ability to reach large numbers of poor clients with financial services. Although specific manifestations differ across programs, virtually all of them share similar features for maintaining viability and outreach.

Key area number one: interest rate policies

The most important key to financial viability, as revealed by the USAID study, is the interest rate policy adopted by microfinance programs. Interest and fee income must cover four basic aspects of costs: the institution's cost of funds; its operating or administrative expenses; losses related to risks incurred in asset management (loan losses); and a return on capital invested in the institution. Microfinance institutions cannot expect to require any less income than commercial banks if they aim to project their operations over a large share of the local lower income economy.

In order for microfinance institutions to grow, they require massive funds. To obtain these funds they may follow any of several strategies, including: raising funds from international donor organizations; mobilizing local savings; and/or accessing local financial markets. The first option, most frequently followed, has obvious limits. In the beginning, concessionary funds are relatively inexpensive, as the amounts are also relatively small. As funding grows, however, so too does the cost of raising those funds through reporting requirements, tied technical assistance, and donor-oriented lending policies. Often, the primary advantage of donor funds ultimately becomes associated with periodic restructuring of the microfinance institution's liabilities.

An institution that seeks to obtain funds from the national savings pool has two basic options: raise funds from institutional investors through time deposits that have low administrative costs but high interest rate sensitivity; or mobilize small deposits from low income clients (taking advantage of the loan distribution infrastructure) which have relatively high administrative costs but low interest rate sensitivity. In either case, it is difficult to imagine how a highly specialized financial institution, whose target population of low income clients will be perceived as higher risk, will be able to mobilize savings at a lower cost than existing financial intermediaries.

The same argument holds true for those institutions that wish to access local financial and capital markets through issuance of bonds, stocks, or by borrowing. It is unreasonable to expect that significant funding could be raised in local markets at a lower cost than that paid by other institutions unless some implicit subsidy such as government guarantees were available to the institution.

An important defect in the interest rate policies of most microfinance programs is their failure to assign an inflation cost to their equity over time. In this regard, equity is eroded in real terms as the institution complacently generates nominal profits, year after year. This problem is particularly pronounced in countries whose experience with inflation is short because both program managers and clients resist imposing inflation adjusted rates that seem to be too high. Indeed, many business activities should not be funded at those inflation adjusted rates if they are only nominally profitable.

Given that administrative costs consume a much higher percentage of earnings in a microfinance institution than in a conventional commercial bank, these programs cannot achieve financial viability unless they either charge higher rates of interest or operate with subsidized liabilities. The ratio of administrative overheads to total costs of even the most efficient microfinance institutions is three times that of commercial banks. Finance companies that specialize in small transactions and credit card operations in these same markets spend about twice as much as commercial banks—about 10% of average annual assets. Although the average loan transaction of finance companies may be similar, most of these businesses are targeted on salaried workers who do not present significant costs to the institution in information gathering and selection processes.

Most of the best microfinance programs maintain loan loss rates of less than two percent of their average annual loan portfolios. These levels are comparable to loan loss rates in the formal banking sector. Although some programs have managed portfolios with virtually zero defaults, the vast expansion that these programs will undertake will naturally increase these levels as they take on slightly riskier clients and penetrate their markets more deeply. Thus, their loan loss levels will more closely reflect those of the formal financial sector and will tend to move in tandem with local economic trends.

If microfinance institutions are to expand at the exponential rates necessary to reach a significant share of their market in the next few years, they must generate a new capital base at each stage of their expansion. In some smaller countries, capital requirements to fund this expansion (US$ 3 to US$ 15 million) may be within the reach of private venture capitalists or donor agencies. In most larger countries and in all of the largest countries, however, the primary source of new capital will in all likelihood be profits from the microfinance programs themselves. In fact, much of the capital that successful programs have generated has been from net profits and not, as might be expected, from donors or governments. Over time, as these programs grow, reinvestment of capital will provide an increasing share of the funding for microfinance growth.

After adjusting for both implicit and explicit subsidies, the better microfinance programs generate real returns on average total assets of between 2% and 5%: rates that would place them in a completely competitive position with commercial banks. In a fully leveraged financial intermediary (i.e., in which risk-adjusted assets are equal to twelve times equity) these returns would be equivalent to between 24% and 60% returns on equity. This would be sufficient to fund growth in all but the institution's first years, when a doubling in size is not uncommon. In order to achieve these rates of return, microfinance programs must charge higher interest rates than those commonly charged by traditional financial institutions to their normal clients.

Key area number two: high loan portfolio standards

The second key to long term financial viability is for programs to maintain very high portfolio quality standards. Late payment problems cause the institution additional expenses in two ways. First, loans that are not repaid pass directly through the profit and loss statement as an expense. Many development credit institutions consider annual loan recovery rates of 90% very good, yet in order to remain self-sustaining, an institution would have to meet this expense out of interest income on its lending. An institution that must add 10% to its interest charges to cover loan losses could find itself priced out of the market for loan funds. Secondly, direct loan losses imply other types of expenses for the institution such as lost interest income and increased staff costs. As a rule of thumb, loan defaults usually run at about one-half to one-third of short-term arrears. Therefore, a 10% default rate implies arrears of 30%. In addition to lost interest payments, the institution's staff must spend more time chasing past dues which leaves less time for appraising new loans.

Most debilitating of all, however, is the decline in an institution's credibility that accompanies loan losses. Instead of being perceived as a program that supports clients in a time of need, the principal experience clients come to associate with them is being pressured to repay loans. The downward spiral accelerates as more clients fail to repay and more time is spent with past due accounts.

Given the very small size of individual loans, the additional cost of chasing past-dues often exceeds the capital amount recovered, even considering late payment penalties and interest. Although programs rarely calculate the full costs of late loan payments in terms of staff time and productivity losses, they are significant and tend to accelerate over time.

Finally, late loan payments can reduce net interest margins by either reducing interest income or by increasing the cost of funds. In the first instance, while penalty interest and fees are often assessed on past due payments, they are also often bargained away in attempts to get delinquent borrowers to repay. In the second instance, if repayment problems are widespread, they may create liquidity shortfalls for the institution. If, due to cash constraints, the institution must borrow short-term funds to meet operating expenses or loan demand, it may not enjoy the lower interest rates applied to longer term loans. This will effectively raise the institution's cost of funds and reduce the interest margin.

In summary, institutions that fail to keep loan losses at low levels (below 5% of their average annual portfolio) will face financial results that move them away from, and not towards, financial sustainability.

Key area number three: strong productivity orientation

Financially viable microfinance institutions all demonstrate a strong corporate culture based on productivity enhancement. All viable programs maintain a fundamental focus on staff productivity and actively seek ways to improve lending efficiency. This emphasis on staff productivity in lending is notable across all successful microfinance programs regardless of the different economic and cultural contexts within which they operate. The lending productivity orientation is manifested in three common characteristics: operating methods which base key functions on community or peer group participation; decentralized administrative structures; and appropriate infrastructure (both human and physical) that generates least-cost productivity.

The most difficult aspects of lending to poor clients are borrower selection and repayment enforcement. The informal nature of their enterprises and the character of their capital assets are such that traditional appraisal and loan chasing methods are worthless for either purpose. Consequently, successful microfinance programs have borrowed the approach of moneylenders in utilizing character-based lending. Under this approach to credit decisions, the borrower's likely willingness to repay is weighted above their visible capacity to repay (Christen, 1992).

Rather than spend time and resources on technical analysis of the borrower's repayment capacity, successful programs base their repayment assessment on prior credit performance. This is often implemented by starting new clients off with small, less risky loans and then moving them into larger loan sizes as they demonstrate a capacity and willingness to repay. These programs also transfer important selection, enforcement, and transaction functions onto the client or his/her peer group. Although many feel that this transfer has some efficiency benefits in terms of cost reductions for the lender, the primary financial benefit to this consolidation lies in its impact on loan repayment ratios.

Successful programs also incorporate community knowledge in the selection, enforcement and transaction processes. The precise form that this takes varies across institutions. In some cases, programs use solidarity groups of four or five participants who band together for the purpose of taking out a group loan that is then divided among the members, each of whom is equally responsible to the program for the entire loan's repayment. Village banking programs utilize groups of thirty clients to generate social pressure and gather necessary information for credit decisions. In other cases programs work through local community structures where village leaders participate in the loan approval and follow-through process, and may even be hired as program staff.

In all of these cases, the systems developed allow individual credit decisions to be made on the basis of information that would not be available to traditional style institutions, and in a way that can be financially sustainable for even the tiniest of loans. Although some interest has been generated by attempts to apply traditional credit scoring and other traditional borrower selection techniques to microfinance, none of the most successful programs have based their programs on them.

The second important aspect of the productivity-based culture of successful programs is that they all, without exception, administer their microfinance services through a decentralized, performance based, modular, operational structure. These operational modules, in turn can be characterized by four common attributes: (1) horizontal organizational decision structures, (2) performance based incentive systems for staff, (3) strong internal controls and ex-post auditing functions, and (4) efficient information systems that permit timely and accurate loan tracking.

Virtually all of the successful institutions manage their operations through modules composed of between four and 12 staff, most of whom are dedicated to client service in either an office or the field. A typical module would consist of one manager, several credit officers or field workers, an administrative support person or two, and possibly cashiers.

These modules normally exercise great operational autonomy in the issuing of loans within the guidelines established by the program. They normally act as their own credit committee, except for particularly large or complex loans which may be remitted to a higher authority within the program. The organizational structure tends to be very flat, with relatively little management superstructure imposed on these units.

Central management tends to focus its efforts on funding activities, general policies, auditing, administration, and institutional development. As much as 85% of the institution's staff work in operational units and central offices frequently operate more as service entities to the branch network.

As a result, the type of control the central office exerts on the operational units tends to be ex-post such as audits and incentive systems. Rather than burden operational decisions with impractical and stifling hierarchical controls the better programs opt for audit procedures which verify, through sampling procedures, that units comply with the guidelines clearly established by the central office. This reduces costs in addition to tremendously enhancing the effectiveness of the resulting operational decisions.

Additionally, successful programs design incentive systems which motivate these operational modules to maintain high levels of productivity. Most financially successful programs have designed incentive systems that tie between 15% and 50% of total operational staff remuneration to the results they obtain with clients. Usually these systems combine some sort of positive compensation for amounts disbursed to both new and returning clients with some sort of reduction for late payments.

In many systems the entire incentive is lost when loan repayment falls below relatively strict thresholds, which may be the key ingredient explaining their consistently superior performance in the face of frequent administrative problems. The importance of incentive systems is so great that cases have even been observed where loan repayment performance has been maintained at above 98% even where centralized information systems have completely failed, management has been ineffective, and staff rotation has been high.

The best programs all generate timely loan tracking information at the module level. Given the very short amortization schedule (60 to 180 days) for many of the loans and the high payment frequency (weekly and semi-monthly), 'timely' usually means that information about payments made during a particular day are provided to the field staff at the opening of the following day's activities. In those cases where payments are made to a third entity such as a bank for security reasons, information seldom takes more than 48 hours to reach the loan officers who then pursue delinquent clients aggressively.

The third main aspect of productivity-based programs is the care taken to seek out appropriate human and physical infrastructure for the nature of the services provided. For example, a program in Indonesia with savings accounts that run average balances of US$ 25, operates out of single room, austere offices that are open only five hours a day. These units are staffed with local community members who work for very low wages since this activity complements their farming and other income-earning activities. This program is among the most successful in outreach and viability, in large part because it has structured itself appropriately for the nature of the services it offers.

Programs born as part of donor-based projects, where outreach, not financial viability is the immediate primary goal, may lock in a relatively expensive human infrastructure composed of university graduates and other highly qualified individuals. In many settings, the basic operational functions of the programs could easily enough be carried out by less prepared individuals at a lower total cost. Those programs whose philosophy has been to base their operational technologies on community staff actually have a great advantage in this area. This has permitted them to reach out with very small unit sized operations in a financially viable manner, while some other programs that reach out to larger clients with more highly qualified staff are less viable.

In the USAID study, the only cost-related variable that proved statistically significant as a predictor of financial viability was the relationship of the program's average annual salary per employee to GNP per capita. This relationship, expressed as a multiple, proved highly significant in a regression equation. Programs that paid a lower multiple of GNP per capita were more profitable than those that paid a higher multiple. Most notable are the differences between the programs with the highest multiples and those with the lowest.

For example, those with the lowest relative salary (multiples of between 1 and 3) were the programs that extensively utilize local community structures and personnel to staff their operations. All hire directly from the communities they serve on the basis of character and basic skills necessary to undertake the program's tasks. On the other end of the spectrum, three programs which only recently have begun to evolve out of donor- and project-based NGO structures have the highest multiples (between 13 and 21).

This conclusion may be somewhat modified by the fact that in some settings, the gap between the educational preparedness of potential community based staff and that required to manage microfinancial services may be too great, leading necessarily to higher multiples. The evidence is intriguing, but insufficient to support broad and definitive generalizations. Clearly, programs that seek financial viability must try to generate a staff structure where employee skill levels are the most appropriate for achieving both operational efficiency and effectiveness. This may not necessarily require individuals with highly honed, academically based skills, as the low multiple programs demonstrate.

Key area number four: effective liquidity management

One of the most complex issues faced by microfinance institutions in the past has been funding. Since most are not savings based, they depend on donor agency and/or government budget disbursements and this gives rise to frequent liquidity crises. In addition, since most of their funds come from these sources, they are pushed to fully disburse before receiving additional funds, making liquidity management almost impossible. Liquidity management in these cases often merely entails pushing money out the door as fast as it comes in.

Frequent liquidity problems can cause costly difficulties that donors often underestimate; costs that, if fully calculated, could even exceed those of a commercial source of funds were it available. For example, liquidity shortages cause programs to delay disbursements, deny credit, and engage in other restrictive policies that indicate to customers that the institution may not be healthy. That perception threatens their future relationship with the institution and provides a strong incentive to default on loans or withdraw savings which in turn provokes more of the same type of crisis.

Programs that try to avoid the costs of this negative cycle by depending on short term commercial borrowing to keep disbursements flowing pay the cost of borrowing the most expensive funds available. Although programs that maintain some degree of liquidity may appear to be losing a chance to be more profitable by lending these resources out at high rates of interest, this cost does not outweigh the cost of being perceived by clients as an illiquid institution.

Both donors and microfinance institutions need to improve their liquidity management in order to enhance financial viability in the long term. This extends to the issues of improving the program's capacity to do adequate financial projections, the donor's ability to disburse on schedule and not impose counterproductive measures such as requiring programs to draw down fully before receiving additional funds, and assistance to institutions to help them restructure liabilities to more completely match their maturities structures with those of their assets.

Some programs are seeking to mobilize local savings as a response to these issues. While the scant evidence available demonstrates that institutions can actually generate a highly liquid position once savings services take hold, the transition from being a lending based to a savings based organization is far more difficult and fraught with dangers than most realize. It requires a fundamental change of mentality. Rather than disbursing rich people's money, microfinance staff must realize that when they mobilize local savings they are in fact protecting and investing poor people's emergency reserves. Long-run financial sustainability of microfinance undoubtedly requires programs to obtain funds from local savings pools, but the challenges that lie ahead in the regulation and supervision of these specialized institutions that cater to the poor and utilize non-traditional operating procedures are great indeed.

Summary consideration: the role of capital in institutions that provide financial services to the poor

Access to capital is one of the most important considerations for private operators of microfinance institutions. Once institutions have devised a way to operate successfully in a given environment, they often experience exponential growth. If indeed, their future lies with the mobilization of local savings as regulated financial intermediaries, their owners will be required regularly to increase their equity contribution to match expansion. Most bank regulators will require that owners contribute paid-in capital of at least one-half the required amount, the other half being funded out of retained earnings. This helps to ensure that the institutions continue to 'belong' to someone who has an important stake in their future.

To the extent that these private ventures consist mostly of NGOs and social investors with limited access to capital, microfinance institutions run the risk of having their very success drive them towards insolvency as they grow. Those interested in the long-run financial sustainability of microfinance institutions must concern themselves with capitalization and not rely exclusively on retained earnings, even when these appear to be sufficient in the early years. Fortunately, as discussed in the opening section, strong financial performance by microfinance institutions potentially increases the interest of commercial investors in this type of activity, which is the ultimate solution to the funding problem for microfinance institutions.

Note

1   This criterion was first proposed by Richard Rosenberg of USAID in a working document that was incorporated in Christen, Rhyne and Vogel, 1994. This typology for classifying microfinance programs according to their self-sufficiency was first proposed by Christen in 1988 in 'Financial Management of Microcredit Programs,' prepared for ACCION and later pub-

lished by them. See Christen, 1990. This typology was further developed by Rhyne and Otero, 1994.

References

Christen, R.P. (1990), *Financial Management of Microenterprise Programs: A Guide for NGOs*, ACCION International: Cambridge, MA.

Christen, R.P. (1992), 'Formal Credit for Informal Borrowers: Lessons from Informal Lenders,' in Adams, D.W and Fitchett, D. (eds.), *Informal Finance in Low-Income Countries*, Westview Press: Boulder, CO.

Christen, R.P., Rhyne, E. and Vogel, R.C. (1994), *Maximizing the Outreach of Microenterprise Finance: The Emerging Lessons of Successful Programs*, IMCC: Arlington, VA.

Rhyne, E. and Otero, M. (1994), 'Financial Services for Microenterprises: Principles and Institutions,' in Otero, M. and Rhyne, E. (eds.), *The New World of Microenterprise Finance: Building Healthy Financial Institutions for the Poor*, Kumarian Press: West Hartford, CT, pp. 11–26.

Yaron, J. (1992), *Assessing Development Finance Institutions: A Public Interest Analysis*, World Bank Discussion Paper No. 174, World Bank: Washington, DC.

12 Other people's money: regulatory issues facing microenterprise finance programs

ROBERT C. VOGEL

Introduction

Throughout the world, most entities providing financial services to microenterprises are informal, that is, they do not fall under the government regulations that are applied to banks and to other formal, regulated financial institutions. Many of those involved in microenterprise finance would argue that this is not surprising, perhaps even highly appropriate. The costs and restrictions implied by government regulations are often said to make it too expensive for banks and other formal financial institutions to deal in small loans to microentrepreneurs, and, in any case, the 'corporate culture' of these banks and similar institutions is too far removed from the informal world of the microentrepreneur. However, perhaps the best-known successful provider of microenterprise finance in the world is in fact a formal bank, the Bank Rakyat Indonesia, with its village units providing small loans and deposit services to vast numbers of microentrepreneurs and other small-scale clients and making a profit to be envied in the process. In addition, a 1994 survey of successful microenterprise finance programs for USAID found that some programs in other parts of the world had already become formal banks (e.g., BancoSol in Bolivia), were in the process of becoming formal (e.g., ACEP in Senegal), or had created or acquired a parallel formal financial institution, such as ACTUAR in Colombia (Christen, Rhyne and Vogel, 1994).

There appear to be two forces propelling successful microenterprise finance programs toward formalization: deposit mobilization and financial leverage, i.e., borrowing by microenterprise lenders to fund their loan portfolios. There can be important economies of scope in finance between making loans and offering deposit services. The reality of this for institutions serving the poor in isolated rural areas was brought home by a pilot study in Peru in the early 1980s that destroyed the myth that the poor cannot or will not save in financial form (Vogel, 1984). But how should informal entities providing financial services to the poor approach the regulatory formalities surrounding deposit mobilization? Traditional views generally posit a tradeoff between institutional viability and outreach to the poor, but the USAID survey (Christen, Rhyne and Vogel, 1994) of successful microenterprise finance programs found a potentially strong complementarity between the financial viability of these programs and their outreach to the poor through the use of financial leverage. However, leverage is achieved by borrowing, if not from other financial institutions then through deposit instruments that are often focused, for the reasons of economies of scope noted above, on the program's microenterprise client pool. Such borrowing implies the need to consider formal regulatory norms.

This chapter attempts to begin to explore issues surrounding the formalization and regulation of informal microenterprise finance programs that wish to borrow from other financial institutions or take deposits from the public, often their own microenterprise clients. First, the provision of more adequate information by microenterprise finance programs is explored. Second, typical features of most microenterprise finance programs (e.g., characteristics of clients, types of loans and capital structures) are examined to see what implications these might have for an appropriate regulatory approach. Third, some realities of prudential regulation and supervision are considered, in particular that even in the richest countries where major resources have been devoted to regulation and supervision, costly failures have nonetheless occurred (e.g., BCCI) and, further, that in poorer countries adequate regulatory and supervisory resources often do not exist to cover fully even the commercial banking sector. Finally, a few tentative conclusions are drawn that tend primarily to suggest that a careful balancing will be required of the potential benefits from prudential regulation and supervision against the costs of inhibiting innovation and outreach by microenterprise finance programs.

Data availability and information problems

A surprising finding from the USAID survey of successful microenterprise finance programs was the difficulty of obtaining the necessary information to carry out the required analysis. Since outreach to the poor can be defined in a variety of ways, it is not surprising that measures of outreach varied across programs. However, financial viability is a much more clearly defined concept, with generally accepted accounting practices existing in most countries (and even widely agreed-upon international standards). Likewise, professional accounting and audit groups as well as government officials develop and enforce standards and provide the requisite services, with a host of special rules and regulations applying specifically to financial institutions.

Thus, it could be considered surprising indeed that the information needed to make the required judgements about the financial viability of the microenterprise programs being analyzed could rarely be found—and never easily. In fact, a number of the microenterprise finance programs initially reviewed as potentially providing good examples of success were rejected primarily due to their inability or unwillingness to provide the requisite information regarding financial viability.

Since most microenterprise finance programs are informal, they are not subject to the rules and regulations that require certified external audits and other forms of external supervision. Therefore, it is perhaps not so surprising that the required information on financial viability was unavailable for most programs. This view, however, neglects the fact that external entities funded these programs in the form of donations or grants rather than commercially-based loans or deposits. Apparently, the suppliers of these funds, mainly governments, donors and international agencies, did not consider financial viability an important issue. Perhaps it was because, until recently, almost no one thought that financial viability was even a remote possibility for microenterprise finance programs, so that it was considered pointless to ask for such information.

However, it is difficult to understand how any serious evaluations of microenterprise finance programs, which one would suppose the providers of funds would have required, could have been carried out without considerable attention to measures of financial viability. In any case, the focus of this brief chapter is not on the political economy of the funding of microenterprise finance programs, and this question is not considered further here.

Three aspects of the informational requirements of the recent survey of successful microenterprise finance programs are worth noting briefly. First, some presumably successful microenterprise finance programs refused to provide information about financial viability, offering a variety of reasons (excuses). This clearly runs counter to current thinking on financial sector development that places high value on the widespread availability of transparent information (e.g., accurate, understandable, timely, pertinent, etc.). Second, the quality of information available varied widely, from near chaos and without what would be necessary for even rudimentary information systems for management and control, to quite sophisticated management information systems complemented by comprehensive external audits.

Third, in all cases, three basic types of adjustments had to be made to the financial statements provided in order to draw meaningful conclusions about financial viability. These three adjustments related to: (1) the quality of assets and appropriate provisioning for assets of doubtful value; (2) price level changes (inflation) and the need to bring balance sheet items into consistent terms (either real or nominal) and then to make the implied adjustments to the income statement; and (3) the need to make allowances for donations and grants (including loans provided on non-commercial terms) so that continuing profitability would not be a function of continuing donations and grants. It is important to emphasize that these were not arcane adjustments serving only certain specific needs of the recent survey, but were rather basic adjustments that anyone making meaningful judgements about the profitability and solvency of a financial institution would need to make.

A core of potential agreement

One area of potential agreement about the formalization of informal microenterprise finance programs could thus be a major improvement in the provision of information. Supporting entities (e.g., governments, donors and international agencies), potential depositors and other types of potential creditors all need fairly standard information about financial viability in order to make informed judgements. Otherwise, the allocation of funds becomes little more than a lottery. Collection and dissemination of information is costly, but some collection and organization of information is necessary in any case for internal management and control systems for any institution that claims to be a serious, albeit informal, financial entity.

External audits imply further costs, but for those microenterprise finance programs that want external funds from depositors, other creditors, or donors that require a certain level of performance, the costs implied by external audits would seem unavoidable. Those microenterprise finance programs that do not want external audits, because of expense or for other reasons, can continue as pure charities, for which donors must make a leap of faith rather than require information about performance. (In the United States even charities must be audited, though mainly for tax reasons.)

Some successful microenterprise finance programs have leveraged themselves through deposit mobilization, while others have borrowed from other financial institutions. Although the former approach has certain important benefits in terms of providing additional services to microenterprise clients and taking advantage of potential economies of scope, the latter may provide an easier and less controversial approach to initiating the leveraging process. Other financial institutions should be 'knowledgeable consumers' so that a 'buyer beware' approach can more easily be justified when informal, unregulated microenterprise finance programs wish to borrow from other financial institutions. These financial institutions should certainly know what information is needed to make an informed judgement about a microenterprise finance program's potential as a borrower without requiring assistance from government regulators and supervisors. In this case the main role of the government may simply be to enforce standard penalties against fraud when microenterprise finance programs provide false or misleading information. However, the difficulty and importance of strong enforcement should not be underestimated, especially when microenterprise finance programs engaging in fraud are simultaneously seen to be 'doing good', by helping poor microentrepreneurs.

Several successful microenterprise finance programs have begun to leverage themselves through bank loans. These loans are often initially guaranteed by standby letters of credit, as in the case of ACCION International's programs in various Latin American countries, but eventually some loans have tended to be unsecured as programs have demonstrated their capacity to bank lenders. Some programs are even exploring the possibility of issuing debt instruments in local markets, including securitization of their loan portfolios. To the extent that unregulated microenterprise finance programs can fund themselves in local credit markets, they demonstrate that they can subject themselves successfully to market-based quality control mechanisms.

A major aspect of this is the provision of the type of information discussed above, as lenders require complete and audited financial statements, often supplemented by special audit certifications of portfolio quality. To support this kind of expansion further, AC-CION's monitoring system is designed to detect possible problems in its microenterprise finance programs in advance, so that potential lenders can have additional information to assure themselves that adequate quality control mechanisms are in place.

Microenterprise finance programs that supply deposit services to their microenterprise clients can benefit from whatever economies of scope exist between lending and providing deposit services. In most countries, deposit mobilization can be carried out only by formal, regulated financial institutions. The reasons for this are well known: the supposed lack of sophistication of depositors, especially small depositors; the costs of analyzing information even when appropriate information is available and depositors are sufficiently sophisticated; and the fear that if a deposit-taking institution fails, depositors will 'run' to withdraw their deposits from otherwise healthy institutions and thereby destabilize the entire financial system.

The issue that occupies most of the remainder of this chapter is whether successful microenterprise finance programs that wish to mobilize deposits should be required to formalize themselves and be regulated like banks and other formal financial institutions or whether there is some more appropriate regulatory approach. Because of the newness and potential importance of deposit mobilization for microenterprise finance programs, an annex to this chapter examines in more detail the key technical challenges of deposit mobilization.

Characteristics of microenterprise finance programs

Government regulation to attempt to assure safety and soundness is the norm in almost every country for institutions that capture savings from the public. Even if agreement can be reached on appropriate standards of information for microenterprise finance programs, and even if a 'buyer beware' approach is deemed appropriate for knowledgeable financial institutions lending to microenterprise finance programs, the issues surrounding government regulation must still be confronted for microenterprise finance programs that would like to become full-fledged financial intermediaries by taking deposits from the public. The issues are complex, not only in establishing an appropriate set of regulatory norms but also in deciding what types of entities might be most capable of supervising microenterprise finance intermediaries effectively. Experience can sometimes be a guide, but in this case no country in the world has significant experience in the prudential regulation and supervision of deposit-taking intermediaries dedicated primarily to microenterprise finance.

Most would agree that microenterprise finance intermediaries are significantly different from commercial banks, but they would not necessarily agree whether this implies more strict regulation, more lenient regulation (including no regulation at all) or identical regulation because of an overriding concern with creating a 'level playing field.' Most promoters of microenterprise finance, once they have discovered the substantial demand for deposit services that exists even among the poor, and once they have recognized that leverage is essential for significant expansion of loan portfolios, are likely to argue vigorously for a highly flexible approach to the regulation and supervision on terms far less stringent than those applied to commercial banks. Others might argue that, given the inherent riskiness of microenterprise finance, regulation and supervision of such intermediaries should be especially stringent. Commercial bankers, on noting the potential competitive advantage of loosely-regulated microenterprise finance intermediaries, might fall into this latter group, or at least argue for identical regulation and supervision to create a level playing field.

To approach this issue analytically, it is first necessary to understand clearly the key differences in riskiness between traditional commercial banks and microenterprise finance intermediaries. Microenterprise finance intermediaries are likely to be different from banks in three specific ways that can make them potentially less stable. These three differences, explored below, concern volatility, systemic threat and recapitalization.

Volatility

If a substantial portion of any intermediary's loans become uncollectible, it will be unable to honor its obligations to depositors. Loan delinquency at successful microenterprise finance intermediaries tends, if anything, to be lower than loan delinquency at a typical commercial bank. However, microenterprise loan delinquency can be much more volatile, in particular because of the usual absence of tangible guarantees and the short term of most loans. Marked deterioration in loan delinquency at microenterprise finance intermediaries has been observed in a matter of months. Furthermore, microenterprise finance intermediaries have much higher administrative costs than most banks. Successful microenterprise finance intermediaries have been able to cover these higher costs by charging higher interest rates. Nonetheless, when a microenterprise finance intermediary is suddenly beset with a high level of loan delinquency, it can lose a higher percentage of its equity more quickly than a bank with a similar level of loan delinquency because of high administrative costs with no interest income to offset them.

The potentially greater volatility of delinquency rates at microenterprise finance intermediaries, together with the greater threat to equity capital, suggests a possible need for more frequent reporting than for banks. It may also suggest closer attention by supervisors to the monitoring and control mechanisms that a microenterprise finance intermediary has in place to detect delinquent borrowers early and to deal with them quickly. On the other hand, regulators of commercial banks automatically penalize loans without tangible guarantees or extensive documentation including audited financial statements. This would tend to eliminate most of the potential clients that microenterprise finance intermediaries are trying to reach.

Systemic threat

A second potentially important issue is whether default by a microenterprise finance intermediary, with resulting losses for its depositors, would have more serious consequences for its sister institutions than default by a traditional commercial bank. When a bank fails, even a fairly sizeable bank, a significant contraction of the overall financial system rarely occurs as long as depositors have adequate confidence in the government's macro-financial policies and especially in the government's commitment to bank depositors.[1]

Depositors in many countries have observed that banks fail from time to time, but that depositors rarely lose their savings. However, there is unlikely to be any such history of government commitment to depositors at microenterprise finance intermediaries. Moreover, depositors using microenterprise finance intermediaries might well be new to such intermediaries if not to depositing in general. It is thus plausible that the failure of a single microenterprise finance intermediary might lead depositors to desert other microenterprise finance intermediaries *en masse*, possibly producing a collapse in a country's entire microenterprise finance system. In spite of this possible danger, there is little likelihood of significant damage to a country's overall financial system, even though the damage to the microenterprise sector could be substantial.

Recapitalization

A related and third potentially complicating factor is that most microenterprise finance intermediaries have much more limited capacity than banks to increase their capitalization levels quickly. This may seem ironic given that most microenterprise finance institutions are heavily capitalized, but most of them have been capitalized by grants from governments, donors or international agencies and not by private investors. If a microenterprise finance intermediary runs into difficulty, it has no clear and solvent owners who can quickly rescue it with inputs of additional capital. Even if a government, donor or international agency were disposed to rescue a microenterprise finance institution, its capacity to do so quickly, before irreparable harm had been done, would be unlikely given the long process that is typically required for approval and disbursement. Bank superintendencies throughout the world have grown increasingly insistent that bank owners be independently solvent and capable of making capital contributions quickly to avoid potential bankruptcies.

On the other hand, donor agencies and NGOs that provide technical support to microenterprise finance programs may have a continuing interest in the solvency of the particular programs that they have supported. Bankruptcy of a microenterprise finance intermediary may adversely affect the image of the supporting donors or NGOs. Moreover, the approach of some NGOs has been to recruit leading local citizens to serve on the boards of directors of the microenterprise finance programs that they support, and these individuals may be especially eager to avoid the damage that an insolvency might do to their image. In addition, while donors and NGOs may not be able to act quickly to provide capital to microenterprise finance intermediaries that are suddenly found to be in serious difficulties, they may act beforehand to try to prevent such problems. However, microenterprise finance intermediaries would do well to consider incorporating investors who have the potential and direct financial interest to increase their equity participation quickly. To do so may require changes in the legal structures of some programs—and will certainly require programs to provide credible information on financial performance.

Some guidelines for realism in regulation and supervision

The three key differences between the risk characteristics of microenterprise finance institutions and those of traditional commercial banks provide some basis for approaching the prudential regulation and supervision of microenterprise finance programs that wish to become full-fledged intermediaries by mobilizing deposits from the public. The main point is that banks and microenterprise finance intermediaries have fundamentally different risk characteristics; applying the same prudential norms and supervisory procedures to both would be a serious mistake.

Loan delinquency can increase quickly at microenterprise finance intermediaries and can erode equity rapidly, on one hand, so that it is especially important to have up-to-date information provided frequently and to pay particular attention to the effectiveness of the mechanisms through which microenterprise finance intermediaries monitor and control loan delinquency. On the other hand, in dealing with small-scale clients, successful microenterprise finance intermediaries have developed efficient and effective lending techniques that seek to avoid the use of costly information (e.g., audited financial statements) and the formalization of tangible guarantees. The standard approach of a bank examiner would therefore inappropriately classify most microenterprise loans as problematic.

A microenterprise finance intermediary just embarking on deposit mobilization is likely to be highly capitalized for its size, so that the adequacy of equity would seem to be of little concern for regulators. However, deposits have grown rapidly for many intermediaries targeting the unexploited market of low-income clients. The need to increase equity beyond what can normally be expected from retained earnings may soon become an issue for regulators, especially if loan portfolio problems are noted. Bank examiners operating under a standard regulatory approach could be hard-pressed to find potential sources of additional equity because the ownership structure of most microenterprise finance intermediaries is so unlike that of a typical for-profit commercial bank. However, other types of support, which can be just as important as immediate injections of new funds, may be forthcoming from the typical owners of a microenterprise finance intermediary. While examiners may need to be especially alert to a range of complexities in judging the actual and potential capital adequacy of a microenterprise finance intermediary, they will be unlikely to face problems of portfolios concentrated in loans to owners and other related parties, which have often been among the most difficult problems to uncover and deal with in the case of commercial banks.

It is clear that individuals charged with the examination of microenterprise finance intermediaries will need to have skills and attitudes that differ from those of a bank examiner. Similarly, agencies supervising microenterprise finance intermediaries will need to have a unique orientation.[2] A bank supervisory agency is oriented toward discovering and dealing with excessive risks that could cause depositors and other creditors to lose their money—but especially toward preventing runs against otherwise viable institutions that could destabilize the entire financial system. As noted above, runs against viable microenterprise finance intermediaries could result from the failure of a single such intermediary and thereby severely constrict the financial services available to microenterprises, but such an event is highly unlikely to endanger the overall financial system. It may thus be difficult to convince bank regulatory agencies to take the supervision of microenterprise finance intermediaries seriously.[3]

The credit union experience

Experiences with credit union regulation and supervision in developing countries provides useful examples of the options realistically available for the oversight of microenterprise finance intermediaries. Bank supervisory agencies do not tend to be enthusiastic about undertaking responsibility for credit union supervision. They tend to recognize that credit unions are quite different from commercial banks, usually expressed in terms of comments about lack of sophistication and technical competence, and will thus require different examination techniques. But, more importantly, they note that resources in developing countries are usually quite scarce even for bank supervision and that credit union failures are unlikely to endanger the overall financial system.

Looking elsewhere for sources of credit union supervision is often no more promising. Other government agencies responsible for credit unions typically have three major shortcomings: (1) they usually deal with cooperative entities in general and thus lack the specialized skills necessary to understand financial institutions; (2) they are often focused at least as much on 'promotion' of cooperative entities, a function that is incompatible with serious supervision; and (3) they commonly have fewer resources than bank supervisory agencies. Turning to the private sector, to credit union federations in particular, for the supervisory function has equally serious shortcomings. In addition to complications arising from a promotional orientation and a lack of resources, credit union federations often have a conflict of interest in dealing with problem credit unions because of their own financial exposure to these credit unions.

The Bolivian experience

Some attempts at regulation and supervision of microenterprise finance intermediaries are nonetheless being made. Bolivia provides perhaps the best example of a serious approach to the regulation and supervision of non-bank financial intermediaries that wish to capture deposits. Although BancoSol demonstrates that appropriate financial services can be delivered to microenterprises with a regular commercial banking license, the minimum capital requirements for such bank licenses in Bolivia (about US$ 5 million) are too high for some of the promising microenterprise finance programs that also wish to capture savings from the public.

The following parameters are among those discussed for licensing microenterprise finance intermediaries in Bolivia: (1) significant minimum equity, probably about US$ 2 million (an amount which, in Bolivia, does not pose a substantial problem for the six best programs, which could probably cover most of the microenterprise finance market once they reached their fully leveraged size);[4] (2) a track record of three years of successful operations (e.g., maintenance of consistently low loan delinquency rates and the achievement of at least near financial self-sufficiency) and a detailed business plan demonstrating the feasibility of leveraging external funds, assuming full commercial costs for these funds; and (3) a gradual path toward full leverage, as microenterprise finance intermediaries would not initially be allowed full Basle commercial bank leverage (roughly 11 or 12–to–1) but would instead be restricted to about 5–to–1 for the first two or three years, with subsequent gradual increases toward the Basle limit, based on their track record and the capacity of their owners to increase capital when required.

Technical capacity and political independence

The ability of regulatory agencies to determine the risk characteristics and capital adequacy of the intermediaries that they examine is a crucial aspect of supervising deposit-taking institutions, but it is not the only aspect. The inability of regulatory agencies to act—because of legal, political or technical limitations—even when they know or at least strongly suspect that intermediaries are insolvent contributed greatly to the costs of the savings and loan crisis in the United States and to banking crises in a number of developing countries. A regulatory agency needs a broad range of legal powers to deal effectively with potentially or actually insolvent intermediaries; to be presented with the choice of either imposing an insignificant fine or closing an intermediary are not adequate alternatives. Regulatory agencies must also have the technical capacity to deal with insolvent intermediaries; that is, they must actually be able to liquidate them, to merge them or to administer them on a day-to-day basis. Moreover, and perhaps most importantly, regulatory agencies must be free from political intrusions that allow intermediaries owned or run by influential individuals to avoid compliance with regulatory norms.

The ability of regulatory agencies charged with supervising microenterprise finance intermediaries to deal effectively with these intermediaries when they are insolvent is by no means assured. Given the experience of regulatory agencies in many developing countries with insolvent banks, it is not clear that they will automatically have the political mandate and technical capacity, especially given the scarcity of individuals who have actually run successful microenterprise finance institutions.

Some tentative conclusions

Successful microenterprise finance programs will and should leverage themselves by obtaining borrowed funds to expand outreach to their low-income clients. Attention to accurate financial information for effective management and control is clearly a key starting point for microenterprise finance programs wanting to transform themselves into financial intermediaries. It is also likely to be easiest to begin leveraging with loans from other financial institutions assumed to have the technical expertise to make informed judgements about the quality of a microenterprise finance institution so long as they have access to accurate information. The accuracy of information can be promoted by external audits and by appropriately enforced penalties for fraud, but without the need for detailed government regulation and supervision.

However, for reasons of economies of scope and the desire to provide deposit services to their low-income clients, microenterprise finance programs are likely to wish to become full-fledged intermediaries by taking deposits from the public. It is at this point that issues surrounding government regulation and supervision must be faced: applying commercial bank regulatory norms and supervisory approaches to microenterprise finance intermediaries is clearly not an appropriate beginning.

One of the apparently surprising findings of the survey of successful microenterprise finance programs sponsored by USAID was the relative unimportance of the policy environment. Except for cases of high and unstable inflation, and the regulatory environment considered here, microenterprise finance programs were not significantly impacted by the policy environment. Microenterprise finance programs were able to succeed even when economies were not growing rapidly or steadily, when governments and donors supported competing subsidized credit programs directed at microenterprises, when interest rates in the formal sector were controlled at rates substantially below market, and when the legal infrastructure for collecting loans was weak.

Successful microenterprise finance programs were able to flourish because they relied on effective informal and innovative approaches to reach their informal microenterprise clients. They were not effectively constrained by controls over interest rates in the formal sector, and they knew that recourse to the formal legal system was an ineffective and inefficient approach to collecting overdue loans. Government and donor loan programs based on subsidized interest rates could never achieve adequate outreach to compete more than marginally with successful market-driven microenterprise finance programs. One danger of government regulation of successful microenterprise finance programs that transform themselves into formal deposit-taking intermediaries is that innovation and the flexibility that comes with informality will be stifled.[5]

This chapter does not conclude with a recipe for how governments around the world should regulate and supervise successful microenterprise finance programs that decide to transform themselves into formal financial intermediaries by taking deposits from the public. The village units of the BRI have been extremely successful at providing financial services to microenterprises in Indonesia on a highly profitable basis. However, this does not imply that all successful microenterprise financial programs can easily subject themselves to government regulation and supervision in every country. In fact, the recent history of commercial bank regulation in Indonesia itself suggests that government supervision may not always contribute significantly to the transformation of microenterprise finance intermediaries.

A main danger of government regulation everywhere is that the public assumes that deposits are automatically guaranteed and no longer demands market tests, thereby leaving taxpayers with very large bills to pay when government supervisors are unable to handle excessive risk taking effectively (cf. BCCI and savings and loan associations in the United States). The danger in the case of microenterprise finance intermediaries is not that the bill for taxpayers will be especially high, but that the market will cease to discriminate between successful and unsuccessful providers of financial services to microenterprises.

Annex

Some lessons on deposit mobilization for microenterprise finance programs

For microenterprise finance programs that have not yet begun to mobilize deposits, the first challenge is to change the specialized lender mentality of their staffs to that needed to mobilize local deposits successfully. The corporate culture needed to mobilize deposits successfully is quite different from that required to channel credit to microenterprises. While incentives for loan officers to select good microenterprise clients and to take the necessary steps to secure loan repayment are widely recognized to be important, performance-based incentives are absolutely crucial for successfully capturing deposits. Even well designed deposit instruments with highly attractive rates of return will not attract deposits if customer service is poor. Liquidity has everywhere proven to be an essential element of successful deposit mobilization, and without good customer service there is no liquidity. In addition, deposit services, unlike the demand for microenterprise loans, must be promoted—often in the face of program staff who are convinced that there are no savings to be mobilized from microentrepreneurs or from the poor in general.

A program in Peru in the late 1970s first demonstrated conclusively how easy it could be to mobilize deposits even in the poorest rural areas and under highly adverse economic circumstances (e.g., high inflation, declining real incomes and controlled interest rates) if appropriate approaches were used. In a matter of months, BANCOOP, a cooperative bank not even fully licensed to capture deposits from the public, with a largely untrained and skeptical staff, and with very limited funding for training, technical assistance or promotional campaigns, managed to mobilize well over US$ 1 million in deposits at two local branches in the Sierra (Vogel, 1984). Even with negative real rates of interest on deposits due to government controls, excellent service provided by highly motivated BANCOOP staff, together with promotional campaigns well-targeted to a clientele of limited economic means, produced dramatic results. Relatively small incentive payments for staff based on clearly-defined performance criteria, together with low-cost prizes and lottery tickets for depositors (all underscored by highly effective publicity) basically produced these dramatic results.

Extensive work by Robinson has demonstrated more fully that the poor save even in the absence of financial instruments to do so (Robinson, 1992). They save by accumulating real assets such as gold jewelry, livestock and seed, or building materials. They also save by keeping cash in their homes 'under the mattress.' They must save to meet the inevitable cash demands generated by family emergencies, major events such as weddings and funerals, and cyclical expenses such as the start of the school year. They also save in liquid form to take advantage of unforeseen opportunities that may emerge and require quick action. Almost all poor families save in some form.

Robinson's path-breaking work with BRI in Indonesia established that poor clients would save in the form of deposits at financial institutions if the instruments they were offered provided greater returns, security and liquidity than their traditional vehicles for in-kind savings. Physical assets are frequently difficult to sell quickly at a good price. Cash under the mattress is not always safe, subject not only to theft but also to requests by family and friends for loans. Livestock and seed can deteriorate through disease or insects. Building materials deteriorate due to inclement weather or can be stolen. Therefore, offering effective financial savings mechanisms to poor families can have more potential outreach than credit. Effective savings instruments can enhance financial management by poor clients and ultimately increase the productivity of their limited assets (Burkett and Vogel, 1992).

In order to provide financial services to small-scale savers, institutions must be able to provide the three features that Robinson and Vogel have identified as critical. The easiest, but probably least important of the three, is returns. Since microenterprise finance programs can pass on their costs of funds to borrowers, offering a competitive interest rate to attract depositors is not difficult. Moreover, the administrative costs of handling small deposits can easily outweigh the financial costs. In fact, some institutions have found that the administrative costs of offering checking deposits were prohibitively high.

The second feature critical for service for depositors is liquidity. Not only is liquidity essential to satisfy small-scale savers, but the sensitive nature of liquidity management has also been difficult for most traditional specialized lending institutions to understand when these institutions have tried to depend on deposits to fund their loans. Such institutions have often become accustomed to rather lax attitudes with respect to liquidity management. If, for whatever reason, an institution runs a little short of cash, it can simply postpone loan disbursements a week or two with various kinds of excuses. Although this deterioration in service hurts a lender's image and can eventually lead to higher levels of loan delinquency, the effect is nowhere near as serious as what would happen if savers were not immediately satisfied when they came to withdraw their deposits. Any delays in deposit withdrawals can easily destroy an institution's credibility and lead to a run on deposits.

Effective liquidity management requires more sophisticated financial administration than normally associated with specialized lending programs. Related to this is the more sophisticated financial administration necessary to manage a full range of financial services, which requires an understanding of maturities matching, interest rate risk management, spread and gap analysis, and service pricing. These are among the basic skills necessary for successful banking. Specialized lending programs often display weak financial administration skills since these are not generally required when the only function is to channel funds to microenterprises. For example, there is no need for special concern about loan maturities (other than the impact on ultimate repayment) when loans are funded by donor-provided equity. However, the risk of having too many long-term loans funded by short-term deposits needs to be understood by managers of microenterprise finance programs that mobilize deposits. Moreover, the risk is not only of being caught short of liquidity but also the potential losses from suddenly facing much higher interest rates on short-term liquid deposits that are funding long-term loans with lower fixed interest rates.

The third critical feature, and often the most difficult challenge for microenterprise finance programs in attracting new depositors, is to establish that they are safe places to put savings. Credit unions, for example, have had their credibility seriously damaged by frequent failures where depositors were not protected. State owned banks, in spite of government guarantees, have sometimes been discredited because government officials in charge of funding these banks saw no need to be in a hurry to cover liquidity shortages, just as the banks themselves saw no need to reduce depositor transaction costs. Private finance companies have been involved in questionable activities in many countries, thereby discrediting a broad range of non-bank financial intermediaries.

To convince new depositors to bring in their savings, microenterprise finance programs must change fundamental internal attitudes. Instead of viewing their fundamental task as one of financing poor microentrepreneurs, they must understand that their fundamental role is to be custodians for the savings of the poor first—and lenders second. Therefore, instead of creating incentive systems focused primarily on disbursing loans, incentives must be placed mainly on generating deposits and administering these funds in the safest manner consistent with the rates of return necessary to make the system function. Loan officers, used to being sought after by clients as sources of funds, must be supplemented by staff whose orientation is go out and seek funds.

In some successful deposit-driven microenterprise finance programs, savings promoters actually outnumber credit officials. Whereas most specialized lending programs have never had to develop a sales function, given their quasi-monopoly position as providers of a scarce and highly desirable service (loans for microenterprises), programs seeking deposits have to create a new institutional image based on sales techniques that create higher levels of confidence within the target audience. Programs that provide high quality credit services in particular markets will be well positioned to build on that reputation when undertaking deposit services, but such a reputation alone is not sufficient. The entire message of the program must be changed, which can be difficult.

Notes

1   This is not meant to suggest that such commitments to bank depositors are a good thing. In fact, widespread confidence in implicit government insurance of bank deposits has often forced governments to bail out failing banks at considerable cost to taxpayers, and with increased likelihood of similar events in the future.

2   External auditors for microenterprise finance intermediaries, and for other types of non-bank intermediaries as well, have often expressed considerable frustration in trying to carry out audits of such intermediaries, and the intermediaries themselves have likewise expressed difficulty in understanding what the external auditors are supposed to be doing.

3   Discussions by the author with bank supervisory officials in a number of
         countries reinforce this view.
4   One of the concerns expressed by Bolivian regulatory authorities is the need
         for time to gear up to take care of the supervision of any significant number
         of microenterprise finance intermediaries. Although the authorities may
         thus be pleased by the relatively small number of microenterprise finance
         intermediaries apparently needed to cover the potential market, supervisory
         capacity would hardly seem to be the correct parameter to determine the ap-
         propriate number of microenterprise finance intermediaries.
5   In addition, as ACTUAR discovered in Colombia when its finance company
         was subject to more stringent reserve requirements, formal financial institu-
         tions are inevitably taxed.

References

Adams, D.W and Fitchett, D.A. (eds.) (1992), *Informal Finance in Low-Income
    Countries*, Westview Press: Boulder, CO.
Burkett, P. and Vogel, R.C. (1992), 'Financial Assets, Inflation Hedges, and Capital
    Utilization in Developing Countries: An Extension of McKinnon's Com-
    plementarity Hypothesis,' *Quarterly Journal of Economics*, Vol. 107, No. 2
    (May), pp. 773–784.
Christen, R.P. (1990), *Financial Management of Microcredit Programs: A Guidebook
    for NGOs*, ACCION International: Somerville, MA.
Christen, R.P., Stearns, L. and Castello, C. (1991), *Interest Rates: Their Significance
    for Microenterprises and Credit Programs*, Discussion Paper No. 6, ACCION
    International: Somerville, MA.
Christen, R.P., Rhyne, R. and Vogel, R.C. (1994), *Maximizing the Outreach of
    Microenterprise Finance: The Emerging Lessons of Successful Programs*,
    IMCC: Arlington, VA for USAID/CDIE.
Gadway, J. (1991), 'Financing Micro-Entrepreneurs and Rural Smallholders:
    Diagnosis and Prescription for Peru,' report for the UNDP and the IDB.
Gadway, J., Gadway, T. and Sardi, J. (1991), 'An Evaluation of the Institutional
    Aspects of the Financial Institutions Development Project in Indonesia,
    Phase I,' GEMINI Technical Report No. 15, Development Alternatives,
    Inc.: Bethesda, MD.
Gadway, J., Wieland, R., Horn, N. and Eysinga, F.V. (1989), 'Impact Evaluation of
    the Lesotho Credit Union Development Project,' report for the
    USAID/Africa Bureau.
Otero, M. and Rhyne, R. (eds.) (1994), *The New World of Microenterprise Finance:
    Building Healthy Financial Institutions for the Poor*, Kumarian Press: West
    Hartford, CT.
Patten, R.H. and Rosengard, J.K. (1991), *Progress with Profits: The Development of
    Rural Banking in Indonesia*, International Center for Economic Growth: San
    Francisco, CA and the Harvard Institute for International Development:
    Cambridge, MA.
Rhyne, E. and Rotblatt, L. (1994), *What Makes Them Tick? Exploring the Anatomy
    of Major Microenterprise Finance Organizations*, ACCION International:
    Somerville, MA.

Robinson, R. (1992), 'The Role of Savings in Local Financial Markets: The Indonesian Experience,' GEMINI Working Paper No. 33. Development Alternatives, Inc.: Bethesda, MD.

Robinson, M. (1992a), 'Rural Financial Intermediation: Lessons from Indonesia, Part One,' Discussion Paper No. 434, Harvard Institute for International Development: Cambridge, MA.

Robinson, M. (1994), 'Financial Intermediation at the Local Level: Lessons from Indonesia, Part Two,' Harvard Institute for International Development: Cambridge, MA.

Robinson, M. (1995), 'Indonesia: The Role of Savings in Developing Sustainable Commercial Financing of Small and Micro-Enterprises,' in Brugger, E.A. and Rajapatirana, S. (eds.), New Perspectives on Financing Small Businesses in Developing Countries, International Center for Economic Growth (ICEG) and Fundacion para el Desarrollo Sostenible (FUNDES): San Francisco, CA.

Rosenberg, R. (1994), 'Beyond Self-Sufficiency: Taking Another Look at Microfinance,' Unpublished manuscript USAID/Bolivia.

Vogel. R.C. (1984), 'Savings Mobilization: The Forgotten Half of Rural Finance,' in Adams, D.W, Graham, D.H. and Von Pischke, J.D. (eds.), Undermining Rural Development with Cheap Credit, Westview Press: Boulder, CO, pp. 248–265.

Vogel, R.C. (1990), 'Successful Rural Savings Mobilization: The Incentives Required and the Discipline They Provide,' Symposium on Mobilization of Rural Savings, The Asian Productivity Organization: Tokyo, Japan (November).

Vogel, R.C. (1993), 'Basic Strategies for Savings Mobilization in Rural Areas,' Rural Financial Markets Seminar: Mexico City (September).

Vogel, R.C. and Burkett, P. (1986), 'Deposit Mobilization in Developing Countries: The Importance of Reciprocity in Lending,' Journal of Developing Areas, Vol. 20, No. 4 (July), pp. 425–438.

Vogel, R.C. and Burkett, P. (1986a), 'Mobilizing Small-Scale Savings: Approaches, Costs and Benefits,' World Bank Industry and Finance Series, Volume 15, World Bank: Washington, DC.

Von Pischke, J.D. (1991), Finance at the Frontier: The Role of Credit in the Private Economy, World Bank: Washington, DC.

Wellons, P., Vogel, R.C. and Shipton, P. (1994), 'Manual for Assessing the Legal Environment of Financial Reform,' Report prepared for AID by HIID and IMCC under the CAER project: Cambridge, MA.

Yaron, J. (1992), 'Assessing Development Finance Institutions: A Public Interest Analysis,' World Bank Discussion Paper No. 174, World Bank: Washington, DC.

Yaron, J. (1992), 'Successful Rural Finance Institutions,' World Bank Discussion Paper No. 150, World Bank: Washington, DC.

Yaron, J. (1994), 'What Makes Rural Finance Institutions Successful?' The World Bank Research Observer, Vol. 9, No.1 (January), pp. 49–70.

13 Measuring the performance of small enterprise lenders

J.D. VON PISCHKE

The first theme of this chapter is that a microenterprise or small business lender's performance is definable in financial terms. The second is that clarity in measurement of financial performance can contribute greatly to sustainability of systems benefiting the poor. These propositions are fundamentally incontrovertible and mundane. However, there is no official of any donor organization with a regional or global reach who can sit at her screen, punch in a few commands, click or hit return, and scan timely financial information and historic trends in the financial performance of the small enterprise lenders in her portfolio. It is also probably quite safe to say that no smaller donor or multinational NGO has a data base that permits use of similar commands to review auditors' reports indicating the quality of accounting data produced by each of its field level lending operations. How can this apparent inconsistency be remedied?

First, it is useful to define what constitutes financial results. They go beyond the usual reporting of numbers of subborrowers and of subloans[1] made, subloan purposes and funds disbursed. They include measures of lender liquidity in the form of cash and bank balances, short term investments and debt service collections; capital-to-asset ratios after realistic provisions for bad debts as an indicator of lender solvency; operating costs as proportions of loans outstanding and loans issued as measures of lender efficiency; and net profit after tax, return on assets and return on equity as measures of lender profitability.

Microenterprise project reporting bias

There are occasional ad hoc reviews of lender financial performance by development assistance agencies, but these often have considerable difficulty assembling a coherent picture—too many pieces of the puzzle are missing at the field level. (See the Annex for a more detailed description of this.) This has remained the typical case throughout more than 20 years of microenterprise lending. At the same time, the literature on microenterprise finance abounds with heroic stories of the performance of microentrepreneurs who borrow and successfully build their businesses and reconstruct their lives.

Financial results are a necessary indicator of a lender's health, but clearly not a sufficient measurement if subsidy is involved. This is because subsidies are targeted and the results expected from targeting reside largely with borrowers rather than lenders. The lack of meaningful financial performance information suggests that these programs must be heavily subsidized, which would explain the one-sided concern for numbers of loans issued and their purposes and funds disbursed. From this perspective, subsidies in effect permit lenders to be less than forthcoming about their financial performance. The lack of financial performance data may not even reflect opportunistic behavior: lenders to microentrepreneurs may never have been asked by their sponsors for financial data in any comprehensive form that would permit application of the standard tools of financial analysis to determine liquidity, solvency, efficiency and profitability.

This state of affairs need not be alarming or controversial if flows to lenders are expected to continue unabated in perpetuity, if microenterprise lenders generally were an infant industry aggressively struggling to grow up, if it were possible to reach all aspiring tiny entrepreneurs in more than 100 poor countries with the funds at donors' disposal, or if the sustainability of lenders were viewed as a trivial consideration. However, these possibilities either do not apply or have been foreclosed by aid fatigue and by the creation of 'sustainable development' policies and departments in donor organizations.

A conclusion that can be drawn from the lack of financial data on credit programs is that donors have not really cared whether these activities are financially sound. Therefore, stewardship of donor funds can be measured or reported in ways that have little to do with financial soundness. It follows from the conditions cited immediately above that sustainability has not been a formalized part of donors' agendas for microenterprise development (Krahnen and Schmidt, 1994; Abugre, 1994; and Adams and Von Pischke, 1992).

Correcting the gap in developers' perceptions offers a tremendous opportunity to contribute to the creation of sustainable systems. To begin to provide more balanced incentives today through attention to measurement would yield an overwhelming amount of information about risk and cost. This information would eventually transform discussions about how financial services and delivery mechanisms or institutions contribute to or undermine development. Attention to measurement of the financial results of lenders to the poor would create incentives for better performance, reducing cost and opening new avenues for risk management to benefit the poor. Fortunately, there are two extremely positive recent developments emphasizing accounting profits and subsidy dependence, which are noted below, that suggest that sustainability is moving up the microenterprise development agenda. Much more needs to be done.

Using financial analysis to enrich the quest for sustainability

Financial analysis offers four concepts and definitions that can portray degrees of lender sustainability: (1) the value of project cash flows to the institution providing services, (2) accounting profit, (3) independence from subsidy, and (4) sources of funding, in that order of analytical detail and soundness, defined with reference to the number of assumptions that have to be made to construct them and the breadth of the story they tell. These are complemented by a fifth analytical tool, the 'constancy' of a lender's outreach. All five measures, outlined below, should be applied to test program and institutional viability.

Each requires valid accounting data as a starting point. Accounting data are customarily organized into balance sheets, income statements and funds flow statements, which provide the building blocks of financial analysis. Tests of liquidity, solvency, profitability and efficiency can be conducted with data found in these statements. The four measures in addition to accounting profit given here provide further insights into sustainability.

The value of project cash flows

Is the subloan portfolio a remunerative use of funds?

The primary financial proxy for sustainability is positive net present value. To be considered sustainable, any donor activity or development initiative should recover the capital invested and produce a surplus that is sufficient to increase the value of capital available for reinvestment, which can be measured by its net present value. This test should be applied to each donor-funded credit operation, focusing on the financial result achieved by the intermediary making subloans and bearing subloan credit risk.

Any financial intermediary using donor funds loses money, breaks even or makes a profit as a result. Financial analysis can easily and routinely quantify which of these outcomes is achieved and which may be reasonably projected to occur. The analytical methodology for calculating the financial impact of a project on the financial institution(s) implementing it is explained in readily accessible literature (Von Pischke, 1991).

It follows that the outcome for a financial intermediary from any transaction with a donor has an impact on the intermediary's capital: losses deplete intermediary capital, break-even results have no impact on capital but fail to create capital to support further growth, and profit increases capital. This is an important and highly relevant focus because financial intermediaries require capital to continue in business. Growth usually requires additional capital. From the perspective of sustainability an indispensable objective of any credit project is that it increase the capital of intermediaries participating in the project.

Attention to increasing and protecting capital facilitates innovative project design. As a starting point, it takes time and experience to create a viable financial intermediary. Many new banks formed in the United States do not expect to break even for five years, and Grameen Bank in Bangladesh has had a similar expectation for each new branch. One means of dealing with this and with the continuing demands of sustainability is to view the net present value of an intermediary's operations at several levels. Three are proposed here, the subloan portfolio, after direct costs and after indirect costs. These levels are applications of activity-based costing. They are substantive building blocks in the overall valuation of the lending institution. The objective of project design clearly should be to add value to the lending institution making subloans and bearing subloan risk.

Sustainability level 1—the value of the subloan portfolio: The core of a lender's operation is the subloan portfolio. If an institution is to be sustainable its portfolio should be sound. If the financial flows in and out of a subloan portfolio are not generally remunerative, the lender is weakened and financial development is undermined because of a failure to create confidence and because funds are less likely to be used productively.

The flows to and from the portfolio can easily be subjected to the net present value test. Flows to the portfolio consist of receipt of the project loan or grant and debt service payments received from subborrowers. Flows from the portfolio consist of subloan disbursements and debt service paid on the project loan. These should be measured purely in cash terms for clarity and simplicity, avoiding the assumptions of accrual accounting. These flows produce a net source or use of cash; annual or other periodic successions of these net flows and a discount rate provide the net present value.

A useful test of how loan terms, conditions and delivery mechanisms contribute to risk management is to distinguish between contractual flows and actual flows. Contractual flows are defined by repayment schedules contained in loan and subloan contracts. Contractual flows are usually not fully realized because of delinquencies and bad debt losses and also because prepayments are not unusual. Defections or variances from agreed behavior result in actual flows. The difference between the net present values of contractual and actual flows quantifies the impact of risk on the subloan portfolio. Good risk management can increase returns by opening new frontiers and creating market niches, increasing potential returns. In almost any situation some risk escapes management, making it impossible to realize potential fully and consistently.

Projections are often required for calculations of profit and net present value. The best basis for these is analysis of the performance of each period's cohort of loans. The period may be a week, month, quarter or year, depending on congruency with specified repayment schedules. What proportion of these were paid on the due date, within a week, 15, 30, 60, 90 and 180 days, 1, 2 and 3 years following the due date, etc.? This analysis yields a collection curve that tends to rise steeply and then flattens over time (Meyer and Srinivasan, 1987). Analysis of each cohort of loans provides trends that can be used to make projections of future recovery profiles.

It appears that collection performance tends to decline over time in many donor-funded credit programs (Meyer and Srinvasan, 1987 and Hossain, 1988): the curve for loans issued in project year 4, for example, will probably be less steep and flatten sooner than those for loans issued in project years 1, 2 and 3. This suggests operations that are unsustainable. But, much more analysis of loan recovery performance is required before a general rule of credit project entropy can be cast.

Sustainability level 2—direct noninterest costs and revenues of credit operations: A subloan portfolio is not free-standing: the costs incorporated in the portfolio net present value test described above are only the cost of funds and the cost of risk reflected in amounts falling due that remain uncollected. It requires resources to create and operate a subloan portfolio. Direct costs of operations include those required to generate loan applications, screen loan applicants, document financial stocks and flows, enforce contracts, and monitor and report results. Many of these costs are payroll costs for the people who directly implement and manage the credit program. A portfolio may also generate non-interest income in the form of application fees and other charges. The test is whether any surplus from the portfolio flows described above can cover the net costs of these operations. If they cannot, the lender is losing money or benefiting from a subsidy, or both.

This type of analysis, subjecting different levels of flows to net present value calculations, helps to focus attention and to frame incentives. Suppose that a portfolio has a positive net present value but fails to generate sufficient surplus to cover its direct operating costs. Suppose further that the program is a femimicroenterprise effort that reaches poor women and measurably helps them to increase their incomes and wealth, improve their family health and living conditions, and educate their children. Most people in wealthy countries would probably not object to a subsidy of US$ 10 per subborrower per year to achieve this result. Fewer would be willing to do so at US$ 30, fewer still at US$ 100 or US$ 200.

Certain other direct costs may not have to be included in the calculation. John Magill offered a useful technique that isolates an agency's 'core' activities from its other activities. Magill posits that sustainability occurs when internally generated income covers 100% of core costs (Magill, 1987). Interpretations of what constitutes a core activity require assumptions. For example, the experience of the Carvajal Foundation in Colombia indicates that trained microentrepreneurs are much better credit risks than untrained ones (Carvajal, 1989). This suggests that when training is essential to program success its cost should be included in credit program costs. However, it may also be an area in which subsidized technical assistance can pay off.

Likewise, the cost of expatriate managers may not have to be fully included in direct costs when these are supposed to work themselves out of their jobs by training locals to be just as or more effective than they are. For the purpose of analysis, these managers' costs could be assumed to be the salaries at which local replacements could be hired.

Sustainability level 3—indirect costs of credit operations: The next level of sustainability analysis reveals the extent to which surpluses created by a credit portfolio, after covering direct operating costs, contribute to indirect costs consisting of other overheads, such as buildings and senior staff of large, multifunctional agencies, for example. The procedures applied to direct costs and the discretionary basis for cost allocation would apply also to indirect costs. Once again, disclosure is fundamental. Data should be sufficiently transparent so that several skilled analysts using the same data independently would come to roughly similar conclusions.

Modifications of this approach would be required where other activities related to credit, such as contractual savings arrangements, are included in a program and have revenue and expense implications for the intermediary. Incorporating these flows can be easily accomplished by applying commercial accounting practices commonly found in countries supplying substantial amounts of funds to donors.

Accounting profit

Does the subloan portfolio generate a profit or a loss?

One highly encouraging development emphasizing the financial requirements for sustainability consists of a very clear and strong statement by two of the foremost promoters of microenterprise lending (Rhyne and Otero, 1994, p. 17):

> Financial self-sufficiency is a prerequisite for making finan-
> cial services widely available to microenterprises. Yet debate
> continues on whether it is feasible for most institutions. A fi-
> nancially self-sufficient credit operation must cover the fol-
> lowing through fees and interest charges: operating costs, in-
> cluding loan loss reserves; the cost of funds; and inflation. To
> achieve genuine commercial viability, it must also show a
> profit.

Some analysts indicate that the effects of inflation should be included in this analysis because it is important to maintain the real or purchasing power value of microenterprise lenders' portfolios.

Rhyne and Otero (1994) go on to define four levels along the way to sustainability. The first includes complete dependence on soft funding for subloans and to cover operating costs. They indicate that the portfolios of lenders at this level tend to be vulnerable to decomposition from inflation and bad debt losses, and that an organizational culture develops that is unlikely to seek independence from grants.

Institutions at the second level borrow funds at subsidized rates but their interest income covers their interest costs and some operating expenses. Level three institutions eliminate most of their dependence on subsidy but tend to retain some behavior requiring hand-outs. This results in part from impressive results in outreach to the poor, which attracts soft funds from willing donors. Grameen Bank has been in this position for more than a decade.

Level four occurs when a program is funded entirely by the savings of its clients and funds obtained at commercial rates from formal financial institutions. This is highly unusual among microenterprise programs, but it appears to have been achieved by credit unions in some countries and by Bank Rakyat Indonesia's village units (Rhyne and Otero, 1994 and Chapter 3 of this book).

The performance of any microenterprise program according to the criteria specified by Rhyne and Otero can be demonstrated by income statements suitably arranged. Donors have often passed up or ignored opportunities for adjusting customary financial reporting formats and conventions to tell the financial story of their client credit institutions most effectively.[2] Small changes in presentation can be quite powerful in identifying a salient relationship.

Accounting profit can also be derived from the methodology for calculations of net present value at different levels of income and expense (Gittinger, 1982). In fact, the statement of the net present value test in *Finance at the Frontier* is accompanied by a second measure, residual net worth. This is the cumulative accounting result at the end of a project's life, when virtually all the subloan debt service that can be collected has been collected. If the project loan has also been paid off, a cumulative profit for the intermediary on the closing project balance sheet would be balanced by a positive cash balance, a break-even result would produce a balance sheet full of zeros, and a loss would be reflected in negative capital offset by a corresponding liability to the rest of the intermediary's operations, consisting of funds consumed by the loss.

The decision-making utility of a distant, undiscounted profit or loss figure may be debated, but it is still a useful test. Most people would not want to see their pension funds exhausted of resources at some distant date within their life expectancy, for example, even if the fund's investment performance were exemplary. Accordingly, project design or microenterprise lending strategy should be revised whenever projected or actual net present value or residual net worth are negative.

Independence from subsidy

Does the lending program require hand-outs to survive?

A second ray of financial light is found in a measure of sustainability that has gained rapid popularity: The Subsidy Dependence Index (SDI), devised by Jacob Yaron at the World Bank (Yaron, 1992, 1994). This useful measure of sustainability demonstrates the extent to which a lender requires subsidy to earn a return equal to the opportunity cost of capital.

This measure responds directly to the World Bank's long-standing concern about the economic rationality of subloan interest rates. Focus on the subloan interest rate as the key variable also reflects the fact that this rate is the variable over which the lender making subloans has the greatest control. The SDI also addresses bad debt losses. It relies on accounting data but goes beyond these to reveal subsidy in a form of public interest analysis. A rationale behind the SDI is that accounting profitability may not be meaningful in distorted economic environments. It is also important to note that the net present value measure proposed above does not test for subsidy and that accounting profit may also fail to identify subsidies.

The SDI formula is $S/(LP * i)$. It is applied to a lender's financial results for one accounting period, generally a year. S is the subsidy received by the lender, LP is the average outstanding loan portfolio, and i is the portfolio's weighted average on-lending rate. The subsidy is defined as:

$$A(m-c) + [(E * m) - P] + K.$$

A is the average volume of concessional borrowed funds in use by the lender, m is the market interest rate the lender would have to pay if concessional funds were not available, c is the weighted average concessional rate of interest actually paid on A, E is average equity or net worth, P is reported annual before-tax profit (adjusted for loan loss provisions, inflation, etc.), and K is the sum of all other subsidies received by the lender.

The SDI is expressed as a percentage and denotes the percentage increase in the subloan interest rate that would be required to break even if the subsidy were removed. An SDI of 100% indicates that lending rates would have to be doubled. An SDI of zero indicates that a lender is achieving a return equal to the opportunity cost of capital, which connotes sustainability.

Agricultural finance institutions surveyed by Yaron (1992) showed varying levels of subsidy dependence: more than 200% for the Agricultural Credit Corporation in Jordan (requiring a trebling of subloan interest rates), 180% for Grameen Bank in Bangladesh, around 60% for the Agricultural Development Bank of Pakistan, and almost zero for the village units of Bank Rakyat Indonesia. It would probably be unusual to find donor-supported lenders that were not subsidy dependent. Krahnen and Schmidt (1994) explain why this is likely to be so with NGOs:

> NGOs are almost never truly self-reliant. Consequently, their operations are bound to be relatively short-lived: after all, they have to ensure that they will continue to receive regular support from their financiers, who, in turn, press for innovative approaches rather than assigning priority to stable and continuous day-to-day work (Krahnen and Schmidt, 1994, pp. 47–48).

The wider application of the SDI now underway should help to identify the degree to which subsidy-free sustainability is not likely to be achieved. The World Bank considered applying the SDI to all its credit projects, but unfortunately declined on the grounds that differences in accounting practices around the world would produce inconsistent results.[3]

Sources of funding

Does a lender create sufficient confidence among its clients to mobilize their savings?

There is some evidence, from Indonesia and Kenya, that suggests that credit programs last longer to the extent that they are funded with savings deposits mobilized in the areas in which they lend (Von Pischke, 1991). Accordingly, financial analysis could usefully highlight the relative importance of different sources of funds and trends in their composition. A donor dependency ratio, similar to but simpler than the SDI and applied to stocks rather than to flows, could be calculated by relating donor funding to total funding.

Retail financial institutions that develop both sides of the financial market are likely to have better information, better incentives and better practices and attitudes toward their clients than those that only lend (Vogel, 1984). They also have to gain the confidence of their clients in order to attract savings. Interaction with clients on a number of levels also tends to make clients value their relationship with the financial institution more highly, motivating them to enter into good contracts on a businesslike basis. Thus, diversification of financial services, combining savings relationships and lending relationships tends to create mutually reinforcing incentives for responsive behavior.

Does this mean that all lenders should offer savings services? The answer is clearly 'No!' The basic reason for caution is that unsustainable programs could rob the poor of their precious savings. The bad debt losses of unsustainable lenders may erode their capacity to safeguard their depositors' funds and to meet normal withdrawal demands. Deposit mobilization also requires good financial house-keeping so that records are accurately maintained. Lenders often do not have effective systems that report financial condition in a timely and accurate manner. In the typical situation, lots of attention would have to be devoted to accounting systems and controls on the lending side before solicitation of deposits could be prudently undertaken.

Lender 'constancy'

Does the lender balance outreach and financial sustainability?

Emphasis on financial analysis and financial viability could logically lead to subordination of outreach in order to become profitable. One means of doing this, found in directed agricultural credit, is to abandon the original target group (Gonzalez-Vega, 1978). This generally occurs through subtle migration, not as an abrupt change in course, possibly through an increase in average subloan sizes or through development of new services that appeal to a clientele that is more wealthy than those whom the lender originally undertook to engage.

A measure that provides a check on the possibility of abandonment of the target group in favor of profit or of rent-seeking through inefficient administration is proposed by Mommartz and Holtmann (1996). They use the term 'efficiency' to denote a lender's profitability and hence sustainability and also its target group orientation (Mommartz and Holtmann, 1996). 'Constancy' is used here because efficiency has such a specific meaning in economics, and in deference to Roy Bergengren's admonition to the staff of the Credit Union National Association in its formative years during his tenure as president: 'Keep purpose constant!' This orientation is demonstrated by three criteria: credit services that are (1) comprehensive, reflected in part by the range of subloan sizes, (2) easily and quickly accessed and available repeatedly to good subborrowers, and (3) inexpensive as measured by total costs, including subborrower transaction costs.

Mommartz and Holtmann (1996) provide no overall index of efficiency, but it is clear that measures of financial performance over time could be plotted on a graph along with indicators of target group orientation in order to illustrate trends for a lender or to provide comparisons among lenders. Thus, this new measure neatly reconciles, at least analytically, the emphasis on sustainability with concern for service to target groups.

Sources of reporting reform

People measure what they value. This explains why pages carrying pictures of smiling, poor women microentrepreneurs outnumber those devoted to financial performance in descriptions of microenterprise finance programs. This suggests that sustainability may be viewed as more of a matter of continuous cultivation of photogenic, smiling poor women than of financial performance. Where this is the case, financial reporting is not likely to be detailed, transparent or directed toward testing the sustainability of subloan portfolios and financial service delivery systems for microentrepreneurs. Lenders are likely to come and go, thrive and falter based on their nonmarket niches, consisting of their attractiveness to donors, lobbies or charities.

Sustainability, in contrast, requires market niches created through the delivery of risk management mechanisms and other responsive services to microentrepreneurs at prices that enable the lender to survive. Finding these prices, perfecting risk management mechanisms and designing other useful services often require and are generally assisted by attention to liquidity, solvency, profitability and efficiency. These in turn have essential quantitative dimensions that can be explored and revealed through financial analysis.

Pleading for serious financial reporting by microenterprise lenders and the donors funding many of them will not be rewarding unless incentives change for these lenders and donors. Little seems likely to happen unless those who provide the funds ask for meaningful financial information continuously and routinely, not just for occasional ad hoc reviews. The possibility of a sweeping change in focus in this direction currently seems remote. It is unlikely to be achieved by delegating the task to regulatory agencies such as bank supervisors, as their incentives are complex and their institutional position and effective powers often somewhat tenuous.[4]

However, the emphasis given to sustainability by Otero and Rhyne and the application of Yaron's Subsidy Dependence Index are encouraging steps. In addition, national credit union movements have developed what might be loosely described as reporting norms, and these are being improved and applied more widely through technical assistance from the World Council of Credit Unions and from the international outreach of credit union apex organizations in wealthy countries.

Annex

An early example of the paucity of financial data in development finance is found in the Inter-American Foundation's *They Know How...* published in 1977 (available from the Superintendent of Documents, US Government Printing Office, Washington DC 20402, stock no. 022–000–00137–0, reprinted in 1986). The Foundation reports that, 'out of 21 projects...sufficient data (are) available on eight projects to make general statements on loan repayment (rates).' Twelve projects had been in operation long enough to have expected loan collections, but no data were on hand (p. 42). More recent entries include Joe Remenyi (1991), who pleads for more financial data, followed by Thomas F. Carroll (1992), who notes a paucity of data, and by G.B. Thapa et al. (1992).

A major study that encountered considerable difficulty assembling and conducting meaningful analysis of financial data for 'successful' donor-funded microenterprise credit operations is Christen et al. (1994). (See the chapter by Vogel in this volume.)

However, there are some notable exceptions to the reporting bias cited here. These include an early effort by ACCION to measure the degree of self-sufficiency achieved by its programs in Latin America. (See Otero, 1989, pp. 211–223). Suggestions for systems and methods of evaluation have been around for many years, as found in DAI's comprehensive analytical guide, Chapter 6 in Goldmark and

Rosengard (1985). A recent entry is Mommartz and Holtmann (1996).

Acknowledgments

An article titled 'Measuring the Trade-Off Between Outreach and Sustainability of Microenterprise Lenders' by the same author and containing material similar to parts of this chapter was published in the *Journal of International Development*, Vol. 8, No. 2, 1996.

Notes

1   *Subloan* refers to credit issued to the ultimate beneficiary of the project, in this case a microentrepreneur, who is the *subborrower*. Subloans may be funded by the proceeds of a project loan made by donors to the lender issuing the subloan, although much of this lending is funded by grants.

2   Certain innovations in this area were proposed in Gittinger (1982).

3   This might have been only the third innovation in credit project financial analysis adopted by the Bank in 20 years. The other two were presentation of farm budgets before and after financing, pioneered in the Economic Development Institute by Jack Upper and the author, and time-adjusted farm budgets, covering harvest-to-harvest rather than the traditional planting-to-planting cycle, promoted by Walter Schaefer-Kehnert, also at EDI. The only other analytical innovation known to the author that has been developed in small scale credit operations is PERLAS, a method for analyzing credit unions. It was designed by David Richardson and others at the World Council of Credit Unions' Guatemala project funded by USAID. PERLAS incorporates the CAMEL bank and credit union rating system used by regulators in the US and adds features especially applicable to credit unions. (See the chapter by Richardson et al. in this volume.)

4   See the chapter by Vogel in this volume.

References

Abugre, C. (1994), 'When Credit Is Not Due: A Critical Evaluation of Donor-NGO Experiences with Credit,' in Bouman, F.J.A. and Hospes, O. (eds.), *Financial Landscapes Reconstructed: The Fine Art of Mapping Development*, Westview Press: Boulder, CO, pp. 157–175.

Adams, D.W and Von Pischke, J.D. (1992), 'Microenterprise Credit Programs: Deja Vu,' *World Development*, Vol. 20, No. 10, pp. 1463–1470; reprinted as chapter 9 in Bouman, F.J.A. and Hospes, O. (eds.), *Financial Landscapes Reconstructed: The Fine Art of Mapping Development*, Westview Press: Boulder, CO, pp. 143–156.

Carroll, T.F. (1992), *Intermediary NGOs: The Supporting Link in Grassroots Development*, Kumarian Press: West Hartford, CT.

Carvajal, J. (1989), 'Microenterprise as a Social Investment,' in Levitsky, J. (ed.), *Microenterprises in Developing Countries*, Intermediate Technology Publications: London, pp. 202–207.

Christen, R.P., Rhyne, E. and Vogel, R.C. (1994), 'Maximizing the Outreach of Microenterprise Finance: An Analysis of Successful Microfinance Programs,' IMCC: Arlington, VA.

Gittinger, J.P. (1982), *Economic Analysis of Agricultural Projects*, 2nd ed., The Johns Hopkins University Press: Baltimore, MD and London.

Goldmark, S. and Rosengard, J. (1985), *A Manual to Evaluate Small-Scale Enterprise Development Projects*, Development Alternatives, Inc.: Washington, DC.

Gonzalez-Vega, C. (1978), 'Credit-Rationing Behavior of Agricultural Lenders: The Iron Law of Interest Rate Restrictions,' in Adams, D.W, Graham, D.H. and Von Pischke, J.D. (eds.), *Undermining Rural Development with Cheap Credit*, Westview Press: Boulder, CO and London, pp. 78–95.

Hossain, H. (1988), 'Credit for Alleviation of Rural Poverty: The Grameen Bank in Bangladesh,' Research Report 65, International Food Policy Institute: Washington, DC (February), pp. 50–53.

Inter-American Foundation (1976), *They Know How... An Experiment in Development Assistance*, Inter-American Foundation: Rosslyn, VA.

Krahnen, J.P. and Schmidt, R.H. (1994), *Development Finance as Institution Building: A New Approach to Poverty-Oriented Banking*, Westview Press: Boulder, CO.

Magill, J. (1987), 'League and Confederation Self-Sufficiency,' *Credit Union World Reporter*, Vol. 2, No. 2 (May), pp. 4–9.

Meyer, R.L. and Srinivasan, A. (1987), 'Policy Implications of Financial Intermediation Costs in Bangladesh,' Economics and Sociology Occasional Paper No. 1389 (October), Agricultural Finance Program, Ohio State University: Columbus, OH.

Mommartz, R. and Holtmann, M. (1996), *Technical Guide for Analyzing the Efficiency of Credit-Granting NGOs*, Saarbrucken: Verlag fur Entwicklungspolitik Saarbrucken GmbH.

Otero, M. (1989), 'Benefits, Costs and Sustainability of Microenterprise Assistance Programs,' in Levitsky, J. (ed.), *Microenterprises in Developing Countries*, Intermediate Technology Publications: London, UK, pp. 211–223.

Otero, M. and Rhyne, E. (eds.) (1994), *The New World of Microenterprise Finance: Building Healthy Financial Institutions for the Poor*, Kumarian Press: West Hartford, CT.

Remenyi, J. (1991), *Where Credit is Due: Income-generating Programmes for the Poor in Developing Countries*, Intermediate Technology Publications: London.

Rhyne, E. and Otero, M. (1994), 'Financial Services for Microenterprises: Principles and Institutions,' in Otero, M. and Rhyne, E. (eds.) (1994), *The New World of Microenterprise Finance: Building Healthy Financial Institutions for the Poor*, Kumarian Press: West Hartford, CT, pp. 11–26.

Richardson, D., Lennon, B. and Branch, B. (1993), 'Credit Unions Retooled; A Roadmap for Financial Stabilization,' (March), World Council of Credit Unions: Madison, WI.

Thapa, G.P., Chalmers, J., Taylor, K.W. and Conroy, J. (1992), *Banking with the Poor: Report and Recommendations Based on Case Studies Prepared By*

Leading Asian Banks and Nongovernmental Organizations, The Foundation for Development Cooperation: Brisbane, pp. 49–50.

Vogel, R.C. (1984), 'Savings Mobilization: The Forgotten Half of Rural Finance,' in Adams, D.W, Graham, D.H. and Von Pischke, J.D. (eds.), *Undermining Rural Development with Cheap Credit*, Westview Press: Boulder, CO, pp. 248–265.

Von Pischke, J.D. (1991), *Finance at the Frontier: Debt Capacity and the Role of Credit in the Private Economy*, The World Bank: Washington, DC.

Von Pischke, J.D. (1996), 'Measuring the Trade-Off Between Outreach and Sustainability of Microenterprise,' *Journal of International Development*, Vol. 8, No. 2, pp. 225–239.

Yaron, J. (1992), 'Assessing Development Finance Institutions: A Public Interest Analysis,' World Bank Discussion Paper 174, World Bank: Washington, DC.

Yaron, J. (1992), 'Successful Rural Finance Institutions,' World Bank Discussion Paper 150, World Bank: Washington, DC.

Yaron, J. (1994), 'Successful Rural Finance Institutions,' *Finance and Development*, Vol. 31, No. 1 (March), pp. 32–35.

14 A road map for financial stabilization of credit unions: the Guatemalan experience

DAVID C. RICHARDSON, BARRY L. LENNON &
BRIAN A. BRANCH

Introduction

Under the strong leadership of the National Credit Union Federation (FENACOAC), affiliated credit unions in Guatemala enjoyed nearly two decades of prosperity and growth. Toward the end of the 1970s, however, the political and economic climate changed and credit unions were confronted with the challenge of surviving in an increasingly hostile environment. By 1987, credit union growth was stagnant, services were not responding to members, and the long-term viability of the credit union system was threatened.

In 1987, the World Council of Credit Unions, in cooperation with USAID, began a new project in Guatemala in conjunction with FENACOAC. The Cooperative Strengthening Project (CSP) instituted a plan to recapitalize and reorient credit unions through financial and technical assistance to achieve institutional reform.

The stabilization program was both preventative and proactive. It provided a new model that replaced the traditional credit union model. The stabilization program established new discipline, policies, and procedures within the credit union movement. Financial assistance was provided to help restore asset values and accelerate the write-down of credit unions' uncollectible loans and losses. Technical assistance and training were provided to upgrade staff and leadership skills, and to establish financial discipline.

All 20 participating credit unions experienced significant increases in membership, loans outstanding, deposits, savings, and retained earnings. In aggregate terms, the total five-year growth of participating credit unions after inflation from 1987 to 1992 was most impressive:
(a) total assets up 126%,

(b) total loans up 98%,

(c) total deposits up 504%,

(d) total shares up 23%,

(e) total capital, up 443%.

Other results of the CSP program between 1987-1992 include:

(a) dramatic increase in provisions for loan losses and delinquencies,

(b) increase in liquid funds from 13% to 22% of total assets,

(c) increase in savings deposits from 24% to 48% of total assets: from 1991 deposits replaced shares as the main source of financing for credit unions,

(d) decrease in delinquency rates from 19% of the total portfolio in 1987 to 7% in 1992, and

(e) compound annual growth in total assets of 18% per year.

The cumulative effect has been significant real growth, accelerated capitalization, strict financial discipline, and an improved professional image. Every major area of credit union operations has been strengthened in a significant way for the system as a whole.

A major component of the CSP was PERLAS. Although similar to the CAMEL system used by regulators in the United States (Capital adequacy, Asset quality, Management, Earnings, Liquidity), PERLAS was developed to help credit union managers improve financial administration.

In response to the success of the CSP programs, the board of directors of FENACOAC approved the creation of the Central Liquidity Fund (CLF) to help credit unions manage their liquidity effectively. Its main purpose is to protect credit unions against large unanticipated withdrawals of cash by providing access to short-term, emergency loans. The CLF also provides high yields on short-term deposits by member credit unions, intra-system funds, transfers, and rapid information on interest rate fluctuations.

The Cooperative Strengthening Project has been an historic initiative in the modernization of the credit unions in the FENACOAC system. The experiences of credit unions in Guatemala can be a road map for carrying the principles, policies, discipline, and tools developed here to help credit union movements around the world.

Financial stabilization

The objective of the stabilization program was to help credit unions become competitive in the marketplace, financially independent, secure in their capitalization, and economically viable.

Financial stabilization is not deposit insurance, but it is preventive. It provides technical and financial resources aimed at improving credit union operations and averting insolvency or losses of member capital. It works behind the scenes to rebuild or maintain credit union strength and solvency. No guarantee of support is implied. Stabilization was used in Guatemala to establish new discipline, policies and procedures. Financial assistance was provided to help restore asset values and accelerate the write-down of uncollectible loans and accumulated losses.

The traditional credit union model

Guatemalan credit unions traditionally relied on international donors for external capital as a source of loan funds for their members. The model was based on a theory that the rural poor lacked the resources necessary to save and fuel their development potential. The traditional model discouraged savings, encouraged borrowings, and forced those who saved to subsidize those who borrowed. Members who deposited shares in their credit unions often could not withdraw the shares until they terminated their membership and they received no direct return or yield on their shares. The amount of a loan which could be obtained was dependent on the number of shares held in savings. Loan size was a multiple of the member's shares outstanding, such as 1:1, 2:1, or 3:1.

The result of these policies and practices was a chronic shortage of loanable funds. In addition, credit analysis was largely based on the multiple and the member's savings balance. Repayment capacity was not considered.

Other significant problems for Guatemalan credit unions were runaway delinquency rates and the absence of real loan guarantees. Credit unions' financial statements often overstated asset values, accompanied by inadequate provisions for loan losses, low earnings, and low levels of institutional capital or net worth accessible only in liquidation.

The new credit union model

The new credit union model helped credit unions become more competitive, financially independent, and secure. The cornerstone of the new model has been the gradual reduction of reliance on member shares for capital, and an emphasis on member deposits yielding a competitive rate of return while offering unprecedented ease of withdrawals. The results were dramatic: deposit savings grew rapidly and the credit unions experienced excess liquidity.

The image of credit unions changed significantly in the communities they served. New members joined because they could receive a competitive return on their savings. Credit union membership was no longer dominated by borrowers who demanded and expected to receive preferential treatment. Delinquency rates dropped dramatically.

With money to lend, credit unions became able to finance larger loans. Average loan size increased, which revealed the importance of better loan documentation and improvements in loan analysis and decision-making. Re-education and training initially were slow but improved as staff gained experience in reducing risk through proper loan analysis and underwriting.

The new model implemented steps to evaluate asset quality more accurately. This included three principal reforms governing how delinquent loans were measured, the adequacy of provisions for loan losses, and requiring automatic write-off of loans delinquent for periods of greater than 12 months at the end of each calendar year.

Credit unions paying market rates of interest on deposits began to raise interest rates on loans to cover the costs of their savings mobilization programs. They also decided to pay dividends on share capital, much like the interest paid on savings deposits.

The new market-oriented model adopted by Guatemalan credit unions represented a radical departure from the past, necessitating:
(a) a shift from share savings to deposit savings,
(b) market rates on loans,
(c) capitalization of earnings,
(d) repayment-based credit analysis,
(e) market-based, results-oriented business planning, and
(f) improved financial information, reporting, control and evaluation.

The process of financial stabilization

The financial stabilization methodology used in Guatemala was developed over several years. The technical package was accompanied by external financial assistance. As credit unions modified their outdated policies and controls, they earned the financial support which helped them to write-down non-performing assets and replenish their institutional reserves.

Stabilization assistance was given to credit unions that agreed to adopt the basic tenets of the new model. These included:
(a) long-term economic potential and viability,

(b) financial discipline in all areas of credit union operations,

(c) leadership and management commitment to operate the credit union as a business,

(d) providing significant in-kind contributions of time, manpower, and financial resources,

(e) formalizing the commitments and condition of the stabilization program with legally binding agreements,

(f) annual audits and supervisory visits by FENACOAC, and

(g) quarterly evaluations of all credit unions to identify problems.

Implementing institutional change requires changing the way that people who work for the institution do their jobs. This holds true at each institutional level and, for a member-owned financial institution, includes the clients of the institution. Thus for every change adopted by participating credit unions, inertia had to be overcome in convincing staff, members and directors that the changes were needed and beneficial. While the stabilization fund provided a significant incentive for participation, serious institutional change required continuous technical assistance lasting more than three years. Early participation by a few credit unions provided a case study for other, potentially participating credit unions and, following the successful performance of early participants, the institutional change required for stabilization became much easier to sell.

The design and implementation of the stabilization mechanism was time-consuming and complex. First of all, the mechanism had to avoid a 'bail-out' attitude. It could not give cash directly to credit unions without introducing discipline, policies and procedures for financial intermediation. It also had to preserve and protect the original capital provided by USAID and provide instant liquidity.

Financial assistance for stabilization purposes was provided to the credit unions in the form of non-interest-bearing one-year loans. The loan principal was invested in high-yielding certificates of deposit (CDs) with the strongest and most reputable finance company that was regulated by the Guatemalan Superintendency of Banks. Stabilization loans were renewable annually provided that the credit union complied with all the terms and conditions of the stabilization agreement. Compliance was measured quarterly. Continued participation in the stabilization fund was contingent upon the adoption of new policies and financial discipline, as well as the continued achievement of aggressive growth targets. As a result, the credit unions actually gave more to the process than they received. As of December, 1992, participating credit unions had contributed an average of Q4.63 for every

Q1.00 they received from the fund. (Q is the abbreviation for Quetzal, the Guatemalan currency unit.)

The stabilization process had eight steps for all participating organizations. The first step was the diagnosis by a team of technicians which evaluated the credit union's financial situation, administration and control, and marketing. From this diagnosis, a credit union business plan was prepared. Budgets and performance indicators were also developed. Written plans, goals, and commitments were then incorporated in legally binding documents. The agreed amount of stabilization funds were used to purchase a CD issued by the finance company in the name of the credit union. As capital, these funds were applied to write-down loans in liquidation and to replenish depleted provisions for loan losses.

Credit unions were also required to participate in technical training events conducted by the Federation and Stabilization Fund personnel. Formal training was followed up with visits to individual credit unions to address specific problems.

Each credit union was required to conduct an annual self-evaluation of its achievements. The evaluation was a key factor in determining whether to terminate or renew the stabilization agreement for another year. Stabilization assistance was terminated for two reasons:

(a) failure of a credit union to achieve its goals and objectives; or

(b) interest earned on the finance company CD equaled the original principal. (At this point the interest income was credited to the credit union and the principal was returned to the stabilization fund.)

During the early implementation of the stabilization process, it was necessary to excuse several credit unions from the program due to poor performance. While this was unfortunate for those credit unions and their members, willingness on the part of FENACOAC and the implementation team to stick to agreed standards of performance served to reinforce the importance of these standards.

Financial stabilization program tools

Once the conceptual design and mechanisms for the stabilization program were established, implementation began. The first step was the immediate application of a series of key institutional policies designed to change the way leaders, credit union staff, and members viewed their institutions. These included:

(a) The credit union is first a business.

(b) Credit unions are savings institutions.

(c) Credit unions do not depend upon subsidized international donor loans.

(d) Credit unions must build institutional capital.

(e) Credit unions offer competitive market pricing.

(f) Credit unions are professional financial institutions.

(g) Credit unions' employees are capable, well-trained, and competitively paid.

(h) Credit unions are for everyone.

Financial discipline

The second step in the implementation plan promoted financial discipline in day-to-day operations. Since credit unions in general suffered from a public perception of mistrust and insider abuse, it was necessary to adopt rigid standards to regain public trust. The first was a strict methodology of reporting and classifying delinquency. Under the new discipline, if one loan payment was late, the entire loan balance was reported as delinquent in the month immediately following the due date of the first delinquent payment.

A strict discipline for creating provisions for loan losses was also instituted. Loans delinquent for more than 12 months had to be provisioned by an amount equal to 100% of the delinquent loan outstanding. Loans delinquent for periods between one and 12 months were required to have a provision established equal to 35% of the outstanding principal balance.

Other new policies included eliminating non-performing loans and maintaining 10% of credit unions' savings deposits in a liquid reserve account with FENACOAC. An additional 10% was also required to be deposited in a local commercial bank. Credit unions were also required to reduce their nonproductive assets to a maximum of 5% of total assets.

Another important discipline required credit unions to analyze loans on the basis of a repayment capacity. This entailed analysis of income and expenses and helped to reduce the practice of approving loans equal to the standard multiple of the member's share balance. Most credit unions adopted a blend of the old and new system. They analyze income and expenses to see if sufficient repayment capacity exists and then apply the loan-to-share relationship to determine the actual loan amount. An important sub-component of this policy is the requirement of solid guarantees such as real estate or chattel mortgages for all loans above a specified amount.

Entrepreneurial business plans

New institutional policies were supported by a new annual planning format focusing on specific balance sheet improvements and goals. The plan included developing *pro forma* financial statement projections and income statement projections. Then, detailed work plans were established to indicate how the credit union was going to achieve its goals. The entrepreneurial business plan became a key tool for achieving reforms.

Uniform accounting system

One of the greatest barriers to accurate and understandable credit union operations was the lack of a standardized credit union accounting system. Thus, a new accounting system was designed. Standardized general ledger accounts were established to make it much easier to compare credit unions with each other and to establish meaningful performance and reporting criteria. This accounting system improved the calculation of yields. A uniform financial reporting format was developed to present the critical areas of credit union operations, and a series of indicators were developed for evaluating the financial performance directly from the accounting system data. The accounting system became a powerful new tool. That quickly improved the accuracy and reliability of financial information and reduced the time needed to prepare monthly reports.

Marketing

Internal changes to operations were accompanied by a comprehensive marketing program. In-depth marketing studies were completed with each participating credit union. The studies identified niches of opportunity where credit unions could offer more competitive products and services. Credit unions then began to systematically improve the quality of their products and services. Improving the physical facilities of credit unions was an important element of the marketing program. The marketing program also recommended improvements in the dress standards of personnel and provided training on how to be courteous and helpful when dealing with members. Publicity and promotional campaigns were introduced and armed guards were placed at the entrance of credit unions to instill confidence and security. These marketing tools resulted in significant increases in local deposits and membership.

Financial stabilization monitoring, evaluation and results

The financial stabilization program was centered on the PERLAS monitoring and evaluation system. PERLAS is a management tool that goes beyond the simple identification of problems. It uses standardized financial ratios and formulas, creating a universal financial language that everyone speaks and understands. The standardized accounting system and PERLAS made comparative credit union rankings possible for the first time Guatemala. In addition, PERLAS provided the framework for a supervisory unit at FENACOAC.

While inspired by the CAMEL system employed by credit union regulators in the United States, PERLAS is different. CAMEL was created as a supervisory tool; PERLAS was designed as a management tool and only later became an effective supervisory mechanism. Each letter of the name PERLAS focused on a different, critical aspect of the credit union:

P = Protection
E = Estructura (financial structure)
R = Rendimientos y costos (yields and costs)
L = Liquidity
A = Activos improductivos (nonproductive assets)
S = Senales expansivas (growth)

PERLAS permitted credit unions to analyze their own operations, set specific goals, and then achieve them. This reinforced the concept that when performance was measured, results are multiplied.

The cooperative strengthening project worked with 20 credit unions. On an aggregate basis, the results of the stabilization have been significant. Some of these achieved between 1987 and 1992 include:

Protection:

(a) Since 1989 credit unions established provisions equal to 100% of their loans delinquent for periods greater than 12 months, and
(b) an expansion in provisions for loans losses to cover 58% of all delinquency, up from 33% in 1987.

Financial structure:

(a) An increase in the percentage of liquid funds from 13% to 22% of total assets,
(b) an increase in savings deposits from 24% to 48% of total assets: from 1991 deposits replaced shares as credit unions' main source of financing,
(c) a decline in dependency on external credit,
(d) a decline in share capital from 47% to 25% of total assets in 1992, and
(e) an approximate doubling of institutional capital (consisting primarily of annual surpluses retained) from 5% to 9% of total assets.

Investment yields and operating costs:

(a) An increase on the credit unions' interest spread (gross margin) from 8.7% in 1987 to 10.8% in 1992,
(b) an increase in operating costs, as a percentage of average assets, from 6.4% to 7.9%, and
(c) a tripling of earnings available for retention as institutional capital.

Liquidity:

As affiliates began depositing the required liquidity reserves equal to 10% of their deposit liabilities in FENACOAC, the average percentage increased from 3.8% to 9.9%.

Non-productive assets:

(a) A decrease in delinquency rates from 19% of outstanding loans in 1987 to 7% in 1992, and
(b) due to strong growth of productive assets, credit unions reduced their non-productive assets from 14.5% of total assets in 1987 to 10.8% in 1992. In most cases, the credit unions also increased their expenditures to remodel their physical facilities.

Growth: (All figures are adjusted for inflation and compounded.)

(a) An overall annual growth rate of 18% per year,
(b) loans increased by 15% per year,
(c) savings deposits increased 51% per year,
(d) shares increased 4% per year, and

(e) institutional capital increased 40% per year.

The cumulative effect of the new institutional policies, financial discipline, and program tools has been accelerated real growth, significant capitalization, strict financial discipline, and improved professional image. Overall, every major area of credit union operations is significantly strengthened.

Beyond financial stabilization

In response to the success of the stabilization program, FENACOAC is working to provide three new services to help credit unions become even more competitive in financial services. In January, 1993 the board of directors of FENACOAC approved the creation of the Central Liquidity Fund to help the credit unions more efficiently manage their liquidity. Liquidity by its very nature is volatile and FENACOAC has found it necessary to streamline operating procedures to respond immediately to requests for high volume deposits and withdrawals. The Federation's ability to communicate with credit unions in outlying areas is very important. Credit unions seeking liquidity management assistance are required to obtain access to a telephone, fax machine and a computer.

The Central Liquidity Fund will provide four key services to credit unions:
(a) short-term emergency lines of credit,
(b) high yields on short-term deposits,
(c) intra-system funds transfers, and
(d) periodic bulletins on interest rate fluctuations.

FENACOAC is creating a new Cooperative Financial System (SIFFE is the Spanish acronym) for its affiliates. The goal of the SIFFE is to polish the tarnished image of cooperatives in Guatemala and regain the public's confidence. The SIFFE membership is composed of credit unions that adhere to the strict operating policies, financial discipline, and performance standards established by the new credit union model. These credit unions will be linked through common products and services that members can use in different geographic areas of Guatemala. Compliance will be evaluated annually.

The Cooperative Strengthening Project has built a basis, using sound financial practice, that should be replicable elsewhere and that should permit credit unions in Guatemala to develop independently of outside assistance.

For Product Safety Concerns and Information please contact our EU
representative GPSR@taylorandfrancis.com Taylor & Francis Verlag GmbH,
Kaufingerstraße 24, 80331 München, Germany

Printed and bound by CPI Group (UK) Ltd, Croydon, CR0 4YY
08/05/2025
01864391-0004